VISTULA R.

DNIEPER R.

DON R.

N

DANUBE R.

BLACK SEA

alona

DIOCESE
OF DACIA

DIOCESE
OF THRACE

Adrianople

Constantinople

Sinope

DIOCESE OF PONTUS

Thessalonika

DIOCESE OF
MACEDONIA

DIOCESE OF ASIA

EUPHRATES R.

Athens

Ephesus

Antioch

DIOCESE OF
THE EAST

Damascus

SEA

Jerusalem

Berenice

D1260268

NILE R.

RED
SEA

palacias

D363.A585   95177

LIBRARY
EMORY & HENRY
COLLEGE

EMORY, VIRGINIA

ONE EUROPE

ONE EUROPE

The Historical Background of European Unity

BY RENÉ ALBRECHT-CARRIÉ

WITHDRAWN

Doubleday & Company, Inc., Garden City, New York, 1965

Library of Congress Catalog Card Number 64–19293
Copyright © 1965 by René Albrecht-Carrié
All Rights Reserved
Printed in the United States of America

D
363
.A585

To Cybèle

95177

EMORY AND HENRY LIBRARY

PREFACE

The idea of this book was suggested by the developments taking place on the European scene at the present time, more particularly the one, so far most successful, that goes under the various names of European Economic Community, Common Market, the Europe of the Six.

Within the short span of three decades the world has twice been involved in well-nigh universal conflict, to the extent indeed that the phrase Second Thirty Years War has been used to characterize this passage. Both wars arose out of essentially European issues, and the fact that they encompassed the whole planet is tribute to the place filled in the world by that smallest of its continents. But if it is true that Europe conquered the whole world, in the broad sense at least of originating the pattern that the whole world endeavors to adopt, the influence of Europe was transferred piecemeal, by her various individual units rather than in collective fashion, the European nations often involved in violent dispute among themselves over the process of conquest and transferral.

These internecine struggles have proved nearly suicidal, till in the end Europe had to be liberated, saved from herself in a sense, through the agency of extra-European forces, most prominent among them the American. In the most literal sense there appeared little remaining of Europe and European power in 1945, especially if one excludes the peripheral entities of Britain and Russia.

Yet Europe has not died, nor even abdicated, but on the

contrary displayed astonishing recuperative powers. But also it would seem that the near suicidal effect of intra-European quarrels has convinced many Europeans that such strife was too costly a luxury. Simultaneously, the common demotion of all the European states, the great powers of the past, has created a bond of common interest vis-à-vis the outside. From Coal and Steel Community to Common Market, to a large and authentic federation, lies a hopeful and clear course of evolution which has captured many a European imagination.

But much of this is also negative in motivation: fear of the dismal record of the past, regret of lost position, attempted rejection of the impinging forces rooted outside of Europe. Fear, to be sure, has been called the beginning of wisdom; yet it is questionable how solid a foundation it is for the construction of positive achievement.

This is the point at which the present discussion comes in. For there is more to Europe than common fears and shared regrets of a loss of power and position. And it is precisely the purpose of this book to look into the positive aspects that make up the common heritage of Europe. This implies first of all definition, and reference has been made to the marginal or peripheral British and Russian cases. The unique island position of Britain has made the British people and their record correspondingly unique, and Russia lies athwart the great Eurasian land mass of which Europe proper is but a promontory.

Any attempt to define Europe is soon bound to lay stress on a factor distinct from geography and culture. Europe, it has properly been said, is an idea. And here, through the vicissitudes of history, one finds much common ground and the true bases and meaning of Europe's unity. These will be sketched in the initial section, which for that reason is called "The Meaning of Europe."

Even when it appeared that Europe's fate was fragmentation, especially in the more recent centuries after the Reformation and the emergence of the modern nation-state, the old vision of unity, Roman or Christian, never lost its attraction for all; and not even the most blatant aberrations of nineteenth- and twentieth-century nationalism succeeded in destroying it. But, undoubtedly, for some centuries the trend was toward a disintegration that reached its climax in our day. The so-called Concert of Europe was but a feeble reed, whose inadequacy was finally revealed beyond peradventure.

But even while this was happening and the idea of Europe seemed to be in retreat, new forces were emerging whose divergent effects did not all fit into the narrow exclusiveness of the nationalist ideal. Not only Utopian, but also more concrete influences, rooted mostly in economic development, fostered unity. Capital and even more the socialist doctrine, child of technique and industry, are no respecters of national boundaries.

This, to be sure, raises another possibility, that of unity on a scale larger than merely European. One World has been advocated. But the realization of such an ideal, if at all possible, lies in a fairly distant future and one reason for this is the current wide discrepancies in stages of development. Nevertheless, there are at the present time various possibilities of evolution.

The overwhelmingly important role of the United States in the last war, the subsequent clash between it and the Communist world and ideal, the consequent close co-operation between the United States and that part of Europe free of Communist control, have led some to advocate the creation of an Atlantic Community. America in many ways is an extension and a synthesis of Europe and America has been the engineer of the North Atlantic Treaty Organization (NATO).

But NATO has a limited purpose, and here one comes to what may seem an ironical turn of events. The very success of the physical recovery of Europe, to which America contributed so much, Europe's own past historic record, in combination with the divisive forces which have been breaking through the unity of the Communist world, would seem to point to other lines of cleavage and to the emergence of several, roughly comparable, centers of power.

Of course we do not know the future, and what appear at present like reasonably established lines of development may break and alter their course. Nevertheless, the possibility exists that, in part because of her historic heritage, Europe may emerge in some unity as one of the world's centers of power. Fully aware of the pitfalls, and without venturing possibly rash predictions, it is the prospects of that possibility as it is currently unfolding that are examined in the last section of this book, especially in the light of the previously analyzed historical background.

Even within this prospect there are possibilities of diverse outcomes and many unanswered questions. For an appreciably long time the crucial element in the story of Europe has centered on the relations of three peoples: the British, the French, and the Germanic. Out of this has grown the overwhelming importance of the Franco-German relationship, source of so intense strife in the past. The present Little Europe of the Six may be taken as the authentic core of Europe. But, granting her peripheral position, Britain cannot be called anything else but European, certainly in face of the rest of the world. Hence the equal importance of her relations to the Six. Britain has been going through a very difficult adjustment of position, but what happened in January 1963—the French veto on her acceptance by the Six—should rather be taken as a measure and an expression of a passing situation than as a final answer, which it is not. Here a large question exists.

And what of Europe's restive Soviet satellites, or for that matter what of the Soviet Union itself? Despite the clash of

East and West, of Communism and Democracy, Marxism can hardly be regarded as other than European. Surely to view coexistence as established and to assert that Europe reaches to the Urals are very long-term and still premature views. These are all questions which are simmering in the caldron of history in the making. To repeat, while firmly eschewing prediction, the purpose of this essay is to throw some light on possible unfolding, especially in the context of the influence of the never-to-be-ignored or minimized historic past.

RENÉ ALBRECHT-CARRIÉ

CONTENTS

PREFACE   vii

PART ONE. THE MEANING OF EUROPE   1

Introduction. America and Europe: A Contrast   1
  I.   The Components of the European Past   6
       The Legacy of Ancient Times: Greece, Rome, and
            Christianity   7
       The Medieval Contribution   14
       Two Special Cases, England and Russia   24
  II. The Unity of Europe in the Early Modern Age   27
       The Divisive Effect of the Reformation   29
       The Sovereign State   33
       The Century of the Enlightenment   50
  III. The Impact of Revolution   56
       Revolution in France and War in Europe   58
       The Rise of Bonaparte   67
       Napoleon Confirms the Revolution but Fails to Unite
            Europe   69
Conclusion   76

PART TWO. FROM VIENNA TO SARAJEVO: CONFLICTING
TENDENCIES AND TRENDS   81

  I.   Europe in 1815   84
  II. The Disintegrating Force of Nationalism   92
       Belgium and Poland   92
       Mid-Europe   95
       The Balkan Peoples   104
  III. The Contradictory Effects of Economics   109
       Free Trade and the Social Question   110
       The Second Industrial Revolution   117
       Europe Overseas   120
  IV. The Impact of Ideas   130
       Socialism, Utopian and "Scientific"   134
  V.   The Actual Record   142
       The Concert of Europe   144
       The Powers and the Eastern Question   147

The Mid-Century Readjustment   152
The Balance of Power   155
   The "Reign" of Bismarck   155
   Wilhelmine Germany   159
Conclusion: The Closing of an Age   164

PART THREE. THE BREAKDOWN OF THE CONCERT OF
EUROPE AND THE SEARCH FOR AN ALTERNATIVE   171

  I. The Meaning of the First World War   171
    Europe and the German Problem   174
    The Classical War   177
    The Intrusion of Ideologies   179
 II. A Critique of the Peace   192
III. The Long Armistice: Continued Failure of the
    Forces of Cohesion   202
    The Anglo-French Divergence   206
    The Organization of Europe   211
    European Union   221
    The Collapse of the European System 228
    Europe and the German Problem Again 238
Conclusion: The German Bid for European Unity   248

PART FOUR. AN IDEA THAT WILL NOT DIE   253

  I. The Defeat of the German Bid: The Second World War 259
    Nazi-dominated Europe   261
    The Impact of External Forces   267
    The Looming Shape of the Future: One World? 270
 II. The Defeat of the Russian Bid   276
III. The Reconstruction and Integration of Europe   282
    Britain and Europe   283
    France, Germany, and the Franco-German
      Relationship   286
    The Common Market—and the European Free
      Trade Association   296
 IV. Prospects and Possibilities   302
    The British Position   304
    The French Position   311
      The Fifth Republic   314
    Britain, France, and Germany   320
    Europe in the Larger World   327

BIBLIOGRAPHY   337
INDEX   339

Part One

THE MEANING OF EUROPE

Introduction. America and Europe: A Contrast

On December 13, 1918 President Wilson landed at the French port of Brest. He was on his way to attend the great gathering that was to seek to reconstruct a world shattered by four years of destruction and slaughter, the First World War of our century. But as some time had to elapse before the formal opening of the peace congress of Paris, President Wilson used the interval to visit some of the other allied countries. Everywhere he received a rousing welcome from the masses of the people, who, fully of their own accord, came out to express to the American President two things: their gratitude for the crucial role that his country's contribution had played in procuring the victory of allied arms; their hope and faith in the promise of lasting peace founded on justice that the New World Messiah brought with him. Those in the seats of power were more reticent; more cynical—or wiser— they were skeptical of gospels and nostrums, but they fully acknowledged the attractions of the New Order and its bearer, and were even concerned lest his appeal constitute a challenge to their own authority. Wilson understood this quite well, reciprocating with suspicion of Old World wiles, diplomacy and politics, conscious that he was bearer of new promise, and even thinking that he was a more authentic representative of the masses than their own governments, whether freely chosen or not. To a degree he was quite right and it is difficult after nearly half a century to reconstruct the expectant climate of 1919; our own day has become familiar with frustration, and whatever hopes we may have are more modest.

Why should President Wilson have been in so exalted and unique a position? That of his country was indeed unique, a fact which had been registered in the insistence upon calling itself the "associated" power, instead of an "ally" like others. It is equally true that the power of ideas is great; all had expressed their adherence to the American program for the future, and the American position of leadership in this endeavor was commonly acknowledged. But there is also no denying that had the same initiative stemmed from a country like Belgium, for example, it would hardly have been likely to command the same attention and carry the same weight. For behind American wishes stood the fact of American power, material power in the last analysis; like them or not, American wishes must be heeded. Whatever may be thought of power, it is a reality which is crucial in the relations among states; it may never be ignored with impunity, and much will have to be said in the following pages on the role and the operation of power.

At the end of the First World War the power of the United States stood unrivaled, a condition of established fact not open to dispute. What was this American giant? It had grown rapidly, and it was the concrete test of war that brought the widespread awareness of a condition that in effect had been in existence for some time; the relative lack of participation of the United States in world affairs had alone prevented its weight from being felt at an earlier time. The bases of American power were of course the dimensions and the resources of an immense continent that the American people had transformed into the effective instrument of power. It is worth looking for a moment at the make up of this people.

The first and basic fact that stands out is that of the foundation of the United States as an extension of England. The final exclusion of France from the North American continent had opened the way to the eventual expansion of the initial thirteen colonies into the entire space that stretched between the two oceans. But that exclusion of another European power, although it had also helped sever the link between the colonies and the mother country, had not resulted in an alteration of the fundamental British base of American institutions and culture. Allowing for important differences in the technique of government, allowing for the fact that long before the twentieth century an authentically distinct American nationality had come into existence, there is no denying that on the whole American culture, institutions, and language were—and still are—a modification, if one will, of the British. But the fact must also be stressed that by the time of the First World War the ethnic composition of the American people could hardly any longer be called British. The flood of immigration had for some time been pouring increasing quantities of other European strains into the original British mold. What is of interest, however, is that, important as this admixture was and marked as its contributions may have been, the fundamental shape of the mold was unaltered; with remarkable rapidity and effectiveness Germans, Irish, Italians, various Slavs, and others became Americanized, and, especially in view of their size, the role of "national" elements in the operation of the American complex may fairly be described as minimal.[1] The American capacity for assimilation has been extraordinary, mainly as a result of the mobility, free-

[1] Much has been written about the various strains of immigration into the United States and the role of various "national" groups in politics is well known. Nevertheless, taking a broad view, the above judgment is justified. The case of the Negro population obviously constitutes a problem of a special nature, that the episode of the Civil War did not succeed in resolving, as current tensions clearly show.

dom, and openness of the American milieu, making the use of the phrase melting pot fully warranted.

The significance of that phrase must be emphasized, for it constitutes the most effective demonstration of the possibility of integration of the various European national strains, and it is equally significant that in their native habitat, in Europe herself, the record has been the contrasting one of persistent diversity. Why this should have been so this is not the place to examine, though it will be desirable to look into the nature of the diversity of Europe and the manner in which it developed. One thing, however, must be noted at this point, one aspect of the difference between the unity of America and the diversity of Europe.

American unity was threatened on two occasions. Once the emancipation from British control had been successfully accomplished there was a doubtful passage when it appeared for a time as if divergence might prevail over union. But this was overcome. More serious was the trial by fire that was the Civil War. That, too, more painfully and with much harshness, was overcome, and thereafter the possibility of severance of any part from the whole disappeared from the domain of the probable.

By the time the American colonies emerged into separate existence Europe had long crystallized into distinct entities. Strife and competition among these was the normal law of existence, and the increasing power that technical progress brought to all had the ultimate effect of seeming mutual destruction, a not unfair summation of the twentieth-century wars of Europe. Yet destruction is a relative term, and Europeans have survived these fratricidal struggles; indeed it may be credited to this same technical progress that the separate units of Europe seem to share at present a climate of unprecedented economic well-being. But from the standpoint of the position of power that had belonged to the nations of

Europe until the opening of the present century, self-destruction or suicide is an adequate characterization.

This demotion has come hard to Europeans and one disastrous war—the First World War—was insufficient to produce adequate registration of it. But it may be that repetition of the first performance on an even grander scale and in a more effective fashion within the span of a quarter of a century has had novel effects on the consciousness of the European peoples. There are those, in Europe and outside, who are reconciled to the passing of the power of Europe, sometimes making comparisons with the fate of ancient Greece. The city states of ancient Greece may be said to have succumbed collectively to external interventions—first Macedonian, then Roman—because of their inability to submerge their internecine differences in the face of a common threat. But across the span of the centuries their demise rather appears like a transformation and was in some respects a contribution to the greater spread of the Greek influence outside its native home. The glory that was Greece has never died. Similarly, Europe, having given the modern world its shape and the impulse to the direction of change, whatever the fate of her power, one may expect her contribution to live on, integrated into whatever shape the course of the future may take.

But there are also those who think that, granting that there is no prospect of Europe's resuming the position of mistress of the planet in purely physical or political terms, a very large store of power remains in Europe. Even if this view is accepted it has become quite clear that the internecine quarrels of Europe can only be damaging to all her parts. It follows that the rivalries of Europe are in the nature of a luxury that Europe can no longer afford, and that place and power can have meaning only if one think of the collectivity of all Europe, or at least of a substantial portion of that subcontinent. Thus it is that there has arisen in Europe, since the

Second World War, an integrating movement which is in process of development and to which substantial accomplishments can already be credited. The unity of America is an accomplished fact, that of Europe remains a problematic possibility.

The future is of course unknown, but such a development could hardly have occurred unless it had had roots in the past, and it is precisely the purpose of this essay to make an examination of these roots, to analyze the precise nature and meaning of unity for Europe. Having done this, essentially an historical task, it will then be possible to examine the specific accomplishments that are contemporary events, and finally to make a survey and appraisal of the divergent forces that operate in Europe, with an eye to a clarification of present tendencies and problems and therefore of prospects. Prediction is not the intention, an activity that ill suits the historian; the so-called lessons of the past have a very dubious validity for the future, for, allowing the truth of the platitude that the same causes produce the same effects, human affairs are too tangled a skein in which but rarely is complete repetition encountered. The stress of this discussion will therefore be on analysis and description, followed by a critical appraisal.

I. The Components of the European Past

Perhaps it might be well to raise the preliminary question of what and where precisely is Europe? The term is used very freely, but little reflection is needed to show how loose it is. The British when crossing the Channel speak of "going to Europe"; if Russia is European, she reaches to the Bering Strait; and what of the relative similarity or difference between, say, Sicily on the one hand and Tunisia or Scandinavia

on the other? But the question of precise physical location
and dimensions, simple and fundamental as it is, will best
be examined after consideration has been given to the nature
of the European complex, the elements that go into its composition, from which it will then appear that the "where" is
closely tied to the "what."

The Legacy of Ancient Times:
Greece, Rome, and Christianity

The division of the history of the West into periods, ancient, medieval, and modern is familiar. It has much arbitrariness in it, and for that reason has been criticized with some
justice, but it will serve for our purpose. It does bring out
the fact that the roots of the West are in the Mediterranean,
especially the eastern portion of that sea with which the ancient period is concerned. The first important observation to
make in this connection is that the West, or Europe, is Greek.
The Greek world had many connections with the Asiatic and
African portions of the eastern end of the Mediterranean, but
subsequent developments, presently to be mentioned, resulted in a severance, with the consequence of making the
more narrowly Greek contribution the peculiar property of
the West. The nature of that contribution must for a moment
be examined more closely.

The fact is often stressed that Greek disunity bears much
of the responsibility for the collective loss of independence
of the Greek states. But disunity may be called by a different
name or seen as a consequence of another characteristic,
namely diversity, diversity of so intense a nature that it im-
peded the common purpose of survival in face of common
mortal danger. One may, if one wishes, seek for the roots of
this condition in the variety of the Greek land, broken up by
nature, mountainous, difficult of inland communication. With-

out unduly dwelling upon that uncertain aspect of the matter, we may rest content with taking diversity as a fundamental trait of the Greek character and history.

This diversity is not unrelated to another basic characteristic—the sources of which again will not be dwelt upon—the emphasis placed by the Greeks on the use of the rational faculty. Here is in fact the greatest single component of the legacy of Greece to the West, one which also distinguishes it from the rest of the eastern Mediterranean. This cannot be overstressed; one consequence of it and one outstanding contribution of Greece is the beginning of the scientific endeavor. This is not the place to go into the details of what the Greeks accomplished in this domain, most markedly perhaps in the mathematical section of it. But the name of Aristotle and his encyclopedic achievements stand out, the influences of which have been as profound as they have been durable. Be it in mathematics or philosophy the stress on the use of reason is dominant.

We often think of science as a characteristically modern activity. This view is fundamentally correct; despite the thriving endeavors of historians of science in tracing continuity of development, the broad judgment is not unfair that the Roman and the medieval worlds did not carry the impress of the cultivation of science in the same manner that the Greek world did; much of the time the opposite in fact was the case; and even the Arabs, who indeed deserve much credit for having brought about the revival of scientific activity in Europe, were essentially carriers rather than innovators or makers of original contributions. The view of man as a rational being is essentially of Greek derivation, and if we now incline to think that view too limited, having lately come to emphasize the importance of the dark places in his soul, it is nevertheless by the use of the rational faculty that science has made progress. Modern science is a distinctly European development. It was first cultivated in Italy from where it spread to other European lands. The rational faculty is, to be sure, no exclusive prerogative of European man, but until almost our own day the home of scientific development has remained European and so has the impact of its more concrete manifestations. The expectation that the practical applications of science will transform and mold the shape of our lives and our society has only begun to affect the world outside of Europe. Even America, an extension of Europe in the present context, did not begin substantially to insert itself into the mainstream of contributions to scientific development until the present century.

Whatever one may think of its quality, its virtues or shortcomings, science and its impact are both unprecedented and European phenomena, for the initial Greek beginning was followed by a long interruption. Nevertheless, the seeds were Greek, and it is wholly appropriate, as well as symbolically significant, that so much of our scientific and technological terminology should be of Greek derivation, for those who have developed modern science are rightly conscious of their debt and of the fact that they were picking up a thread long submerged. Now scientific activity is broadly human and does not recognize boundaries of nation, race, color, or sex. Operating in the cold light of reason, it is predominantly objective, even ruthless, in its appraisals and judgments, naturally in proportion to the degree to which it deals with the exact and the measurable. There is a far greater degree of agreement as to who is a good physicist or mathematician than in regard to the merits of historical work, for example. To sum up and repeat, the view of man as a rational entity and the application of the rational faculty to the understanding and control of the universe is a great contribution of Greece to Europe which long remained a virtually exclusive European possession. This is the reason for asserting that *Europe is Greek.*

But it is Greek in other ways as well. This remarkable and unique legacy may or may not have been related to that other Greek characteristic, the stress on individuality, perhaps best seen as an aspect or a source of the earlier mentioned diversity. It might be expected that the use of abstract reason would be conducive to agreement; the truth presumably is one. In a limited domain this is so, but as the Greeks themselves well knew—witness their literature—man is not exclusively reason, so that the multiplicity that is man is productive of difference. The combination of these elements can thus easily lead to the assertion of the value of individual freedom. In the political domain the ancient Greeks are credited with the fatherhood of the democratic idea and practice, incidentally a point of distinction with their contemporary oriental world, near or far. And this is true despite the fact that slavery was practiced among Greeks. The democratic practice is recent in the West, where it is still much honored in the breach, but of the potency of the idea there can be little question. In modern times the democratic impulse has also unquestionably been of European origin, largely British and French, and the clearest expression of it to be found in bills of rights and declarations of the rights of man. Much has been added to the Greek contribution, which none the less remains fundamental in its assertion of the value of the individual.

Everybody knows what happened to the Greeks after they lost their independence and how Greek culture spread and leavened much that was not initially Greek. The Hellenistic age centered as much as anywhere in Egyptian Alexandria, where many of its exponents were Jews. But Greece herself, like Alexandria and much else, fell under Roman domination. Where culture is concerned the Roman age and world are decidedly less attractive than the Greek, whose mastery in that domain Rome quite rightly acknowledged. The Roman bent was concrete and added little to the Greek contribution in the scientific realm, manifesting itself in more practical applications such as give scope to the craft of the engineer.

But in another field, that of society and politics, the accomplishments of Rome were impressive and lasting, expressing the same genius for organization. Much of the politics of Rome may not be very inspiring, and Caesar is in many ways an unattractive figure; but the stamp that he left was of unusual duration. Rome more than anything meant empire, and for a time, a long time by the standards of the durability of human accomplishment, Rome brought under her sway the totality of civilized Western mankind. A glance at the map of the Roman world at the height of its expansion is instructive; it shows that the empire was essentially Mediterranean: Hadrian's Wall marked the limit of its northern extent, while on the Continent the Rhine and Danube were its boundary, thus excluding much that we now consider European, while on the other hand North Africa and the Near East fell within its confines.

In that very large area Rome enforced unity and order, and the duration of her rule implanted the idea that it was an aspect of the proper and normal order of things that the totality of civilized mankind should have but one political allegiance. Here was a great, indeed a noble, conception, in marked contrast to the outcome of Greek disputatiousness. Both Greece and Rome tended to think of man primarily from the standpoint of his "humanness," but it fell to the latter to effect in practice the union of the Western human race. The management of the vast Roman domain meant a considerable measure of uniformity in administration, and much emphasis on the preservation of order, best maintained by exalting the conception of law. Here is precisely where the great legacy of Rome is to be found; unity, order, and law are what Rome gave to the world, and for that reason one is justified in saying that *Europe is Roman.*

But Rome eventually also fell upon evil days; the outer Barbarians successfully breached the border defenses and overran the whole Roman world, save for a very much reduced domain around the second Rome, Byzantium, where the Greek cultural influence, rather than the Latin, continued to prevail. Long before this came to pass and while Roman power was in its heyday, out of a small Near Eastern people there arose a Messiah. The early story of the Christian sect is tangled and confused, and that of its eventual success is at once marvelous and strange; out of it one thing alone need be retained here, the fact that the Roman world became Christian, thus giving us the third major component of Europe or the West: *Europe is Christian.*

This last fact warrants a little consideration and some explanation. The Messiah no doubt was born among the Jews and much has been said about the Judaic component of Western civilization. This may be granted and there is also no doubt that the holy book of the Jews, the Old Testament, has become the holy book of the Christians. Yet this is also misleading. For one of the fundamental characteristics of the Jewish people was the element of exclusiveness, best expressed in the conception of the chosen people. Whatever qualities of distinctiveness the Jewish people may or may not have is irrelevant at this point; what is significant, however, is that the new religion, born of the Hebraic milieu as it may have been, stressed the precisely antithetic principle of the salvation of the totality of mankind, hence of inclusiveness in place of restrictiveness. This element appears from the very beginning, and, quite appropriately, Christianity spread among the Gentiles.

But there is more to the tale. Whatever the original teachings and intentions of the Messiah and his early followers may have been, the new religion was born in a world that was culturally Greco-Roman. As it spread and succeeded, and precisely because it spread and succeeded, it could hardly do other than absorb the impact of that dominant culture. The result was integration or fusion with consequences that are very clear. In the shaping of Christianity the influence of St. Paul was very great, which was largely a Greek influence; there is indeed a characteristically Greek flavor to the disputations of the early Church. The passage of more than a millennium saw that other aspect of Greek influence, the annexation of Aristotle by Thomas Aquinas. In between, as Christianity prospered while the Empire went into decline, followed by complete disintegration and collapse, it was the Christian Church which, more than any other institution, fell heir to imperial Rome, which became the capital of Christendom. In more senses than one the Christian Church became the heir of ancient Rome, and thus Christianity was itself a consequence of the two great influences, Greek and Roman, that have given Western culture much of its identity.

But Christianity was more than a mere synthesis of older things, for it added elements of its own. However worldly it may have become in actual practice, the Church could not deny its primary function, the stress on salvation, in other words the unworldly or the spiritual; also, because of the Christian view of the nature of man, it brought into a place of prominence the conception of the value of the individual person as well as that of equality. This, to be sure, was not a simple matter, in the sense that modern democracy has asserted the universal equality of rights that all individuals possess; yet it is no exaggeration to say that the seed of the democratic idea was embedded in Christianity. No doubt by placing the stress on the other-worldly aspect of its functions and by resorting to such sayings of its founder as "render unto Caesar that which belongs to Caesar," Christianity could easily accommodate itself to any political system; in effect the structure of the Church was strongly hierarchical, monarchical, and authoritarian rather than democratic and egalitarian; yet it is also true that for a long time it was in entering orders that lay the best possibility for the individual to overcome the handicap of unfavorable social conditions.

The Medieval Contribution

What has been said so far has stressed that the European world is Greek, Roman, and Christian, and that these are the common qualities, integrated and fused with each other, that distinguish it from others. It will be noted that these are all traits which derive from antiquity. The millennium usually known as the medieval period and which some prefer to call the Dark Ages, in many respects doubtlessly was, at least in the context of the present discussion and despite such accomplishments as the Gothic cathedrals and the appearance in it of certain outstanding intellects. Certainly there was a long period of decline, more marked in the Latin than in the Greek section of the Roman world, before the slow and painful reconstruction could be initiated. The Barbarians who overran the Roman structure did not on the whole contribute any elements of comparable importance and depth to those derived from antiquity; the feudal system can hardly be called such a contribution and, for that matter, the roots of feudalism are no less Roman than Germanic. The Germanic invaders became Christian, for one thing, and they were duly awed by the splendor and might of the Rome they had conquered and of which they even sought to pose as heirs.

Nevertheless, if, broadly speaking, no new elements of comparable significance to those of ancient derivation were brought into the European world, that world did not remain unchanged during a thousand years, and some things must be noted that occurred in the course of that period.

Perhaps the first and most fundamental of these is the final taking shape of Europe as we have come to think of that part of the planet as a geographical and political entity possessed of a certain cohesion. In one respect the whole medieval period may be characterized as the age of invasions or of peoples' migrations. It opens with the influx of the Germanic peoples, Goths, Burgundians, Lombards, Franks, and others, and closes with the coming of the Asiatic Turks. Some of these peoples settled in permanent abodes, others, like the Huns and the later Mongols, merely came as raiders and went. The most significant fact about those who remained is that, although they destroyed much, they were eventually absorbed and integrated. Their conversion to Christianity was the clearest manifestation of this absorption; the consequence of that conversion was that the domain of the influences originating in antiquity, Greek, Roman, and Christian, was extended considerably beyond that over which the rule of Rome had held sway. Beyond the Danube and the Rhine, into present-day central, northern, and eastern Europe, the same culture was spread. The process was long and full of vicissitudes, but the intensified division along the lines of Greekdom and of Latinity, the separation between the churches of Rome and Byzantium, another aspect of the same cleavage, and the consequent extension of Christianity in two different forms, all these may, from the present stand-point, be regarded as relatively secondary differences; whether in the Eastern, Greek Orthodox, or in the Western, Roman, form it was Christianity that spread. Thus Europe was expanded to her present boundaries *in Europe*.

But simultaneously there was a shrinking of the regions under former Roman control. Six centuries after the coming of Christ, out of the same Near East, which seems to be fertile ground for the growth of religion, another prophet came. The spread of the Mohammedan faith was far more rapid and sensational than that of the Christian, from which it differed also by being in part military conquest. Within less than a century of the Hegira (622) the Arabs crossed the straits named after them at Gibraltar (711), thereafter to raid deep across Spain into France, where the first great Islamic offensive was checked by Charlemagne's grandfather. For centuries the Arabs maintained themselves in the Iberian peninsula, the story of which during that time can nevertheless be summed up as that of their gradual eviction. As a consequence, while the Arab occupation has left important traces in Spain, that country and Portugal have essentially remained Western and Christian.

But it was otherwise along the southern shore of the Mediterranean which became and has since remained part of the Arab Muslim world. Especially in view of the difference in religions and of the divergent roles that Islam and Christianity have assumed in the ordering of society and the state, the coming of Islam had the effect of splitting the Mediterranean world, the European portion of which was definitely severed from the Asiatic and African. The fact that in its earlier period Arab civilization was higher than that of the West, a situation subsequently reversed in the more recent period, has served if anything to confirm the separation.

The Eastern, Byzantine, or Greek Empire was also more civilized than Western Europe when Islam first appeared upon the scene. It, too, maintained itself against Arab onslaughts, and even contrived to retain a portion of Asia Minor. That was not finally lost until the coming of the second great Islamic offensive. The date 1453, when Constantinople finally fell to the Ottoman Turks, used to be taken as that of the formal closing of the Middle Ages, in the manner that the year 476 is taken as their opening. The Turks had for some time before the fall of Constantinople already established themselves in the Balkans, and after their capture they launched a powerful drive into the heart of Europe. But Vienna in 1526, like Poitiers in 732, marked the high point of their success. It is not one of the less interesting "ifs" of history to speculate on what the shape of things might have been had Europe fallen to Islam; as it was, Christian Europe successfully resisted, free to pursue her independent course, the fact of her successful resistance to Islam itself becoming a contribution to her awareness of unity, on a religious basis be it noted.

Just as the Arabs long maintained themselves in the Iberian peninsula, so likewise the Ottoman Turks for some centuries kept control of an appreciable portion of Europe, roughly the Balkan peninsula. That story, through alternating ups and downs—the Turks were at the gates of Vienna again in 1683—like that of the Arabs, in the long perspective of time, may be summed up as one of steady recession until they were completely evicted from Europe, save for Istanbul and the Straits that they hold to this day. Also, as in the case of Spain, even the region where they remained established for a substantial period of time retained its Christian religion save for some isolated pockets, as in Albania or Bosnia, where some relatively small islands of Muslim population took root and persist to our day.

What may then be regarded as the closing of the age of invasions, the beginning of the modern period, finds Europe having taken the geographical shape that is now usually associated with her name. The coming of Islam had had the consequence, of great importance indeed, of effecting a severance between Europe and the African and Asiatic sections which in more ancient times had been intimately associated with her, but otherwise Islam had not contributed important elements to the shape of European culture or civilization.[2] Without wishing to minimize the impact of Islamic conquest in Spain and in the Balkans, or the role of the Arabs in transmitting to Europe Aristotle and much ancient Greek lore, there is no denying that this impact was not in the same category of importance as that of the above-mentioned Greek, Roman, and Christian components of that same European culture.

Since human material is in the last analysis the basic stuff of history and since as the result of the closing of the age of invasions the distribution and the composition of that human material has remained essentially unaltered in Europe, it is worth stopping to look for a moment at the nomenclature of the peoples of Europe at the opening of the modern age. This is especially important in view of a much later development, for the concept of the nation-state, one which was eventually to play a role of overwhelming importance in the affairs of European man and a concept essentially alien to the ancient and to the medieval worlds, has its roots in the diversity of ethnic groups. In the stability of these diverse members of the European family of peoples lies the root of much future development; the particular shape that this development was destined to take may not have been inevitable, but it is hard to see how it could have occurred without this stability. And here, in passing, is to be found one of the principal keys to the difference between contrasting aspects of the European and the American course of events. It lies in this: the various ethnic groups of Europe have been compact entities attached

[2] This statement, in the large sense and taking Europe as a whole, is justified for all that may be adduced about the Arab impact in such places as Sicily and Spain. The Arab role in transferring knowledge of ancient Greek lore was also important, but it was after all a transference of things not Arab, but Greek.

to definable territories; the members of these same groups, once they became transplanted in America, have moved with great freedom, have mixed and have found it expedient to adopt the English language, instead of preserving their own, as the inevitable means of communication. Thus with considerable ease diverse European strains have fused into American unity, while retaining in Europe their separate identities.

But to return to Europeans in Europe. Despite some interesting, but also largely fanciful, ideas, mainly of European origin, on the subject of race, that hornets' nest of loose argument, that bog of unverifiable confusion, will be completely avoided in this discussion. Nor is there cause to pay it any heed for we need do no more than deal with the observable and clear reality that ethnic difference is, and in order to make things even sharper and simpler we shall content ourselves with the linguistic criterion of difference. It is not a perfect test of distinction, and there are exceptions to it, but they are not of such magnitude or significance as to affect substantially the validity of the larger classification. We are dealing primarily with a cultural phenomenon.

The overwhelming bulk of Europeans falls into three main language groups, Latin, Teutonic, and Slavic, and the separation between them has on the whole considerable sharpness. The line of demarcation between French- and German-speaking, that between Italian- and either German- or Slav-speaking, and that between German and, say, Polish or Czech would leave only a fairly narrow zone where argument could be honestly pursued. Even if it is pointed out that some Poles have become authentically Germanized, that the prevailing Germanic dialect of Alsace has not prevented Alsatian allegiance from becoming French in the main, that some Croats have been Italianized—here, incidentally, is the source of many petty modern disputes—the emphasis on the whole is on fixity, stability, and clarity of separation. The three main groups fall into further subdivisions, among which the lines of demarcation, because of closer affinity, tend to be somewhat less clear; this is especially the case in the Slavic domain, partly because of the closeness of the Slavic languages to each other and partly because the political independence of some of the Slavs has been more recent. The divisions of Europe to which we are referring are best perceived by a glance at the Europe that resulted from the First World War, for that conflict marked the sharpest success of the principle of self-determination in that continent. We see the Latin peoples in the Southwest—Portuguese, Spanish, French, and Italians, to which isolated Rumanians are usually added. Almost half of Belgium is French-speaking, and so is a section of Switzerland, the rest of which, like that of Belgium, belongs to the Germanic group. That group, in the north center, is mainly constituted by Germany, with Holland, Austria and the Scandinavian countries as well. Britain is a somewhat special case, the English language being a compound of Germanic and Latin, increasingly Latinized with the passage of time, but on the whole still better included in the Germanic group. The rest is nearly all Slavic—Russian, Polish, Czech, Slovak, and South Slavic. There is no need to go into such finer points as the degree of similarity, or the basis of separateness of Ukrainian, for example.

There are some exceptions, but they are small; hence they do not invalidate the larger scheme of classification. Hungarians could not now be called anything but European, but, like their language, represent a survival of earlier Asiatic incursions. There are scattered Celts on the Atlantic fringe of France and of the British Isles; neither do Basque and Finnish belong in the larger divisions. All these languages and peoples, large and small, have been in their present locations for a long time; as pointed out before the ethnic distribution of Europeans has undergone no significant change for some centuries.

But also, to repeat, the fact of ethnic diversity had little meaning, political meaning at least, until quite recently. For even though the unity that Rome had represented was in effect destroyed by her invaders, these invaders, full of admiration for Rome, had no such conscious purpose of destruction. Indeed, had Rome not suffered an internal collapse as well, it is wholly conceivable that she might have assimilated the Barbarians, as she had for that matter been doing for a long time before she fell.

Although this did not happen, the ideal of unity as constituting the proper ordering of society was accepted by the invaders, with the consequence that they strove to resuscitate the Empire. It was a Frankish ruler, Charles the Great, who formally assumed the imperial dignity in the year 800. Apart from the fact that the substantial domain which he ruled was but a portion of the Empire of Rome,[3] the real bases of unity, administration, towns, and a substantial flow of commercial exchanges, had been too thoroughly destroyed. Charlemagne's empire, like the Carolingian revival, was a short-lived phenomenon that soon gave way to continued disintegration; the day of the invasions for that matter was not finished, as the coming of the Normans proved. An attempt similar to Charlemagne's, that of Otto I, in 962, a Saxon this time, had little more effective results. Yet the Holy Roman Empire lived on at least as a title, but the rest of its name "of the German nation," was in itself recognition of the limita-

[3] Actually, there was greater continuity in the eastern section of the Empire. Byzantium, the second Rome, survived the first in independence, and, in many respects, at a higher level of culture, for another millennium. But the subsequent course of European development makes the record of the West of greater significance, especially from the standpoint of this essay.

tions of its scope. It may be said in retrospect that the inner inconsistency that lay in the effective identification of the Empire with the Germanic people on the one hand, together with the continued assertion of a universal claim on the other, producing in effect little more than a German immixture in Italian affairs, is one of the main reasons that delayed the evolution of the Central European area along the same paths as those of the European West. It remains none the less of the deepest significance that the title of Holy Roman Emperor, however much divorced from reality, should have survived; it is telling expression of the depth of the roots that the Roman legacy of unity had struck. Despite the validity of Voltaire's quip that the institution was possessed of none of the attributes that the three words in its name represented, it is of interest to note that the title was not formally abolished until 1806. And even that was done by one who had just assumed the imperial dignity two years earlier and, as we shall presently see, himself, in his own way, subsequently attempted to create unity in Europe. Also Kaiser and tsar are but variants of Caesar, and Moscow has called itself the third Rome, claiming kinship from Byzantium, the second Rome after the first had fallen. The ideal of unity would not die, however much denied in practice.

Some of the consequences of the attempt to revive the Roman Imperial ideal, if not its effective reality, are of interest. When Charlemagne became emperor the ceremony of his coronation took place appropriately in Rome. The Pope was the chief officiator in that ceremony, a fact of considerable significance. The emperor of Rome had been Pontifex Maximus, but one of the fundamental characteristics of the new religion had been to divorce God from Caesar and to assert the supremacy of mind (the spiritual or the soul) over matter (the world, *saeculo*). Out of this separation there grew, not surprisingly, a conflict between church and state. The story of the relations between emperor and Pope is a long and tortuous one the details of which do not belong in this treatment. In so far as a claim to universality could be advanced, the Pope's had sounder standing, for, in the face of political disintegration, his office did in a large sense more authentically embody the legacy of Rome than the limited territorial control of the emperor. That the Pope did in fact become the ruler of a specific section of Italian territory has only secondary significance, save in the limited domain of nineteenth-century Italian history; but for a time he asserted, and for a moment made good, the right to make and unmake kings. However, in the final reckoning, the civil power was successful in establishing its independence, with the highly important consequence that separation of the two spheres of jurisdiction became increasingly marked. Clearly, the domains in which state and church operate cannot be so sharply demarcated; they inevitably have zones of contact, and conflict has continued in the domain of their overlapping jurisdictions, but the European state was destined to become essentially secular. Secularization should perhaps be regarded as a common characteristic of the European scene, one of equal importance to those derived from antiquity, which sets Europe in sharp contrast with the condition of neighboring Islam, for example. Whether one holds the view that the church is of God and the state of the devil, or the contrasting one that the successful assertion by the state of independence from the church and of supremacy within its own domain is the factor that has mainly released the springs of Western progress, the fact is that secularization has been one of the main characteristics of the evolution of the Western state.

Before giving some consideration to what happened to the elements that make for European unity during the centuries that more immediately precede our own—the so-called modern period—one more thing must be said that is essential both to the understanding of subsequent developments and to the definition of what, or rather where, Europe precisely is.

Two Special Cases, England and Russia

England had known Roman rule, but when external pressures became too intense, it was, not surprisingly, from that most outlying outpost that the Roman control was first withdrawn. Out of the subsequent vicissitudes that constitute the history of the British Isles, one is of prime significance for our purpose. Having come, like others, as raiders, the Normans established themselves in Gaul. They were successfully assimilated, and the Norman conquest of England at the end of the eleventh century was another continental invasion, essentially French in this case. This event had the effect of establishing an intimate connection between England and France. England eventually did not become a fief of the French crown, but instead the holder of the English crown could claim a very large section of France; could even put forward a claim to the very crown of that country. There ensued, quite naturally, protracted disputation and much warfare. There is a measure of similarity between the records of Italo-German and Anglo-French embroilments. But there is also a great difference, for the climax of the Anglo-French struggle was the Hundred Years War, the fundamental significance of which was the failure of the English attempt to secure a continental establishment. Here one finds another of history's fascinating "might have beens" had things gone otherwise. In any event the outcome was early to emphasize the consciousness of Frenchness in France—witness that astonishing episode of which Joan of Arc was the center— as well as to assist the distinct consciousness of the Englishness of England. The French Normans, a ruling aristocracy but never large in numbers, became English, and French became displaced as the language of the court although picturesque remnants of it survive in England. By the fourteenth century Britain was not a powerful state; she was rather an island, containing two separate kingdoms, which had no cause to play a major role in European affairs.

That condition was destined to change, but not for a long time, and the result was that England—or Britain—could develop in a state of isolation and separateness that has been unique among Western nations. The fact that England was invaded for the last time in 1066 is the clearest manifestation of this distinctness of historical experience; no European state has enjoyed such immunity, and one must go to Far Eastern Japan for the nearest resemblance. The importance of this special condition cannot be given too much stress. The consequence of a geographical accident in the last analysis is the most important single element that has made for the uniqueness of Britain, a fact which had sunk deep into the consciousness of the British people, and the consequences of which have been, and are, enormous, as we shall see. Surely the British people are Western and European, certainly in contrast to Asiatic, or African, but how European they are is not an unfair question.

Moreover, once England had definitely abandoned the possibility of territorial possession on the Continent—Calais, her last foothold, was not surrendered until 1556—she was free to concentrate her energies on overseas and imperial expansion. This activity she pursued with eminent success, until the Empire and, later, the Commonwealth came to have for her a significance that they had in no other case, thus emphasizing more than ever the separate character of England and of her history. The nineteenth-century phrase "splendid isolation" is misleading if one takes it to mean a lack of British interest and participation in the affairs of other European states; Britain ever watched these with close attention, but it does correspond to the reality of a position that no other country could enjoy. Where the Continent was concerned England's wars could be fought by others whom British wealth would subsidize, and only in extreme cases would British military power be thrown into the scales. Britain's power came to be sea power and the extent of her imperial interests and commitments naturally gave to these even greater importance in her eyes than the international politics of the Continent.

But this is in a sense anticipating our story; for all that even Shakespeare already gave voice to the consciousness of the peculiar quality of the people of the "precious stone set in the silver sea." The moral of it all, to repeat, is that the position of Britain is unique, and this uniqueness was, if anything, destined to increase during the more recent centuries, to the extent that the British themselves have questioned the degree of their Europeanness.

Some of this same quality of distinctness, although for wholly different reasons, belongs to the easternmost section of Europe, the Russian land. Russia was Christian like the rest, having been Christianized from Byzantium of which she eventually claimed to be the heir. But Russia fell and long remained under the rule of Asiatic peoples; only at the beginning of the modern period, and in a small way at that, did the Muscovite principality rid itself of that yoke and that influence, thereafter to embark on a virtually uninterrupted process of expansion which was eventually to make Russia by far the largest state in the world.

Also, the nature of the Russian land is different from most other European countries. Where smallness, a long, indented coast line, numerous harbors, proximity to the sea in all cases, and mountain ranges, are characteristic of the Asiatic penin-

sula that is Europe, Russia in contrast is the great heartland of
unbroken continuity, a distinction that lies at the root of the
contrast between the dimensions of Russia and those of other
European states. The Byzantine origin of her Christianity, the
long subjection to Asiatic influence thus have combined with
the facts of geography to set Russia apart. This distinction has
expressed itself in the long-standing issue, central to the
Russian historic development, of whether to adopt or to reject
the ways of the West, an issue which may be said not to have
finally and irrevocably been resolved until the Russian Revolution of our time—if then, some would say.

Thus we come to a point when Europe may be defined
in geographical terms as well as in cultural. In a narrow sense,
Europe is the area between the Atlantic and, say, a line running from Odessa to Riga. Britain to the West and Russia to
the East are parts of Europe also, but they are borderlands to
which pertain special characteristics. Finally, it might be
pointed out that as the modern period of the European story
opens, neither England nor Russia were states possessed of
any great power; they were not at the time, and for some time
to come, until their power had sufficiently grown, would not
be in a position to have a very great impact on the course and
shape of things European.

II. The Unity of Europe in the Early Modern Age

It has been pointed out before that the chronological division between the medieval and the modern periods of
European history is artificial. The increase of our knowledge
that the work of scholars provides tends to blur the line even
more and perhaps the Renaissance should be called the transition from the one to the other. Italy was the first home of
the Renaissance, where great emphasis was placed on artistic

accomplishment and whence uncouth northern Barbarians were introduced to greater amenities. There was no begrudging by others of this Italian primacy but rather willing and admiring recognition of it; and the case of the "annexation" of Leonardo by French Francis I well illustrates the point, for Leonardo was no part of war booty but an honored and well-furnished guest. But in the present context a more significant aspect of the period than the artistic is what may be put under the humanistic label. In the rediscovery of the ancients Italy led others, though the figure of Erasmus of Rotterdam is no less prominent than that of earlier Petrarch. What is of interest in this is that it was a European phenomenon. The revived interest in the ancients had the effect of confirming the Greek and Roman strands that have been pointed to as fundamental components of the joint heritage of the culture of Europe, a factor therefore that would tend to stress the unity of that continent. It was in Italy as well, more than in any other land, that the beginnings of modern science must be placed, and that activity, too, is one to which the stress on national boundaries is alien.

However, this same period witnessed the emergence of contradictory trends from the standpoint of unity or division. For this was also the time during which the vernaculars began to come into their own. Here, too, Italy led in time. Dante's *Divine Comedy* is still the great monument of the Italian tongue derived from the local usage of Florence as a consequence of the impact of that work, and Petrarch has remained better known for his sonnets to Laura than for his imitative Ciceronean efforts. Somewhat later, Montaigne and Rabelais wrote in French, Cervantes used Spanish, Luther translated the Bible into German, and Shakespeare, of course, wrote in English. Latin was still the common possession of the educated—it was, incidentally, the antiquity-admiring humanists who did much toward making it a dead language

—but from this time on the vernaculars increasingly displaced Latin as the means of written communication. The importance of the diversity of language in creating consciousness of diversity will not be emphasized again.

The Divisive Effect of the Reformation

The fact has just been mentioned that Luther translated the Bible into German, a work destined to become one of the early monuments of the German language. But thereby hangs as well another and a very different tale. A common allegiance to Rome was one of the strongest bonds that held together those Europeans whose allegiance was not to the Eastern or Greek Orthodox Church, but now that bond was to be broken. That part of Europe destined to become Protestant remained Christian indeed, but by its very nature Protestantism could hardly fail to develop, as in fact it has, along the path of increasing fragmentation. Luther, as much as any one individual, may be given credit for initiating the revolt against Rome and may also be fairly charged with having been less consistent than earnest, a situation out of which flowed the ironical consequence that the Protestant revolt achieved in some respects the opposite of its original intention. Luther was not a modern man, but rather medieval in outlook and spirit; his primary concern was to restore the institution of which he was a member to its purity and original purpose, from which he felt that it had deviated. But Luther was a dedicated man, and once he had taken the step of asserting the individual right to interpret Holy Writ against the monopolistic claim of the Church in this domain, he could hardly do other than found his own church in rivalry to Rome. However, having made this claim for himself, he balked before the logic of his own position and denied others the validity of his own criterion when it led to conclusions different from those he himself had reached.

The Protestant Revolt thus introduced an age of intolerance, the expression of which was the Wars of Religion. Yet again, though by indirection, the Reformation may also be credited with having powerfully assisted the eventual success of the opposite tendency. For, in actual practice, what else could be done but accept the condition of "live and let live" once it had been established that the common and logical dedication of all to the destruction of error had regrettably foundered in a stalemate of balanced forces? The practice, once installed, could eventually be exalted until it achieved the dignified status that tolerance was finally to gain. There is no denying that the religious strife eventually did much to implant acceptance of the view that religious belief should be a matter for the private conscience to decide rather than for the state to enforce. This attitude greatly helped to strengthen the trend toward secularism in Europe, but it took a long time for this to happen, and before it did the first effect was the opposite one of wedding more closely the church and the state. But as there was no Protestant Pope the effect was also to stress in those states where the Reformation became implanted the subordination of the church to the state.

This points to another aspect of the matter. The fanatical vigor of religious controversy that, in the last resort, leads to the recourse to physical force is alien to our time. Though it would be quite wrong to deny the authentic religious content of the religious wars, even in the earlier period of the Reformation, political, economic, and social matters became inextricably tangled with the more purely spiritual issues. It is doubtful whether Luther himself might not have met the fate of earlier reformers and heretics if he had not had, at one point, the support and protection of the Saxon Elector. Increasingly with the passage of time the share of politics in the Wars of

Religion became larger. By the time a cardinal of the Church of Rome, chief minister of His Most Catholic Majesty of France, fought in alliance with the great Swedish defender of the Lutheran cause and the Protestant princes of the Empire against the Catholic Holy Roman Emperor, one may well question the religious content of the struggle. That is why the Thirty Years War is generally considered the last of the wars of religion.

The Peace of Westphalia, signed in 1648, put an end to that conflict. By this time it was possible to make an assessment of what the impact of the Reformation on the community of Europe had been. In quite a few respects Renaissance and Reformation are antithetic in spirit, certainly in their divergent stresses on the world of the here and now in the case of the former, on that of the hereafter in the latter. Yet they have also points of convergence. Both, in a sense, were backward-looking movements; pagan antiquity for the one filled the same place as the early Christianity of Paul and Augustine did for the other. Both, in the end, asserted the supremacy of the individual and in that sense confirmed and strengthened an ancient strand of essentially Greek derivation. It was the triumph of that tendency, common to all Europe in varying degrees, that set the European peoples on their common modern path.

An enlightening case is that of Copernicus, who is properly credited with initiating the revolution in astronomy which implanted the modern scientific view of the cosmos. Copernicus, like his contemporary Luther, belonged to the Catholic establishment. His interest, however, was not along lines of religious controversy, and his fame came from his astronomical accomplishments. He, too, as was befitting his time, went to the ancients, and in their writings found the seed that led to his questioning of the prevalently accepted system of Hellenistic Alexandrian Ptolemy. Copernicus did not run afoul of the

Church; his astronomical theories were set down in a work
published in 1543, the year in which he died, and dedicated
to the Pope himself. But Copernicus had initiated a development, truly a case of international scientific co-operation, and
it was not until nearly a century later that Italian Galileo
had to stand trial before the Inquisition for his views on
astronomy. The fact that Galileo recanted, though he remained unconvinced, is of historic interest, but it had no effect
on the development of astronomical science. The particular
work initiated by Copernicus found its culmination in that of
an Englishman, Newton, born in 1642, the very year that
Galileo died. The Newtonian World Machine is, as much as
any one single example, the perfect illustration of what can be
achieved by the application of the unfettered rational faculty.
Coming at the time that it did, still early in the days of modern
science, it had a tremendous impact and was a show piece
in eighteenth-century religious discussions, but Newton, operating in the more flexible Protestant climate, was not involved in these. Newton in fact was a religious man who
spent quite as much time commenting on the Bible as on his
world machine.

The case of astronomy is but one illustration, though in
many respects the neatest, which is the reason why it has
been chosen to point out the change that had taken place
in the course of two centuries and also shows very well that
if the Age of Reason was very different from the Middle
Ages it was a continuation, a renewal, of certain trends deep
rooted in the common cultural inheritance of all Europe.

The political content of sixteenth-century religious change
has been mentioned. The economic aspect of things has also
been much discussed, and the emphasis that has been given
to the significance of the ethos of Calvinism in particular is
well-known; the reader may be referred to such works as
Professor R. H. Tawney's *Religion and the Rise of Capitalism.*

Without entering the controversial domain of the connection between economics, politics, and religion, the simultaneity of changes in these various domains is not open to question; it is a simple fact that the sixteenth century was the time of the Reformation, as well as that in which Europe broke out of her confines, away from her Mediterranean connections, and set out to discover the world. In the sixteenth century may also be situated the beginnings of modern science, though that development is somewhat less amenable to precise location in time; and finally it is the time when the national monarchies took shape and root as initial models of the modern state.

The Sovereign State

This last development merits special attention, for it was destined to have the greatest effect on the issue of the unity of Europe, or rather the disunity that has become so familiar an aspect of her historical landscape. Perhaps the ultimate source of this occurrence resides in technical and economic change. However that may be, the final severance of England from the Continent and the successful termination of the long Spanish crusade that evicted the Moors from that country in the same year that the New World was brought to the attention of the Old by Columbus also had some important effects. Nor should one disregard dynastic connections, a matter of great moment in those days. It was the combination of these things, superimposed upon the deeper reality of the existence of distinct peoples, that made possible the emergence of the Atlantic Monarchies, of which Spain, France, and England are the first and outstanding examples. But there again the role of the accidental should be allowed its place; the union of Ferdinand and Isabella had much to do with the ultimate unity of Spain, and one must delve into the

detailed work of successive French kings to understand how
France became one instead of at least two separate states.

Central European conditions were inimical to this centralizing type of evolution. There was in that region a German
as well as an Italian people. The role of the previously mentioned universalistic Imperial institution must be borne in
mind, to which may be added the fact of religious disunity:
the Germanic world became divided, half Catholic, half Protestant. The Protestant Revolt made little dent on Italy, but,
apart from the intrusion of the imperial connection, it is
perhaps precisely because of the greater wealth and cultural
advancement of the Italian world that the individuality of its
units persisted. How could proud Venice, for instance, the
great naval power of her time, as much imperial as Italian,
renounce her separate entity? The fact is that some centuries
were to pass before the world of Central Europe was to
follow the model of the Atlantic Monarchies. The common
and fundamental characteristic of the story of these states is
the triumph of the central power over the centrifugal forces
of feudal lords and provincialism, thereafter to produce
steadily increasing uniformity and integration.

This then was the large role that was played by adventitious
dynastic connections. The Imperial dignity, unlike the royal,
was elective, but it had, in effect, become a virtual appanage
of the House of Habsburg. The election of 1519 that made
Charles V emperor confirmed this tradition; the prospects
of his rivals, Francis I of France for one, were never very
serious. However, it so happened that the new emperor, as a
consequence of previous marital arrangements, also fell heir
to much that lay outside the strictly imperial domain. Spain
was his, with which went much of the newly discovered world,
as well as the European Netherlands or Burgundy, not to
mention smaller units. Even without his overseas possessions,
his European domain was enormous, raising the question of

the possibility of bringing the totality of Europe under one single control and truly realizing the universal claim of the Empire.

Much of Charles' reign was spent in war, caused in part by the resistance of those who would not lose their separate independent existence. The chief center of this opposition was France, where too much power and too much consciousness of difference existed, and the ultimate outcome was the failure to unite Europe under Charles V. The story is long and involved; France was hard-pressed and for that reason formed an alliance with the infidel Turk, who, on his side, represented another possibility of European union—under Islam. The very fact that the Habsburgs saved Europe from that possible form of unity contributed, through a diversion of their forces, to the failure of their own attempt. For that matter, much of the power that Charles V could muster had to be expended in controlling his Germanic domain, for that was where he had to meet Luther's challenge and the more concrete one of the Protestant princes, whom the French king also helped. This is no place to go into the detail of these struggles, which illustrate the extent to which diversity had taken root in Europe, while showing, at the same time, the degree of the survival of the idea of unity.

The fact and the extent of this diversity were given further confirmation by what Charles himself did shortly before his death. The imperial dignity went to his brother Ferdinand, together with the direct Habsburg inheritance; Spain and the Netherlands went to his son, Philip, a Spaniard, at least by early association and upbringing unlike his Netherlandish father. If there was adequate common ground for fusion at the level of the mass of the people in England, in France, or in Spain proper, the difference between the Spanish world and the Germanic was too great for a similar integration to succeed.

This same consideration applied to the personal union of Spain with the Netherlands, one half of which, the Dutch, aided in its resistance by the successful intrusion of the Calvinist doctrine into it, contrived to make good its severance from the Spanish association. Yet, even without the Empire, Philip's domain and his resources were still great, and his ambition may be seen as another attempt to create unity in Europe. Philip, too, was involved in much foreign strife; his diplomacy was very active, and his intrigues, political, religious, and marital, in England and in France are well known. They brought him mainly grief, and among English-speaking peoples the episode of the Armada has received much attention. It is well to retain a sense of proportion and to realize that at the end of the sixteenth century England was not a very great power and that she did not succeed in breaking the power of Spain. Yet it is in a sense all the more significant that little England, assisted by the elements and by other circumstances as she may have been, did manage to inflict a major setback on the great power that was Spain. The lesson was the same as it had been fifty years earlier: the diversity of Europe was asserting itself with success.

If the decline of Spain may not be credited in overwhelming measure to England, decline nevertheless there was, to the extent that the "Spanish century" came to a close and the primacy of power in Europe shifted from that country to France, a transition that took place in the first half of the seventeenth century. The second half of the sixteenth had been a sorry time for France, torn as the Holy Roman Empire had been by Wars of Religion. Once these were essentially settled with the accession to the throne of Henry of Navarre, recovery was rapid, as it should have been. For the French land is favored and its native resources considerable, rather greater than those of either England or Spain. So that, granted good management, France can easily prosper and be a center of considerable power. The phenomenon has recurred more than once, as we shall see.

Henry IV governed France well, but it would take some time before France could assert primacy in Europe, let alone entertain thoughts of leading her to, or forcing upon her, unity. Henry IV had no such plans, but his Grand Design warrants at least passing mention. The plan, more the Duke of Sully's than his own, was one for the reorganization of Europe on what might be described as a fair balance, and therefore one that might endure in peace. Freed of internecine quarrels, Europe could devote her strength to defense against such common danger as the Turk still represented. The scheme has been presented as a device behind which French aggrandizement could proceed; but it was hardly that, although the House of Habsburg would be diminished, for Henry's aims in foreign policy were very limited indeed. The plan does not in fact deserve too much attention, though it serves as an indication of the significance that the common Christianity of Europe, Catholic or Protestant, held at this time.

It was four years after the death of Henry IV, at a time when it seemed that his work of reconstruction of the French state was threatened, that the French Estates were called to meet. They accomplished little, went home, and were not to be summoned again for the better part of two centuries. An institution which, even though never formally abolished, is not called into operation for 175 years, may in human terms be considered defunct. Hereby hangs an important tale. How the French kings managed to govern without recourse to the Estates is an important part of the story of France during two centuries. The point is that they succeeded and that, as is often the case in matters governmental and social, theory followed practice to which it gave its own added sanction of abstract foundation and standing. This is the age of absolute monarchy, enshrined in divine right. What gives French affairs special significance is that this development took place in France concurrently with the rise of French power to a position of European primacy; which of the two was cause and which effect need not matter here. France is but one among European states, and her own govermental arrangements during this period may be regarded as a pattern or a model, and certainly her success and her power lent added luster to the practice and the theory. Louis XIV's *L'Etat, c'est moi* is the tersest expression of this state of affairs.

If the state is the God-given possession of the monarch whose will and pleasure are the basis of law, it is evident that such a condition is easily conducive to sharp, unregulated competition highly inimical to international order. Louis would brook no higher authority than his own, and, quite logically, in Catholic France, if he was responsible for the attempt to enforce uniformity in religion that was the Revocation of the Edict of Nantes, he also quarreled with the Pope; Catholic as he was, he sought to strengthen his control of the Church—his Church—in his domain and extracted from subservient bishops the Declaration of Gallican Liberties.

Because of his own character and because of the resources and power that were at his command, Louis XIV was the most perfect embodiment of the absolute doctrine and practice. Not surprisingly, his foreign policy was one of aggressive expansion that led to a number of conflicts, and it has even been presented as an attempt to bring all Europe under French domination, another attempt, if one will, to create unity in Europe. But this is an exaggerated view, for his ambition, if great, was not so far reaching, and the achievement of a natural boundary—the Rhine—for his domain is a fairer measure of his limited aims, among which a position of primacy for France in Europe may be fairly included.

He did not succeed in achieving even this limited aim. Mention may be made at this point of an event that coincides with the very beginning of his long rule; it is one of the major landmarks in the story of what, at this point, may better be described as the fragmentation of Europe or the successful assertion of diversity at the expense of those elements that furnished common ground.

Louis XIV formally became king, although a child of five, in 1643. This was precisely the time when the success of French arms was shifting the superiority that had been acknowledged to Spanish power to that country's northern neighbor; when Richelieu's patient work was about to bear fruit. That fruit was to become apparent in the result of the long negotiations, begun in that same year, to bring to a close the Thirty Years War. The last and longest phase of that war is known in the history books as the French phase; and rightly so, for the initial issues that had arisen in Bohemia had long been superseded by the dynastic contest between Bourbon and Habsburg. The latter were on the whole the losers, a fact most evident in the essential voiding of content of the Imperial title. It was the Peace of Westphalia that gave the princes of the Empire that clearest appanage of sovereignty, the control of their own foreign policy. And the fact that the French king, like the Swedish, through the acquisition of imperial territory, obtained a voice in the affairs of the Empire, is a measure of the low estate to which that institution had fallen. Although it continued to exist, it was more like a wraith, a shadow, and a memory of former claims or hopes. Thereafter France was conveniently placed to have a hand in Germanic affairs, and the Austrian Habsburg mattered only because he still possessed substantial resources of his own, and not at all because he continued to be the bearer of an empty title. It was the settlement of Westphalia that justified Voltaire's later quip.

The Peace of Westphalia is usually spoken of as the event that marks the birth of the European state system. This is a fair description even though the condition that is labeled the European state system clearly was the result of a long evolution. The system has endured to our day and influenced much of the world besides Europe. Of its demise in the twentieth century and of the consequences of that demise much will have to be said in the later sections of this essay, but, in view of the duration of the system, its nature and the operation of it through the better part of three centuries must also receive some attention.

The Peace of Westphalia may be said to have registered the final failure of the unitary tendency in Europe. For, if Westphalia registered a French success and a corresponding Habsburg setback, it did not substitute one hegemony for another, but established instead an equilibrium of forces. What is more, this condition of equilibrium came to be recognized and accepted until it was enshrined as the desirable principle which was the strongest guarantee of the liberties of Europe, liberty meaning the equal right of all to separate existence. The attribute of sovereignty is the sharpest expression of this state of affairs, for the sovereign, sanctioned by divine right, clearly may not be lawfully deposed.

Here it may seem that an inconsistency is involved, as indeed in strict logic it is. By the very essence of sovereignty, the sovereign cannot be subject to law; his acknowledgment of a higher authority than his own would be tantamount to divesting himself of the attribute of sovereignty. Strictly speaking, our twentieth-century attempts to organize collections of sovereigns subject to some rule of law is in the last resort a contradiction of terms, and we shall observe the consequences of this dilemma. Theoretically, a collectivity of sovereigns can therefore only exist in a condition of anarchy.

But there is another aspect of the matter. The sovereign

must by definition be free to make whatever use he wishes of whatever power is his. Now, clearly, power is very unevenly distributed so that it appears that nothing exists to prevent the destruction of the weaker by the stronger. This is the law of the jungle, but it is law of the natural, rather than of the legal, kind and it is not exclusive of the law of the balance of nature. But there is, in addition, an automatic regulatory device which will lead several of the weaker to combine against the common threat that a stronger represents to all. This is known as the balance of power, out of which can easily grow an extension of the claim of the attribute of sovereignty to the acknowledgment by all of the right of all to exist. We are thus led to a condition where the collectivity of European sovereigns came to accept this principle as a desirable one, with the result that the logical consequence of anarchy that flows from the sovereign principle did not prevent the European community from functioning and thriving in relatively stable multiplicity. This is the great regulatory principle that Westphalia enshrined: it sanctioned diversity while registering the common ground of principle, the tolerance in the political domain, if one will, into which the stalemate of religious intolerance had developed.

To return to Louis XIV and seventeenth-century France: this is why his aggressive endeavors, on the one hand, failed while, on the other, they did not have the universalistic hegemonic aspect that could more easily derive from Charles V's imperial position. The operation of this state of affairs is clearly evidenced in the wars of the turn of the century. The League of Augsburg is the perfect illustration of a coalition induced by the common threat of French expansionist aims, even if not beyond the Rhine, when the balance of power was set up as a countervailing principle against the claim to natural boundaries. The same situation applied to the War of the Spanish Succession, when the prospect of a union of the

French and the Spanish crowns raised the specter of a new version of what Charles V had attempted. The result in both cases was the same: a compromise based on an equilibrium of forces, and these outcomes went a long distance toward implanting the belief in the merits of the balance of power.

This practice, or doctrine, is sometimes thought of as a peculiarly British contribution, and undoubtedly Britain had been its stanchest upholder. Something must be said of the English role at this juncture. Early seventeenth-century England, even with Scotland added, was not a very great state, certainly not a world empire; one must guard against reading too far back into the past a condition that only came to pass in later times. As far as her domestic arrangements went, seventeenth-century England, like France, witnessed the same attempt on the part of the Crown to assert its unfettered control, and in the early part of the century the stress should rather be on similarity than on difference if one compares the mode of governance of the two countries. It is also well to remember that in the contemporary eyes of Europe it was Englishmen who were considered incapable of devising orderly modes of government, while Louis XIV's France was instead the model of order. The disturbed record of internal seventeenth-century British politics is well known; it will not be considered here, but two things are of interest in connection with it.

English rulers, still style themselves king (or queen) by the Grace of God, even to this day, when monarchs have become the exception. But unless one adheres to the nineteenth-century view that the voice of God is expressed through that of the people, what happened in England toward the end of the seventeenth century, the since enshrined Glorious Revolution, voids the "Grace of God" phrase of any real content. The British ruler was therefore in a weak position in asserting the same divine basis of legitimacy as most of his continental peers. But this had no effect on the sovereignty of England as a state, and it is noteworthy that the violent quarrels that set Englishmen against each other at home had little effect on the enhancement of English power. It is in fact during the highly unsettled seventeenth century that England grew to the dimensions of a truly major European state. Her role in the two wars that have been mentioned, that of the League of Augsburg and that of the Spanish Succession, brings out this English position very clearly. William of Orange originated in the Netherlands, and the French threat to his country gave him sufficient reason to fear and to oppose that power. He, more than any one individual, was the organizer and heart of the coalition that was the League of Augsburg. It was appropriate that he should have been called to the British throne, just as it is a measure of the growth of French power that it was shortly before his time that England shifted from a French alliance against Holland to one with Holland against France. The English role in the War of the Spanish Succession is even more significant, for England, more than any other state had a pivotal function in the conflict. Her power was on the sea while in the land war her contribution consisted primarily in financial assistance to others, Prussia for example, who fought the French armies. But as this aid proved to be insufficient this was the occasion for an early instance of a phenomenon that has recurred again, but only on relatively rare occasions and as a last resort. Britain had to make a direct contribution to the fighting on land; this she did with effectiveness, as the memory of Marlborough witnesses.

The consequence was the initiation of a condition that, having lasted to our day, was to take on the attribute of tradition. England achieved vis-à-vis the continent of Europe the arbitral position that was to remain hers for two centuries. With impartial catholicity of choice England would fight any one who threatened to establish the one condition that she considered inimical to her own interest, namely too great a focus of power on the Continent. For a long time "any one" invariably meant France, hence the fact of Anglo-French enmity could become a seemingly fixed element in the politics of Europe. It could easily graft itself onto the earlier medieval contest, and the eighteenth-century Anglo-French conflict has appropriately been dubbed the second Hundred Years War. The respectability that long duration gives to existing institutions or conditions is what has made this particular relationship so long-lived.

Thus it appears that the Balance of Power, if underwritten by all, came to be a principle of which the English felt they were the very special guardians. It should be mentioned, in addition, that the unique island position of England, in combination with the extent of her power, made the manner of her guardianship different from that of others. She tended to eschew anticipatory commitments, preferring to throw her weight in the balance, if and when necessary, on whichever side seemed desirable for the defense of her own interest. Unlike continental states, England coveted no specific segments of European land; quite understandably, the island kingdom, normally concentrating the totality of its power at sea, embarked on the path of empire-building overseas. England has never claimed an exclusive monopoly of empire, but with admirable steadiness of purpose she went about eliminating other possible rivals. Once Spain, Portugal, and Holland had ceased to offer any serious competition, they could be allowed to keep their own, but England would not rest content until the one serious remaining challenge, the French, had been effectively destroyed. Quite understandably, from geographic necessity, the French always gave the land first priority, and the consequent division of their forces is not the least factor that went to seal their ultimate defeat overseas.

Thus the facts of geography, combined with those of power, contributed to give England a place that was unique. Of Europe, yet apart from Europe, she looked upon the whole of the Continent in a way that no other power could, while the growing dimensions of her overseas empire exerted a pull away from the Continent that obviously no continental state could entertain or feel. In quite a special sense therefore, England became the guardian of the system of equilibrium in Europe. Seen from different angles it may be said that England became either the prime defender of the liberties of Europe—in the sense previously described of favoring the continued independence of all—or the greatest single impediment to any unity of the Continent.

The maintenance of this state of affairs entailed many wars. For, although the principle of the balance of power as the instrument through which the acceptance by all of the right of all to exist could best be implemented obtained universal recognition, it did not prevent an everlasting competition for the enhancement of individual positions. Nevertheless the common ground of general acceptance made for a measure of stability within competition and conflict. This is characteristic of eighteenth-century wars, conflicts of limited aims, so different from our twentieth-century crusades laden with the moral content of right contesting wrong and dedicated to total destruction. As a consequence they were relatively gentle wars, more in the nature of a gentlemanly game, the rules of which all the participants abide by. The courtesy displayed at Fontenoy, where English and French deferred to each other in shooting, symbolizes this to perfection.

The existence of so broad an area of agreement might be expected to reflect itself in some attempt to formalize and codify the commonly accepted rules that prevailed in the relations among states. But the agreement, such as it was, remained essentially tacit. The point was made earlier that an inconsistency is involved in the coexistence of sovereignty and international law. Yet an attempt was made to create some basis for the latter. The concept of international law and its practice are definitely of European origin. The fatherhood of the concept is usually attributed to a seventeenth-century Dutchman, Grotius, whose *De Jure Bellis et Pacis* remains an outstanding monument along the thorny path of this endeavor. Grotius was moved to pen his treatise out of revulsion from the horrors of the Thirty Years War of his day. What was significant about his writing was the expression it contained of common ground in a certain domain, to the creation of which it was itself a contribution. But the central difficulty, then as now, and despite some extension of the field of international law, lay in the absence of an agency possessed of power that is capable of enforcing it. Opinion and a moral climate are feeble reeds when a vital interest, or one thought to be such, is at stake. There will be occasion, later on in this discussion, to consider what progress has been made in this field, especially when we come to the contemporary efforts to formalize the rules of international organization. There is no need to dwell upon it at this point; it is mentioned because of the very fact that the emergence of the concept represents a significant common element of the European community as a whole.

The uniqueness of the British position, which the rise of English power brought into sharp relief, has been explained. This position may be said to have become established and crystallized at the turn of the seventeenth to the eighteenth century. At the opposite eastern end of Europe this was also the time when the seeds were being planted of developments destined to have eventually consequences of a magnitude comparable to those rooted in the British Isles. Asiatic control

had to a large extent severed the Russian land from participation in the unfolding of European happenings. The coming
of the Turks into Europe acted as a further barrier between
Russia and Europe, although their establishment coincided
with the process of Russian emancipation from Asiatic control.
The Russian growth took time, and Poland, or Poland-Lithuania, rather than Muscovy, was the eastern outpost of Europe.
The Poles were in Moscow in 1661. But after some troubled
times, followed by a relatively quiet period, there appeared
on the Russian scene Tsar Peter whose orientation was definitely Western. The picturesque figure, somewhat larger than
life-size, and what he did are well known. The substance
of his accomplishment must be seen as the definite insertion
of Russia into the comity of Europe. From his time, and allowing for occasional recessions, the role of Russia in European
affairs has grown steadily larger. A measure of this increasing
Russian penetration into Europe was the eventual destruction
of the once powerful Polish state, by far the largest part of
which became absorbed into Russia.

That episode,[1] incidentally, may be regarded as a denial
of the principle that all states acknowledged the right to existence of all other states. It was an exception, albeit an important one, and for that very reason was severely criticized as a
serious breach, precisely because it was a direct challenge to
the commonly accepted belief. But, for the rest, with the
extinction of Poland, this meant that all the Slavic lands, other
than Russia herself, were deprived of their independence.
This situation is not unrelated to the eventual collapse of the
three empires, the Russian, the Austrian, and the Ottoman,

[1] Poland, or Poland-Lithuania, had once been a powerful state and
had played a large part in the affairs of Eastern Europe. The vices of its
internal constitution were in part responsible for its decay and ultimate
demise. During the last quarter of the century, beginning with 1772, in
three successive partitions, all Poland was absorbed by her neighbors,
Russia, Prussia, and Austria.

under whose respective subjections they were. That, however, is a later story.

But to return to Russia proper. From Peter's time she was definitely an important factor in European affairs. However, it is a measure of the limited extent of Russia's European role in Peter's own time that she failed to join in the great struggle of the Spanish Succession. In order fully to become European Russia had to first break out of the isolation in which she was confined. This Peter understood, and the counterpart of the westernizing reforms that he sought to force upon his people was the cardinal purpose of his foreign policy, the struggle for access to the sea. He was successful in one quarter, and managed to wrest from Sweden access to the Baltic; but he failed in the South, and the Black Sea was not permanently reached until Catherine's day. The struggle is still going on, because both the Black Sea and the Baltic are really lakes, and access to them is in other than Russian hands.

The reason for the persistence of this condition is that, in her attempts at westward expansion, Russia encountered too strong and too well established a force. It was otherwise in the East, with the consequence that the Russian expansion, in a fashion and to a degree comparable to the American, occurred eastward, settling the relative void of Siberia, until the natural boundary of the Pacific was reached. South of Siberia, in Central Asia, expansion also took place, and this brought into Russia appreciable numbers of Asiatic peoples, establishing a strong Asiatic component, as distinct from the European, in the Russian complex.

In addition, while the prevalent religion of Russia is Christian, it is of the Eastern persuasion. There was in Russia neither Reformation nor Counter-Reformation, and where religion is concerned Russia has remained largely immune to the currents that have agitated and molded religion in the Western World. Also, the Russian Church, again especially since Peter, has been in large degree subservient to the state. Despite this fact, however, the influence of religion in Russia has generally been against such westernizing tendencies as the state has encouraged, and has served to strengthen the aspect of divorce from the West. The neatest expression of this outlook is the feeling that it was the special mission of the third Rome, Moscow, to lead the world along the path of salvation by emphasizing the opposite of those tendencies that have characteristically shaped the modern West. It is not at all inconceivable that the leadership of the West and its giving Europe and the whole modern world their shape will terminate in universal perdition and destruction; but this, in the present context, is irrelevant, when the point at issue is that of the peculiar nature of the Russian milieu in contrast to the rest of Europe. The contrast, to be sure, is only a matter of degree and should not be exaggerated. For example, the view that the ways of the modern world are the ways of perdition has been far from alien to the West itself; the point is that in the contest for leadership of change, this view has been a losing idea to a far greater extent and earlier in the West than it has been in Russia, where its opposite has not finally succeeded in achieving control until the Revolution of our time. The point therefore is emphasized again that, although for wholly different reasons, in the cases of Britain and of Russia, we are confronted with two states which must indeed be called European, yet stand in special relation to the rest.

Catherine of Russia was not herself of Russian origin though she unquestionably and with complete success identified herself with the interests of the land of which she became a ruler. She certainly pursued, and again with success, the western extension of Russia, being as much as any one responsible for the final destruction of Poland. Catherine also lived in the age of the Enlightened despots. The noun fits her well, the adjective is more debatable. To be sure, she conducted extensive exchanges with the *philosophes*, Diderot in particular, who visited her court and expressed himself on her score in highly complimentary fashion. So did Voltaire, another beneficiary of her bounty. This in effect was largely window dressing, and Catherine's interest in improving the lot of her people was minimal, hardly an enlightened approach. But the fact that she felt it desirable to indulge in such association in rather ostentatious fashion, apart from personal predilection, is indicative of her recognition of what constituted the civilized world of her day.

The Century of the Enlightenment

The eighteenth century is labeled in the history books as the Age of the Enlightenment. Certain observations from the standpoint of what that period meant for Europe as a whole are warranted. As far as the relations among European states were concerned some major developments may be noted. The confirmation of the arbitral role of Britain together with the enhancement of her imperial position to one of undisputed primacy is one; the increasing European role of Russia is another. In connection with the second, the definite beginning of the process of Ottoman retreat should be mentioned. The contrast is arresting between two specific events: in 1683 Vienna was besieged by the Turks; in 1699, the Peace of Karlowitz, a great turning point in the Ottoman record, was signed. After this the process of the Ottoman retreat from Europe went on with hardly any interruption because of the internal rot that sapped the vigor of the state. This situation at first—during the eighteenth century that is—provided a common interest and generally a source of co-operation between the Habsburgs and the Romanovs, as did also their sharing of Poland.

The eighteenth century is also the time during which

Prussia begins to rank as an important power, her ruler having risen to royal dignity in the War of the Spanish Succession. The Prussian role was rather greater than warranted by the dimensions, population, and resources of the Prussian state in comparison with others. This situation was best expressed in the observation that war was the national industry of Prussia. It was an industry that flourished and put her in a position to challenge the Habsburg place in the Germanic world of Central Europe. But, for the rest, the Germanic world was more than ever fragmented and the quip, "The sea belongs to the English, the land to the French, to the Germans belong the clouds," is fit expression of the contemporary view of things.

On land France held first rank, a position justified by her size and her wealth, as well as by the fact that her numbers were greater than those of any other European state, Russia not excluded. If French power did not give a better account of itself in this period it was in considerable part the result of deficient domestic management. Louis XV, a neither unattractive nor unintelligent man, if a slothful one, was well aware of this condition. His appraisal of the state of things, as expressed in the famous phrase, *Après moi le déluge,* proved to be an eminently sound forecast of the future.

There was much strife and many wars were fought during the eighteenth century, but again the point must be emphasized that these contests, manifestations of the permanent competition among states or rulers and of the stresses resulting from shifting relations of power, took place within the framework of a broad common understanding of their proper scope and limits. The shared consciousness of Europeanness was not an empty myth: for example, English Gibbon could travel across France while the two countries were at war with each other; the French Navy, under the same circumstances, had instructions not to interfere with the explorations of Captain

Cook, for the higher and supra-national standing of scientific work was acknowledged. These occurrences are far more difficult to conceive in our presumably more advanced time.

Such incidents are illustrations of the degree to which common ground existed at the cultural level. The primacy of France has been mentioned; no better expression of it can be cited than the status achieved by the French language, which was superseding Latin, and in fact did in diplomatic practice. It is difficult to see as an improvement the regrettable twentieth-century departure from so useful a condition. It was not so much that France held a marked leadership in concrete artistic or scientific achievement. Her own contributions were large in these fields, but there is no question that in the latter domain it was the Newtonian synthesis that dominated the day, just as in music the German contribution was outstanding. It was rather the tone and the climate of a civilized society that made Paris the nearest approximation to a capital of Europe. German princelings, for example, with deficient humor sometimes, could think of nothing better than trying to create small replicas of Versailles, stuffy and tawdry as they may have been. France was par excellence the home of the enlightened *philosophes*, not philosophers in the narrow technical sense, but social critics, popularizers of the "enlightened" ideas, although some of them were indeed also scientists in their own right.

The roster of their names is long, and Voltaire more than any one may be regarded as their prince, in himself a synthesis of the age. Voltaire is essentially a literary figure and if undoubtedly an intelligent man, hardly a profound thinker. Voltaire in his youth made a sojourn in England whence he brought back mainly two things which he highly admired. In briefest form they may be labeled Newton and the Whig Revolution.

There is no necessity to delve deeply into Newton's *Principia* in order to grasp and appreciate the beautiful simplicity of the Newtonian World Machine. This final synthesis of a long process that has been mentioned earlier was calculated to instill in man admiration for the power of reason, and, by extrapolation, faith in the possibility of its unlimited future accomplishments—a faith not truly challenged till our day despite the continued scientific progress of our time. The thought of the eighteenth century is dominated by the mechanistic outlook and the belief that the cosmos in all its aspects can eventually be reduced to mathematical formulation. After all, did not the law of gravitation contain the summation of an enormous quantity of superficially unrelated phenomena, the fall of a pebble as well as the rotations of the planets?

The consequences of the successful demonstration that an explanation of the operation of the physical cosmos could be given in terms of rational order had understandably tremendous impact. It led inevitably, among other things, to much religious disputation. The order that prevailed in the universe could be cited to the greater glory of God, the supreme clockmaker, but it would be degrading the divinity to expect the maker of laws capriciously to tamper with His own work, for instance to respond to the wishes, hopes, prayers, or whims of His creatures. If God was still granted a place He was removed from close contact with man. The eighteenth century, like the rational faculty, is highly formal, and in some of its aspects it is rather cold and somewhat inhuman, especially in the more rigid Catholic milieu. Attacks on foolish superstition and on the role of the priesthood attained considerable violence, although there are rare instances of the total rejection of God, as in d'Holbach's pure materialism.

If the unfettered application of the rational faculty could achieve such results as the Newtonian World Machine exemplified, might it not with equal success operate in the domain of society and politics? Voltaire had brought back from

England an admiration for the English system of government.
How deep a political thinker he himself may have been
matters less than the fact that the English system could be
made an effective tool to belabor the French. And for this
there was room, for, even if the monarchy had served a useful
integrating purpose in France, the despotism tempered by
corruption that was Louis XV's régime was open to much
legitimate criticism. The despotism did not press on the
country with a heavy hand, but precisely because it was lax—
censorship may have caused French works to be printed in
Holland, but it interfered little with the circulation of these
works in France—the scope of that criticism was all the
greater. The political as well as the religious institutions came
under attack, and if the view that freedom could prevail when
the last king had been strangled with the entrails of the last
priest is unnecessarily gruesome in cast, its very form bespeaks
the intensity of the existing criticism and tension. *The Great
Encyclopedia,* under Diderot's editorship, was one of the
great vehicles of the Enlightenment. It powerfully contributed to the spread of new ideas, but many of its entries dealing with matters social, political, and historic were heavily
laden with propagandistic content.

In this work of demolition Voltaire had a great rival, an
enemy in some ways, and a man of greater intellectual depth
even if a far less adjusted individual. It is a measure of the
freedom that in effect prevailed in the French intellectual
milieu that Genevan Rousseau should have won a prize in a
competition with an essay written around the theme that
"man is good, it is society depraves him." The sophistication
of over ripe, decadent institutions and societies will often
cheerfully entertain and appreciate gibes at its foibles. If Rousseau's extreme views expressed a reaction against the formal-
ism and artificiality of eighteenth-century society, there was,
behind his exaltation of the noble savage, far more than merely

titillating attacks. The fiction of Rousseau's *Social Contract* and the very modern educational views of *Emile* are still living realities. Rousseau is one of the early romantics; but that inclination, however contrasting with the classical rationalism of the *philosophes,* was also effective in leavening and focusing discontent.

The reason emphasis is placed on French-centered developments is not their Frenchness, but the fact that France was the chief center of ideas shared by the whole European community. The eighteenth-century educated class was highly cosmopolitan, and the climate of the Enlightenment was shared across political boundaries that it did not acknowledge. The case of Russian Catherine has been mentioned; Prussian Frederick is even better illustration. Frederick wrote mainly in French, regarding his own German as relatively barbaric, and when Voltaire congratulated him for his military victory over the French king no one thought of accusing Voltaire of patriotic delinquency. The quarrels of the rulers operated on a level distinct from that of the great international of letters, which was truly the common possession of Europe, at least that portion of Europe oriented toward change and the future, progress as some would say.

The social and political thinking of eighteenth-century Europe was anything but narrowly provincial or national. Its thought was of society and man, not even of European man alone, in which respect it shared the universalistic quality of Christianity, however much it may have berated the prejudices and superstitions that went with the practice of the Christian religion, especially in its Catholic form. And speaking of progress it was fitting that a reversal should occur: hitherto the legend of the golden age of man had invariably been situated in some distant, dimly remembered past; the story of the Garden of Eden is the Judaic-Christian form of that legend. But now the Golden Age was shifted to the future. Man through the use of his rational faculty could understand, then master, his environment, and could organize the perfect society for himself.

The Golden Age was about to burst forth, and, quite appropriately, in France, whose model all could follow.

III. The Impact of Revolution

The virtually defunct Estates General of the Kingdom of France, a potentially representative institution, met on May 5, 1789. Thirteen years earlier, across the Atlantic on the American seaboard, a relatively small group of people, the English-planted thirteen colonies, had risen in protest against what it considered an undue extent of alien control. Its purpose and justification was proclaimed in the justly famous declaration, the heart of which, despite its familiarity, is worth recalling:

> We hold these truths to be self-evident, that all men are created equal, that they are endowed by their Creator with certain inalienable rights, that among these are life, liberty, and the pursuit of happiness. That to secure these rights governments are instituted among men, deriving their just powers from the consent of the governed. That whenever any form of government becomes destructive to these ends, it is the right of the people to alter or to abolish it, and to institute new government, laying its foundation on such principles and organizing its powers in such form, as to them shall seem most likely to effect their safety and happiness.

There is nothing that is per se self-evident about the self-evident truths which did no more than state in forceful fashion certain beliefs or assumptions. Like all political theory this was but the expression of certain views and desires in governmental matters. Nor was there even anything peculiarly American about Jefferson's assertions. Their filiation from

Locke, more broadly their reflection of much eighteenth-century political thought, has been often and sufficiently explained; Jefferson and the founding fathers were steeped in the Enlightenment. It was wholly in keeping with the tone and spirit of the time that the above quotation should be couched in universal terms of claims that could be made by all men at all times.

At any rate the claim at this time was made good by the American colonists to whom applies the Napoleonic criterion, "a revolution is an idea that has found bayonets," some of the bayonets in this event being French. Having emancipated themselves from British rule the thirteen colonies went on to seal their union, and they wrote the intention to make it "more perfect" into a formal constitution.

Living in the twentieth century one may indeed regard the achievement of American independence as a great event, for the seed planted in 1776 has grown into a mighty oak, and the fact that the United States still functions under its original constitution is one of which the significance, for the world as a whole, can hardly be exaggerated. Nevertheless, in the last quarter of the eighteenth century to speak of "the shot heard round the world" may be viewed as an overstatement, for the shot has not really been heard until the present century. There were indeed at the time those, in France and elsewhere, who welcomed the American event for ideological reasons and as an encouraging example, reasons that in fact led some individual Frenchmen and others to lend their swords to the American cause. But if the aid of the French alliance was crucial in procuring the ultimate defeat of Britain, it must not be forgotten that the alliance was concluded by the government of Louis XVI, primarily for reasons of the politics of power. The outcome, registered in the Treaty of Paris in 1783, in some degree was compensation, or revenge, for another signed there twenty years earlier.

Revolution in France and War in Europe

It has been said, not without some justification, that the chief contemporary effect on France of the American war of independence was to seal the final bankruptcy of the French treasury. It was indeed the financial plight of the French state that, as a last resort, induced the calling of the Estates. That event was to have repercussions the reverberations of which are in some respects not yet stilled; it may be viewed as the introduction of the modern age and some of its aspects have relevance to our story.

The Estates did not at first concern themselves with matters financial in any special way, but took up instead the far more ambitious task of reorganization of the realm. The membership of the Estates, the Third especially, was of a high quality. The elections had been held on a very broad base, the discussion had been very free, and the members of the Third Estate consisted in the main of that section of society that was progressive and literate, highly imbued with the enlightened spirit of the century. The adventitious fact that the membership of the Third Estate was equal to that of the other two (nobility and clergy) combined, together with some support it had among the other orders, enabled it very early to transform the entire Estates into a single constitutional assembly. The dramatic occasion of the Tennis Court Oath is well known, appropriate symbol of the revolution that was taking place in France. The acquiescence of the monarch with his well-intended weakness made the initial phase of the revolution surprisingly swift and smooth.

Developments flowed fast. An emotion-charged session in the beginning of August proclaimed the abolition of privilege, or class distinction, and by the end of that month the great document that was at once the death warrant of the *ancien régime* and certificate of birth of the new order had been drafted. The French Declaration of the Rights of Man, which proclaimed, "Men are born and remain free and equal in right," derives from the same inspiration as the American Declaration of Independence, and the Bill of Rights, the progressive political thought of the eighteenth century. It is the central document and the summation of the spirit of the French Revolution, for the bold assertion of the equality of men in terms of fundamental rights was the deliberate condemnation and denial of the hitherto existing structure of European society. It matters little that when it came to establishing criteria for voting, it turned out, in the modern Orwellian phrase, that if all men were equal in theory, in practice some were more equal than others; for once the wedge of the egalitarian principle has been introduced, the censitarian test is a mechanical device that can easily be altered. At first, in France, as had been the case in England, the franchise was very severely limited; the first election in the former country allowed some 100,000 *active* citizens (voters) in a country of 25,000,000. But in the case of both countries, as in others that have subsequently followed their example, the virtually uninterrupted story has been one of a steady reduction of limitations, until practically none are left anywhere in today's world. The introduction of the egalitarian principle is what matters; it is this central fact that gave the French Revolution universal relevance. Quite fittingly, in view of its Enlightened background, the French Declaration of Rights did not speak of French Man, for in the eyes of its drafters what they were doing in Versailles had equal applicability in Berlin or Rome, in Moscow, or even in Peking. The eighteenth century believed in the common humanness of man; it also tended to believe, naïvely perhaps we should now say, in the fundamental goodness of man.

The detailed course of French events in their native milieu

is not, in the main, relevant to our story. But it could hardly
be expected that events in France should long remain confined to that country: the spirit that informed the Declaration
of Rights was European, and France was the most powerful
state on the Continent. Having successfully asserted its purpose, the French National Constituent Assembly went on to
implement it. Within two years it had drafted a constitution
that ineffectual Louis XVI signed with reluctance. France
was to be a constitutional monarchy, and one thing worth
noting about the first modern French constitution is that, in
contrast with the almost simultaneously adopted American,
instead of accepting Montesquieu's system of checks and bal-
ances, it placed in overwhelming fashion the locus of power
in the hands of the legislature. The consequences of this, in
France and elsewhere in Europe, were to be very considerable, and not always for the best.

Another aspect of the shift from the old order to the new
must be stressed. In place of the hitherto prevailing theory
on the Continent of the divine derivation of the monarchical
institution was introduced the principle of popular sovereignty; the people, or the nation, instead of the king, was
henceforth to be the source of power in the state. The implications and consequences of this radical change in political
theory were not long in appearing.

The prevalent theory of divine-right monarchy had had the
effect of creating what might be called an international of
rulers, whose common stake in their position could in the
last resort take priority over their limited quarrels. In June
1791 a dissatisfied Louis XVI attempted to escape from Paris
to the shelter of more congenial surroundings. But the attempt
was a failure: he was recognized at Varennes by some "patriots" and was brought back, in effect a prisoner of his own
people, or of the revolution. Within two months the emperor
and the king of Prussia issued the Declaration of Pillnitz;
granting that their statement of intent was conditional on the

assent of others—an unlikely prospect—there was nevertheless asserted the solidarity of rulers to the possible point of intervention against the revolution, in other words against the French people. Thus the cleavage was sharpening between two antithetic principles; for the answer to the international of rulers could be the international of peoples. The universality of the principles asserted by the revolution in France could easily be used as an appeal to other peoples to emulate the example so far set by the French. It did not yet come to that at this moment, but it is precisely the clear perception of this possibility that brought about a closing of the ranks of the rulers. The internal order of France became a matter of European concern. Either principle expressed an assumption that was common ground for all Europe.

Another aspect of the revolutionary principle led to unintended, if logical, consequences. The people hitherto had been the subjects of their legitimate princes; but if they were to be henceforth the repository of sovereignty, clearly they might choose their own allegiance. In Avignon the people were ethnically French, but Avignon was, within the French realm, an enclave of which the Pope was the legitimate ruler. As early as 1790 there was in Avignon a demand for union with France, a demand to which the French Assembly, after some hesitation, responded with a decree of annexation. In terms of the existing law of Europe here was certainly a breach of the peace and an aggressive act. This was not debatable, at least not unless the fundamental basis of the law of Europe were modified through acceptance of the new revolutionary principle. Not surprisingly, the Pope would not do this.

A similar issue arose in Alsace, an imperial land which had become the possession of the French king in the seventeenth century while remaining part of the Empire. The political and social changes decreed by the French Assembly did to the nobility of Alsace the same injury that had been suffered by the privileged order in France. The nobility of Alsace appealed to imperial protection, bringing into sharp focus the issue of the basis of the right of the people of Alsace.

Small as they were, the cases of Avignon and of Alsace brought out nicely the sharpness of the issue between irreconcilable principles. That issue was a very large one indeed, reminiscent of the sort of issue involved in the Wars of Religion, and could hardly do other than produce an open clash. Thus war broke out in the spring of 1792, and the formal initiative of it was French.

Save for an uneasy truce of a year the war was to last a quarter of a century and to embroil all Europe. It was a new kind of war, where the distinction between the combatants was blurred by the injection of a novel principle. Quite early, in July, the duke of Brunswick, commander of the allied forces, issued his ill-advised Manifesto, the central point of which was the warning to the French people that they would be held responsible for the fate of their king. The answer was too easy and had the consequence of clarifying the issue implied in the earlier Declaration of Pillnitz: apart from the September massacres, an outburst of Parisian mob rage, the French revolutionaries would make the war a universal contest between peoples and kings.

From a twentieth-century standpoint this may seem an unequal contest. That it was not was due to the fact that the implementation of the simple principle of popular sovereignty in terms of state and military organization is anything but simple. On the one hand the masses of the rulers' subjects did not rise against their masters; on the other, not all the people of France were united behind all aspects of the revolution.[1] The immediate result was that control of the revolu-

[1] The quarrel which developed quite early between the state and the church, as the result of the attempt of the former to assert a measure of control over the latter, had the effect of alienating from the revolution much Catholic sentiment, which had initially been favorable to it.

tion in France was diverted, following the path of its inner logic, into the hand of its more radical exponents. In brief, the results were: new elections, a new constitution—that of 1793, the Year I, never enacted—the Republic, the dictatorship of the Mountain, the Terror, and the excesses of the revolution. Under the leadership of dedicated and determined men, humanitarians who would not recoil before bloodshed and coercion to force upon mankind its own salvation, the revolution would fight at once civil and foreign war. That, too, might seen an unequal contest and it would have been but for the enormous energies that were released by the revolution.

For the revolutionaries were not idle. If France was the totality of the French people, all of them had an equal stake in and responsibility for the defense of their own. The principle of universal conscription was the logical corollary of that of popular sovereignty, and this provided a relatively unlimited reservoir of manpower, in violation of the existing practice of mercenary armies. Also, after the initial disorganization of the cadres of the king's armies, the egalitarian opening of careers to talent revealed among the French no dearth of potential military capability. War is a potent instrument of progress, or at least of change, and new techniques, like new weapons, can seldom be resisted save by imitation.

Not only in the field of war or in the domain of general principle did the revolution present a challenge to the Old. From top to bottom the structure of the state was to be renovated: old provinces abolished to make way for new administrative divisions; an entirely novel scheme of administration; education and schools reorganized and created; even the standards of measurement rationalized into a metric system; the very calendar renewed from the Year I of the Republic, one and indivisible. Uniformity and centralization, the trappings of modernity, made what had been the most advanced state of the Continent, also for a time the most efficient. Even without political revolution the new France would have been an example for Europe.

But it was revolutionary France that did all this and was only too ready to export revolution abroad, where there were those quite willing to receive the gift. Thus, when French armies appeared in the Austrian Netherlands or in the Rhineland they found at first not a few who welcomed them as liberators. But war such as this inevitably is tarred with the brush of ambiguity; for, if it was a war between the French people and certain European rulers, it was also a war between states to which the classical pattern of rivalry was not alien. Catherine, the would-be enlightened ruler of Russia, was among the stanchest opponents of the revolutionary principle; she gave much encouragement to the Prussian king and to the emperor, but she found their embroilment with France a suitable occasion to contrive, on advantageous terms, the final destruction of Poland. Not for some years would Russia herself actively participate in the crusade against the revolution.

England preceded her in this role, though in the English case there was a minimum of ideological motivation. In fact the earlier stages of the revolution in France could appear as but the compliment of imitation since constitutional monarchy had long been familiar in England. To be sure, the excesses of the revolution in France, the execution of luckless Louis XVI, soon drove away much English sympathy, and Burke's *Reflections* were penned as early as 1790. But the threat to the mouth of the Scheldt and the Low Countries was a threat to an English interest that was well known to all and of long standing. In 1793 England was at war with France.

The case of the British participation is one of special interest and significance. In one of its aspects the outbreak of Anglo-French hostilities was merely a recurrence of a phenomenon often witnessed before. England could thus resume, or continue, the defense of her own interest against her chief rival, and the method was familiar: control the seas while raising other enemies on land; England was to be the backbone of the ever renewed anti-French coalitions. But in the course of defending herself England was also the defender of the liberties of others, meaning by liberties their separate independent existences. The issue thus resolved itself: was revolutionary France fighting for narrow national advantage or was she fighting for a principle? Was Europe threatened by a particular hegemony, or was she offered the opportunity, under the shield of a new principle, to supersede timeworn, petty quarrels?

If man were fundamentally good, as optimistic eighteenth-century reformers would have it, once he had come into his own, rid of the shackles of kings and priests, the good society established, what obstacle would there be to his living in peace with his neighbor, to creating an all-embracing community of Europe, pending the day of possibly even more universal extension?

This is a dream that will not die, and the idea that had seized control of the French state had in it the possibility of inserting itself into the long background of the common traditions and culture of Europe, which, put in modern form, would even rejoin the true ideal of egalitarian Christianity, however much the revolution in France might quarrel with the Church of Rome.

But as events turned out, national diversity, the other tradition of Europe, developed especially since the Reformation and the settlement of Westphalia, was to receive from the French Revolution its greatest impetus, and in a most dangerous fashion. The view is essentially correct that modern nationalism, the virulent, intransigent product that we have come to know, is a creation of the French Revolution. How this happened is not difficult to understand, but before that outcome became clear, some other unexpected results of the revolution must be indicated.

If principle is not amenable to compromise and the clash of contrasting ideas results in such conflicts as the Wars of Religion, the more pedestrian qualities of man, his attachment to terrestrial life, have a way of evolving accommodations. The high-minded intransigence of sixteenth-century re- formers after a century of strife yielded, through the intrusion of more limited material interest, to the stalemate and com- promise out of which religious tolerance was born. *In abstracto* there was no meeting ground between the two sides in the war of peoples against kings; but out of the imperfect identifi- cations between the democratic principle and the French state on the one hand, between other European states and the monarchical principle on the other, an equilibrium might *de facto* be reached.

After three years of war it appeared that the revolution in France, if somewhat tamed,[2] was in reasonably firm control of the country. But it had not succeeded in overturning the European order as a whole. A measure of success had been achieved by the newly created French armies, success which by the standards of Louis XIV's limited ambitions could be regarded as considerable: the natural boundary of the Rhine had been secured and even a satellite Batavian Republic es- tablished. The new regime of France, the Directory, was the expression of weariness with too much of a too high-minded revolution and was willing to abandon the crusading ardor of the Terror. Peace on advantageous terms was made with some

[2] Internal opposition and the foreign danger had had the effect of orienting the Revolution on an increasingly radical and dictatorial course, the climax of which was the episode of the Terror. When Robespierre was executed, there was a reaction against this, and a re- turn to the more moderate arrangements of the initial constitution of 1791, rather than that of 1793.

of the belligerents, such as Prussia and Spain. The possibility existed that a bourgeois France, governed in the main by a small, propertied class, in a fashion not very different from England, might rejoin the community of European states. Voltaire's democracy had never envisaged government save by the qualified, and French bourgeois and English Tories might have found much common ground in agreeing with the divine-right monarchs of Europe that government was the proper preserve of the competent, chosen more by political mechanics than principle.

The Rise of Bonaparte

However, peace had not yet been made in 1795 with either England or the emperor, and, as a consequence, plans were made for the prosecution of war on the Rhine and in Italy. When war had broken out initially, on French initiative, there had been in the French Legislative Assembly a small radical minority opposing it. The reason for their opposition was the fear that the resort to military action might open the door to the possibility of the rise of a military dictator; the radicals of 1792 were about to be proved right, for Bonaparte was ready to enter the scene. Much has been written about Napoleon Bonaparte and in our time some have compared him to Hitler. In many ways, certainly in personal terms, the stress should be on contrast, for the least that can be said of Napoleon is that he was both a sane and a civilized man. But, allowing for the weight and the influence of personal idiosyncrasy, the ways of history are often mysterious, and the agents of her deeper forces may have little in common besides the strength of personality. Great as the differences are, there are some points of contact between France's role in Europe at the beginning of the nineteenth century and the German attempt in the middle of the twentieth. We need not explain that the historic place of Napoleon is large, but some of the aspects of his influence bear on the present tale.

Bonaparte was a perfect example of the opportunities that the revolution had opened to talent in France and in the most literal sense the claim he always made of being a son of the revolution was true. At twenty-six he had been placed in charge of the ragged army operating on the Alpine front. His first campaign of Italy, in 1796, was a brilliant military performance that gave him an opportunity to reveal his nature. By October 1797 the General of the Republic, far exceeding the proper bounds of his political competence, had forced upon the emperor a peace highly advantageous to France, having meantime dealt in equally arbitrary fashion with some of the Italian rulers, the king of Sardinia and the Pope among them. There is no need to dwell upon the details of these arrangements, highly impermanent ones for that matter, other than to note two things. The creation of a Cispadane Republic, another French satellite, meant on the one hand cavalier disregard of previously existing legitimacy while on the other it transplanted into a part of Italy much that the revolution had accomplished in France. Also, there were in Italy more than a few Jacobins, as they were styled at the time, precursors of twentieth-century fifth columnists or fellow-travelers, ready to welcome the coming of French armies and the reforms they brought in their baggage.

What happened in Italy during the next few years is highly illuminating, a limited illustration of what befell the larger European scene during the next two decades. Peace having been restored on the Continent, General Bonaparte went to Paris where conditions, however, were not yet ripe for the achievement of his domestic political ambitions. England alone still remaining at war, he embarked on the diversion of the picturesque expedition to Egypt, where superior British sea power left him stranded in local victory. Of greater significance was the fact that his absence from Europe enabled England to reweave the web of an anti-French coalition. The conclusion, in December 1798, of an Anglo-Russian alliance brought together the two peripheral powers of a Europe that seemed unable to maintain her liberties against the too-great power of one of her own components, a phenomenon that was to recur again in our time.

The second coalition, in Bonaparte's absence, succeeded in evicting the French from all of Italy, where they had meantime extended their control to Rome and even Naples. What is worth noting is the fact that by this time, 1799, there was in Italy much desire for liberation from the initial liberation that French armies had brought; the latter after all were alien, and the benefits of the modernization that they had introduced were insufficient compensation for the heaviness of their foreign hand. Austrians and Russians were not long in causing second thoughts about the merits of the latest liberation in Italy. In any event, Bonaparte, reappearing on the scene, quickly repeated his original performance in Italy, and once more brought it under French sway. However, this did not happen before Bonaparte had, through the coup d'état of Brumaire (November 1799) first secured mastery of the French state itself. As First Consul he had in effect power to direct domestic as well as foreign arrangements.

Napoleon Confirms the Revolution but Fails to Unite Europe

Napoleon attended first to foreign affairs and for a year there was peace with all, even with England. The respite he used to good purpose and what he accomplished in France during the five-year period of the Consulate, had he done nothing else, would be ample justification for historic fame. The relentless drive of his energy coped with all—religion, law, finance, and administration; with these we are not concerned, and it suffices to sum up his achievements by saying that Bonaparte integrated the revolutionary innovations into the old centralizing tradition of the French state, which he made the most modern and progressive of Europe, a model for others to emulate. He made France by far the most powerful state in Europe; in fact it may be said that his efficient mobilization of the native resources magnified for a time French power beyond its true dimensions.

For that very reason the implied threat that was Napoleonic France—in 1804 the First Consul became Emperor Napoleon I —made the preservation of peace impossible. Before he assumed the imperial title, war had already been resumed, in 1803, appropriately with England, who again responded with the customary fostering of a continental coalition. The coalition did not long resist Napoleon's military genius and tactics; Austerlitz confirmed the supremacy of French arms, but Austerlitz was almost simultaneous with Trafalgar, which established a corresponding position for England on the seas. Thereafter, Napoleon abandoned any thought of challenging the English maritime primacy or of invading the island, and resorted instead to economic warfare where England was concerned.

Thus there arose the situation where a predominant sea power confronts one supreme on land. Unless one of the two adequately develops the weapons of the other, a stalemate ensues or novel weapons must be found. The effectiveness of the economic weapon depended upon control of the Continent, an enterprise into which Napoleon thus found himself drawn. Having defeated in turn the Austrians, the Prussians, and the Russians, he did two things. First, at Tilsit, in June 1807, he met the Russian tsar. The impressionable Alexander fell easy prey to the imaginative wiles of the Corsican. Leaving the fate of the Near East in suitable ambiguity, the two would divide Europe between them and even form an alliance; Europe proper, Europe outside of Russia and England that is, would be Napoleon's domain, to do with as he pleased.

Next, Napoleon proceeded with the task of organizing this Europe, a corollary of the agreement with Tsar Alexander. For some years, amidst occasionally renewed warfare on the Continent, Napoleon was master of Europe within the limits described. What he did is important, although the main outline of it alone need be considered. France herself was very substantially enlarged through direct annexations—Hamburg and Rome became French cities—which produced an extension of the domestic French system of administration to a very considerable domain. For the rest, cavalier arbitrariness and disregard for the past best sum up the Napoleonic treatment of Europe. The Holy Roman Empire, long essentially defunct, at last received formal burial, its ruler re-emerging as emperor of Austria. The Habsburg was severely punished for his defeat and his mistake of prematurely resumed hostilities; in addition to territorial loss he had to endure the humiliation of dependent alliance and the granting of a daughter's hand to the usurper, thus made through marriage a relative-in-law of the ill-fated French Bourbons. Prussia was even more severely treated: territorially mutilated, partly disarmed, reduced to second-rank status as a state, she was also made an allied dependent. A less reluctant ally, for natural reasons, was the Grand Duchy of Warsaw, a segment of the former Poland. Next door to France herself, in mid-Europe, a broad band of territory bore a relationship to France perhaps best expressed in contemporary terms as that of the present-day European satellites of the Soviet Union: a kingdom of Westphalia provided a throne for one of Napoleon's brothers, just as in the newly created kingdom of Italy, his stepson Beauharnais reigned, or in Naples, his brother-in-law, Murat, was king. In more reluctant Spain another brother was

installed. Even in distant Sweden one of his marshals, color-
ful Gascon Bernadotte, became king. Perhaps the most significant characteristic of these often revised territorial arrangements was the arbitrariness of their making. Especially
in the Germanic world and in Italy the cavalier disregard
of formerly existing rulers and boundaries, the breaking of the
old mold of states, was to prove a most useful preliminary to
the accomplishment of the mid-nineteenth century. In the
former especially, the multiplicity of states that had been part
of the Holy Roman Empire could never again be brought
to life.

The benefits of French administration, even when forcibly
introduced, were undeniable, as was the freely adopted imitation of some of them in other parts of Europe; the Prussian
state was modernized, or rejuvenated, and serfdom abolished
in it. Had peace come to prevail, even if at first enforced by
the superiority of French arms, it is conceivable that European
unity might have been realized through the initial agency of
force, the classical manner in which integration had in the
past been achieved. If dependence on French interest or
whim was burdensome, it was not so much because of personal
oppression or the loss of civil liberties; there was relatively
little oppression, and liberty had been hitherto largely unknown.

French rule nevertheless was heavy and for that reason
resented. But it was so mainly because of continuing war,
which in the end meant war with England, the only state with
whom, save for the lull of 1802–3, peace was never made till
the end. The burden of French control was mainly felt in
three ways: it meant heavy taxation, for all that this was
modernized and more efficiently collected; it meant demands
on manpower; and finally it meant irksome economic controls
and deprivations in pursuance of the policy of the Continental

System, designed to bring England to surrender, or at least to terms.

There is little need to explain that these burdens, dictated by purely French, or Napoleonic aims, were resented by those who felt they had no direct stake in the promotion of these aims. Also, the fact that the revolution had so much exalted the nation had the natural consequence of emphasizing the French consciousness of the French at home, and by repercussion, the alienness of French control of others. We know the outcome.

It was because of the continuing war with England, in order to perfect the efficacy of the Continental System, that Napoleon was drawn into overextending his strength at the opposite ends of Europe. It was not very difficult to impose his formal control over Spain, on the throne of which his brother Joseph was placed, but the Spanish war had two effects. From an objective point of view it might be contended that the Spanish people rather gained than lost from the elimination of the sorry figure that had been their Bourbon king and the introduction of French-modeled institutions. But they would not have it so; their attachment to their own ways and institutions, backwardness as it was in some respects, induced in them a reaction of strong opposition to alien French control; Napoleon's armies might be invincible in regular warfare, but guerrilla tactics did not fit their book, and Spain became a running sore that could never be healed. In addition, the attempted extension of French control over the whole Iberian peninsula had the effect of persuading the English that their mastery of the seas was insufficient contribution to the war; following in the steps of Marlborough a century earlier, English land forces made their appearance on the Continent; led by Sir Arthur Wellesley, later Duke of Wellington, they were to give a good account of themselves.

In the East, Tsar Alexander, of his own accord, had participated in the Continental System, an arrangement that brought little but inconvenience to the Russian people. To be sure, the tsar extended his control over Finland and made headway against the Turks, but in the latter case Napoleon remained reluctant to make clear and formal commitments; he could never abandon visions of oriental possibilities, once attempted in Egypt. Thus, with the passing of the years, co-operation between the two emperors shifted to divergence and friction, for which competition over Poland furnished additional cause.

Napoleon, no patient man, decided he must deal with Russia as he had with others; in June 1812 his Grand Army crossed the Polish-Russian border. The make-up of the force that he led is enlightening, for, although its core was French, the greater part of it was not. Both Prussia and Austria were formal, if reluctant, allies who had had to furnish contingents; there were also other German elements, a large Italian contribution, and others. In brief, the Grand Army was European.

There is little reason to doubt that its success would have confirmed the mastery of the French control over Europe, but we know what happened instead; this is not the place to dwell on the epic of the march to, then the retreat from, Moscow. The assets of Russian dimensions and weather, in combination with the Russian refusal to yield, succeeded in destroying the Grand Army; of the 600,000 men who had gone into Russia in June, a mere 100,000 came out of that country the following December. Quite naturally hope reappeared among the unwilling subjects of Napoleonic control, and here the German case is the most enlightening. The Austrian emperor might appeal to his subjects on the basis of personal loyalty, though hardly on national grounds[3]; Metternich's behavior was cautious and he offered Napoleon compromise. But in

[3] Mention may be made of the situation in the Tyrol, where Andreas Hofer may be regarded as an early model of a hero of the authentically nationalist resistance that he led.

the rest of the Germanic world the extent to which national consciousness had taken concrete form now became apparent.

Since Napoleon would not compromise, the war must continue, and so it did; but the last coalition had this time collected sufficient power for dealing with him. As the last stage of his struggle, the campaign of France in 1814, clearly showed Napoleon's military genius had not deserted him; but the odds were too great. During the course of the preceding year the war had swept from Poland to the Rhine; it has properly gone down in German annals as the war of liberation, for indeed such it was. The preparations for it in the hearts and minds of the people had been going on for some time. It may suffice to cite some illustrations. It was in 1807 that Fichte delivered in Berlin the stirring appeal that were his *Addresses to the German Nation;* the response to them has made them a landmark in the German national movement. Kant, in remote Königsberg, still extolling the virtues of revolutionary principle, was by this time a voice in the wilderness. The *Tugendbund,* the League of Virtue, if more symbolic than effective, expression of the same surge of national feeling, dates from 1808, and it was in the following year that King Frederick William founded the University of Berlin. The high distinction that it gained from the quality of intellect it gathered made it all the more telling as the hotbed of nationalism it became. It is not necessary to explain that Prussian, or German, nationalism gained much of its sustenance from the clear and immediate necessity of ousting French control.

The end of the Napoleonic tale need not detain us. Facing the near totality of Europe, including Russia and England (a Europe that had learned much from him), and left to his purely French resources which he had drained for many years, Napoleon could do nothing else than go down in defeat. This was registered in two instruments: the Treaty of Fontaine-

bleau, in April, sealed Napoleon's personal fate in the form
of his abdication; at the end of the following month peace
was restored with France by the first Treaty of Paris.

Conclusion

What is the moral of the twenty-five-year story of the French
Revolution and its sequel, the Napoleonic episode? In 1789
an idea was born, or perhaps better, the seed of an idea
planted long ago, came into flower in France, one of the members of the community of European states. It was an idea of
universal applicability that proposed to organize society on a
new basis and in concrete terms to substitute the people, the
nation, for the king. It was an idea, moreover, that inserted
itself into the long tradition of European culture, for democracy had Greek roots, and the trinitarian slogan that became
the motto of the French Revolution, liberty, equality, fraternity, its last two parts especially, fitted well into the Christian
view of man on earth. It does not matter that the Enlightenment, the immediate source of the revolution, was in large
measure anti-clerical, especially where the Church of Rome
was concerned. The Enlightenment, with no little justification, has been called the end point of the Reformation; the
internecine quarrels among Christians have less significance
in this context than the common ground between them, which
certainly includes that of the brotherhood of man. The possibility existed that a new basis had been found for the
unity of the peoples of Europe.

Because of this universalistic character, and also because of
the power of the French state, the idea could not be long
contained within the bounds of the initial domain where it
became triumphant. War between France and the rest of
Europe ensued, and at this point something happened and

the new force was deflected into unexpected channels. If the kings did not succeed in crushing the revolution in its initial home, neither did the revolution manage to dethrone the kings, and the war became, like past religious wars, an ambiguous contest in which the element of strife among states loomed increasingly larger than that of pure ideological difference. Also, the masses of the peoples of Europe were not ready for a wholesale response to the revolutionary principle. What response there was among them soon tended to dissolve into allegiance to established loyalties, and they welcomed liberation from the boon of French liberation where that had taken place.

The stalemate that ensued was not broken until Bonaparte appeared upon the scene, and the result of his successes was a further deflection. He was indeed the most effective instrument for carrying to most of Europe much that the revolution stood for. But in so far as he stood for the unitary principle (he did for a time recreate in effect something like Charlemagne's empire) the unity was based on conquest. That was a fatal vice. Yet even that vice might have been overcome, for, just as the peoples of Europe were not yet ripe for revolution, they were also not yet deeply infected with the nationalistic virus. But at this point the two eccentric powers of Europe, England and Russia, threw the weight of their influence into the balance. They were primarily fighting for the preservation of their own positions as states, but their positions also contained the elements of either opposing the broad ideology of the revolution, or preserving the liberties of Europe, the separate identity of its component parts. In more limited form they were fighting to preserve the long-honored principle of the balance of power in Europe.

Another aspect of the contest that must be stressed was an even more serious perversion of the initial content of the revolution. It has been pointed out that its original makers were thinking of the remolding of society at large rather than in the limited terms of French society alone. But, as it turned out, one of the products, and one of the most successful exports, of the French Revolution, was the principle of nationality. That, too, inserted itself into the traditions of Europe where the state had taken deep root. But to inject into the state the national idea, in place of the right of the monarch, was to give it a foundation far more recalcitrant to change or fusion. It was still possible during the interval between Louis XIV and the French Revolution for the Germanic people of Alsace authentically to change their "national" allegiance, for the simple reason that the concept had little depth of meaning in that period. But after Napoleon's time such a change would be well nigh out of the question. The irony of this cannot be overstressed. Beginning with a principle of universal applicability, the French Revolution had in the end the effect of giving an enormous boost to the development of Europe along lines of increasing diversity.

The victorious allies, as pointed out, were united essentially by two purposes: their common opposition to the revolutionary principle and their common opposition to the magnification of French power. Their aims they fulfilled in two ways: to France they brought back in their baggage the legitimate Bourbon, in the person of Louis XVIII, brother of the last French king. The restored legitimate ruler of France might be counted upon to join his brother rulers in upholding the common basis of their legitimacy; but just because he was the legitimate ruler of France there was no reason to inflict upon him any such punishment as the loss of territory would have been. The boundaries of 1814 France meant no reduction of those of 1789. In fact, surprisingly in terms of principle, these were even somewhat extended; the Pope, for one, did not regain control of Avignon.

Such a change, small in itself, was highly significant, for

it implied, to a point, acknowledgment of the revolutionary criterion of popular sovereignty. If Castlereagh and the tsar were the most insistent in preventing France from being punished, this was because, in the English case especially, they saw in France a necessary element to the preservation of the equilibrium of Europe. Here was indeed common European ground, if hardly ground for unity or union.

The clock of history may not be set back. However much "Restoration" might be the guiding slogan of the victorious coalition, plus restored France for that matter, too much had happened in the course of twenty-five years for it to be possible to restore the old order. In France most of all, but over an increasingly large portion of Europe as well, the revolutionary principle would continue to assert itself. The story of nineteenth-century Europe is in large measure that of the success of the French Revolution, especially in the form of the extension of the democratic practice and of the intensification of the national consciousness.

The latter is most inimical to unity of any sort. Yet there were also contrary forces at work. The common elements of European culture that have been mentioned before in these pages had not disappeared. To them, new factors must be added, which have mainly to do with technological development. To a certain extent, they worked to simultaneously opposite effects. The record of the contest between these divergent influences, of integration and diversity will be the next part of our story.

Part Two

FROM VIENNA TO SARAJEVO: CONFLICTING TENDENCIES AND TRENDS

In the first part of this book an attempt has been made to find a definition of Europe. In the concrete terms of geographical location, the fact has been stressed of the special positions occupied by Britain and by Russia. From the standpoint of Europe in the world as a whole, they must undoubtedly be classed as European, yet their peripheral geographical situation corresponds to the special position that they occupy in regard to the more limited "little" Europe. No better illustration of this condition can be cited than the role they both played in the Napoleonic episode, and the manner in which they combined to provide the chief motive power that finally defeated Napoleon.

Europe being thus situated in geographical terms, this essay attempts to define the nature of this Europe and to determine whether and to what extent there are common and divisive elements in it. In brief, the purpose is to analyze, by searching the historical record, and with an eye on contemporary developments, the meaning and the prospects of unity for Europe.

What has emerged so far is the fact that what unity existed was essentially a cultural phenomenon. Europe, it has been pointed out, is Greek, Roman, and Christian. These are powerful strands that kept alive the ideal of unity, most simply and correctly expressed by the effective unity that Rome for a time succeeded in creating and maintaining. But the ideal became increasingly divorced from the existing reality. The northern Barbarians on one side, the Muslim Arabs on the other, gave Europe her modern geographical shape, the former bringing the North and East into the fold of common culture, the latter having the opposite effect, severing the Asiatic and African parts of the Mediterranean from the properly European.

Certainly one of the most, if not *the* most, important factor in this separation was the religious one. In Islam the theocratic aspect of the state has been fundamental, while "render unto Caesar" has been characteristic of the Christian view. This attitude led to the success of the secular state, so typical of Christendom, but also to the defeat of a powerful element of cohesion. The adjective "Holy" in the title Holy Roman Empire rather than a source of unity, furnished the object of a running quarrel between the state and the church over an overlapping domain where their jurisdictions contended; if the state won in the end, it was also fragmented into a number of states. These, not surprisingly, differed and quarreled, and the Empire's claim of universality was voided of content. The failure of Charles V may be regarded as the last attempt at recreating unity on the old foundation.

Interestingly enough, one of the many reasons for that failure must be seen in the religious break that was the Reformation. If high regard for the value of the individual is one of the essential traits of Western culture, which Greek as well as Christian traditions embody, it is also no doubt an element that makes for internal disunity. The Protestant Revolt, whatever its initial motivations and causes, gave a great boost to that divisive tendency. Once Charles V had failed, the European state began to take its modern shape; it was a century after his time that the modern state system of Europe was sanctioned at Westphalia. The heart of the system was the assertion of the principle of sovereignty which, when combined with the realities and the competitions of power, resulted in the compromise expressed by the balance of power. The facts and the behavior of power are ancient; certainly they were not discovered in the mid-seventeenth century. Nevertheless the so-called modern state system may properly be said to have enshrined and sanctioned the formal recognition of a novel doctrine and practice.

This put stress on disunity, for the acceptance of diversity, if it was shared by all and thus was a characteristic of the European scene, can hardly be regarded as other than a centrifugal force. Yet to a large degree the unity of culture remained and the cosmopolitan tone of educated eighteenth-century thought and society was in many respects more important than the petty quarrels and wars of the rulers, and the clash of their sordid, limited interests.

Into this situation the explosion of the French Revolution injected a novel component. For if the revolution was an authentic product of the circumstances and thought of the time, its result was in certain respects a deflection of the antecedent trend. Just as the earlier sixteenth-century religious reformers, motivated by the desire to put new life into the universal church, the universality of whose doctrine they did not at first question, ended up by implanting the disintegrating seed that Protestantism became, so likewise the eighteenth-century political reformers, largely concerned at first with man and society in their universal aspects, ended up by vastly emphasizing the consciousness of difference among the various types of European man.

The ideals, or the ideological aspects, of the French Revolution were not destroyed by Napoleon who indeed himself contributed much to their transplantation outside their initial French milieu. They remained a powerful living force after he had been removed from the political scene, but in the process of procuring his defeat, the consciousness of national difference became greatly developed and was itself a powerful tool in the expulsion of the French from other parts of Europe. Thus, this last episode had the effect of contributing, or at least emphasizing, in Europe, two simultaneously contradictory forces. As a consequence, democracy and nationalism are, in the political domain, forces that dominate the whole nineteenth century. That century, from the end of Napoleon to the outbreak of the First World War, is a transitional period which we shall examine from the standpoint of its significance for the concept and possibilities of unity in Europe. We may appropriately begin by looking at the condition of that Europe as it emerged from the turmoil of a quarter century of conflict.

I. Europe in 1815

In the final reckoning, Napoleon's France had succeeded in uniting virtually all Europe, exclusive of herself, because the common threat that she had been furnished sufficient common cause for union of the rest. France herself had to be dealt with, a matter that was arranged with both expedition and ease. The first Treaty of Paris, of May 30, 1814, reduced her to her original dimensions, with the minor qualifications indicated before. The brief reappearance of Napoleon on the scene a year later, the picturesque interlude of the Hundred Days that closed with Waterloo, deserves, in the present context, no more than passing mention, for it had no significant effects. Napoleon himself was more securely eliminated; the English removal and guardianship of him on St. Helena disposed of Napoleon for good, save as a future myth. For the rest, the second Treaty of Paris, in November 1815, differed little from the first: a minor territorial change, an indemnity, and foreign occupation, are of secondary importance; France remained France in France.

The first Treaty of Paris had been preceded by another two months earlier. The chief significance of the Treaty of Chaumont was the reassertion of the anti-French coalition. As on other occasions, the achievement of its main purpose proved in itself the greatest solvent of the coalition, the common danger having been removed. The disappearance of this danger had the inevitable effect of bringing to the surface again and reemphasizing temporarily submerged differences, of which there was no lack. The British in particular set great store by the Treaty of Chaumont. This was at the level of relationships of power and can hardly be called a manifestation of unity in any larger sense than the immediate and concrete.

To be sure, the peculiar nature of the French challenge, laden with ideological content, cemented the coalition more solidly than did the threat of French power alone. To the ideological aspect the other powers were in fact rather more sensitive than the British; it would presumably be dealt with in the gathering provided for in the first Treaty of Paris, and which accordingly met in Vienna the following September.

There is no cause to review the details of the Congress of Vienna but certain observations about it are relevant nevertheless to this discussion. All Europe was at Vienna, for Europe had to be politically reconstructed after so much of it had been so thoroughly and often arbitrarily shuffled into new combinations; but it is worth noting that Europe meant the rulers, not the peoples, hence by its very constitution the Congress asserted one theory of government—the rulers' right to rule—and denied another—the peoples' right to rule themselves. The work that was accomplished at Vienna may therefore be looked upon in two different lights, from the standpoint of power and from that of ideologies or principles.

If the old order was to be restored, in theory as well as in practice, so could the pre-existing practice be restored, characteristic of the pre-revolutionary community of European states, the right of all to exist, of which the balance of power was the sanction. Power was also acknowledged in another way: for the fiction of the sovereign equality of states, enshrined in such twentieth-century practices as the voting procedure in the General Assembly of the United Nations, there was no room at Vienna in 1815; the five Great Powers, without apology or question, kept in their hands the right of ultimate decisions. France, to be sure, was one of the five, and her representative, the seemingly indestructible Talleyrand, who had with skill navigated the whole gamut of regimes from the *ancien* to its return, could play the game with the best. Talleyrand served France well, but he, like his compeers at Vienna, was a European man. Also, as he well understood, France was after all on probation and at the moment defeated. Hence, it behooved him to bide his time and play a quiet role, stressing meanwhile the old principle of legitimacy that he would broadly link with that of justice.

In the circumstances, the temptation to seek special advantage was strong. None was more anxious to do this than the tsar, though the British were not unaware of similar possibilities. The British practice of collecting their gains overseas minimized the possibility of opposition since they sought no advantage *in Europe;* Malta and the Ionian Islands were small coin. But if he had no claims in Europe, Castlereagh was highly sensitive to the balance of power on the Continent; he, more than any one, objected to too great an extension of Russia into Europe, in which objection the British interest and the Austrian coincided. Since the tsar wanted to retain the major portion of Poland, and had to this end, and for the price of Saxony, enlisted Prussian support, the anti-French coalition was riven into two clashing combinations, the Anglo-Austrian pitted against the Russo-Prussian. In a sense it was patient Talleyrand who furnished the solution. It was none other than Castlereagh himself, leader par excellence of the anti-French coalition, who enlisted Talleyrand's support in forming the tripartite alliance that served the purpose, by threatening renewed armed clash, of effecting a compromise. This might appear unprincipled behavior, characteristic manifestation of Albion's perfidy, yet may also be viewed in an altogether different light. Castlereagh was indeed defending British interest, but by equating this with the balance of power, he identified it with the larger European concern for the defense of the liberty of all. Any one overmastering position was what must be avoided, and Russia in that guise was no better than France, or any other power.

Credit for the shape of things, as they emerged in Vienna, goes in fact more to Castlereagh than to any other single individual. There were many issues at Vienna, but the Polish-Saxon problem was the most dangerous of all; once it had been resolved, the Congress could deal with the rest and proceed to restore the old order. Some changes did occur and some things had been killed beyond the possibility of resurrection. This was true of the Holy Roman Empire, though the new German Confederation, presided over by the Austrian Emperor, bore very close resemblance to the defunct Empire; yet it was a modernized and refurbished version, the multiplicity of German states having suffered a nearly 90 per cent reduction in their number. Venice was gone for good, as was the Genoese republic, the former supplying, with Lombardy, adequate compensation for Austria's loss: her Netherlands possessions passed to the king of Holland, compensation in turn for some British imperial acquisitions at his expense. But these, with some other changes, were only minor reshufflings, and the 1815 map of Europe bore close resemblance to that of 1789.

How could it have been otherwise when the avowed purpose of the Vienna gathering was to reassert the validity of the old order, momentarily but in the end unsuccessfully threatened by revolutionary France? Legitimacy was the slogan stamped on the accomplishment of the Congress of Vienna. All the same, none could be quite so innocent as to believe that the military defeat of Napoleon meant the demise of the revolutionary idea. To guard against the possible resurgence of it was, for most of the participants, at least as important, in some respects more so, than the adjustment of limited clashing material interests. For the great issue at stake was what, in terms of political systems, should constitute the proper basis of the governance of all Europe, which is why the Congress of Vienna has such a large place in the annals of Europe.

Here we come to an interesting cleavage. To the ideological aspect of things, Britain was relatively less sensitive than others. That the legitimate Bourbon king should have returned to his legitimate position expressed the reintegration of France into the comity of Europe. But aged Louis XVIII understood that the *ancien régime* could not return to France unmodified. Consequently, most of the changes that had taken place in his realm he did not seek to undo. Even more, out of the kindness of his heart and his love for his people, he granted them a charter that would give them some voice in their own governance. The fact that the charter was "granted" served to maintain the theory that the source of the royal power did not reside in the nation, but the charter was actually a significant wedge that made the governance of France very similar in practice to that of the United Kingdom, a similarity that extended to the size of the respective electoral rosters. The British had found little cause for objection in the initial stages of the revolution in France.

In fact, taking Europe as a whole, and apart from the dif-

ferences in formal constitutional theory, governmental practices offered much similarity: the appanage of ruling belonged
everywhere to the qualified, the educated, the competent, the
upper layers of society, the ruling class; Castlereagh, Metternich, the tsar, and Talleyrand spoke very much the same
language. Yet the difference, especially in the context of the
future, is also highly significant, and the change between the
liberal West, Britain and France, and autocratic conservative
Europe, Austria, Prussia, and Russia, is an important factor
from the beginning of the nineteenth century.

Metternich was aware of this. The relationship and the
balance of power he understood in realistic fashion—he would
have compromised with Napoleon—and the opposition to Russian encroachment he fully shared with Castlereagh. But from
the latter he differed in his attachment to the conservative
principle for the governance of society. To him, therefore, the
alliance had the double purpose of maintaining the domestic
as well as the international order, a view that raises the most
important problem of the propriety of intervention by one
state in the affairs of another. Such intervention was on the
whole repugnant to the British, yet clearly Metternich had
logic on his side, for it is idle to pretend that if a large and
novel conception becomes established in a state it will or can
remain confined to its initial borders; the French Revolution
had convincingly demonstrated otherwise as have again the
events of our own time. Metternich, in addition, had another
special incentive for denying popular sovereignty, for he correctly understood that one aspect of that sovereignty, national
self-determination, constituted a threat to the very existence
of the Habsburg state. Metternich's views have long since
fallen into desuetude, yet must be granted the consistency
and standing of an authentic and not lightly to be dismissed
philosophical position; in these ideas he genuinely believed.
Metternich's role and influence at Vienna were second only

to Castlereagh's, and the arrangements that were embodied in the Final Act of June 1815 have subsequently been criticized for ignoring those successful nineteenth-century forces that were democracy and nationalism. This is true, but it was quite consciously and deliberately done; the settlement of Vienna expressed the controlling forces of the time and the consensus of a large segment of European thought.

However, Metternich realistically put greater trust for the future in common action, in his ability to guide and manipulate the European concert, than in formal expressions of the common purpose. The prospect of subsequent meetings of the powers was as much as planned common purpose could register; curiously enough it fell to the Russian tsar to attempt a more definite formulation of this European agreement. Tsar Alexander is an interesting character, whose shifting moods elude consistency, save in his unswerving devotion to the promotion of Russia's or his own interest. Yet he, too, was seriously concerned with the continued orderly and peaceful operation of the whole community of Europe.

Tsar Alexander's education and personal inclination made him acquainted with and not unsympathetic to eighteenth-century liberal thought. He had fought France, especially Napoleon, but in 1815 he was not bent on revenge and proffered to Louis XVIII advice that was on the whole conciliatory where arrangements for the future government of France were concerned. He preferred the liberal label to the reactionary, and if he wanted the kingship of Poland, he made Poland a constitutional kingdom. But Alexander was also endowed with a mystical streak, and the variety of his interests and predilections found expression in the Holy Alliance. The opening of the instrument in which his hope was formalized warrants quotation:

In keeping with the words of Holy Scripture, which enjoin all men to consider themselves as brothers, the three contracting rulers [Russia, Austria, Prussia] will remain united by the bonds of a true and indissoluble brotherhood, and, considering themselves as belonging to one country, will lend each other in all occasions and places, assistance, aid, and succor; considering themselves in regard to their subjects and their armies as fathers of families, they will guide these in the same spirit of brotherhood by which they are themselves motivated to protect religion, peace and justice.

The view of the Holy Alliance has varied, and debate is still going on about its precise meaning. The initial membership could easily be interpreted as a union of rulers to assist each other maintain their peoples in subjection, and Castlereagh referred to the tsar's proposal as "nonsense." Even Metternich was unsure but felt that the tsar must be humored; there were, after all, no enforcing provisions to give the pious declaration teeth. But it has also been contended that the Holy Alliance was in effect the true reality that guided Europe for some time, and some have seen in it a precursor of more formalized twentieth-century attempts—the League and the United Nations—to preserve the order of Europe. At the very least, here was expression of a common purpose that the tsar hoped all would join in underwriting. As a measure of existing unity one cannot say that, even in the most optimistic interpretation, it went a very long distance to effect that end.

Thus Europe on the morrow of the quarter century of turmoil that had its starting point in 1789 at Versailles seemed to a large extent to have returned to the old order. But the forces unleashed, twin aspects of the assertion of the right of peoples to choose their mode of government and their allegiance, if momentarily suppressed, would soon begin to reassert themselves. We shall deal with one of them first in an attempt to trace the impact of the national idea on the unity of Europe.

II. *The Disintegrating Force of Nationalism*

That people of similar ethnic background should organize themselves in separation from others of different background is hardly a matter to be connected with abstract good or evil. Syrians and Gauls could share alike in the characterization *civis romanus sum,* and the congeries of peoples over whom the Habsburgs had long ruled fared no worse for owing allegiance to the same ruler. It is however a fact that the tendency of diverse nationalities to separateness has struck deep roots, has been enshrined as a good, and the contribution to this state of affairs of the French Revolution need not be mentioned again. We are now, in our day, and have been for some time, much concerned with the more nefarious effects of this situation, and it is in fact a purpose of the present essay to look into the possibilities and the background of its alteration, where Europe at least is concerned.

Perhaps the simplest way to observe the effects of the nationalistic force in nineteenth-century Europe is briefly to follow the changes in the map that can be credited to it. There are very few that cannot, and the significance of the exceptions—instances of resistance to or violation of national feeling—is, for that very reason, no less.

Belgium and Poland

The union of the Low Countries into a single state was one of the accomplishments of Vienna. This was but a return to an earlier situation, though one that had not been in existence since the successful revolt of the Dutch against Spanish rule in the sixteenth century. During the intervening three centuries Dutch nationality had become firmly rooted while the southern part of the Netherlands had remained under first Spanish, and then Austrian, control. Whatever else they may have been the people of this territory were certainly neither Spanish nor Austrian. Nor by this time were they Dutch. Whether or not they were a distinct people might, in 1815, well be debated, for, standing astride the meeting line of Germandom and Latinity, half of them were Flemish (Germanic), the other half Walloon (French-speaking).

Though distinct from the Dutch, their union with the latter might have been acceptable had the Dutch king not treated them somewhat like conquered people. Trouble might have occurred even sooner than it actually did had it not been for political differences between the Catholic and Liberal tendencies that delayed united action. The events of July 1830 in neighboring France were the signal for trouble in Brussels, where the persistent obstinacy of King William of Holland in refusing moderate reforms led to a declaration of complete independence. As King William, unaided, failed to put down the revolt, once the powers had given the revolt their sanction, which they did in London, independent Belgium was born. Belgium is of especial interest, for it was initially a case of nationalism only to a degree; and in fact the subsequent story of Belgium has been considerably troubled by the existence in that country of the two distinct ethnic groups that have been mentioned: the Flemish have struggled for and increasingly secured cultural parity with the French-speaking Walloon. Yet Belgium still exists and it is easier to conceive of its becoming severed into two parts than of the whole or either part becoming merged into its neighbors. No doubt the birth and the continued existence of Belgium were due in considerable measure to the state of the international politics of Europe, but these could not have created the ethnic situation in the Belgian land, the emergence of which into separate existence was favored by the nineteenth-century climate.

It has been said sometimes that Belgian independence was secured in Warsaw. The quip arises from the fact that the tsar was willing to lend to the Dutch king armed assistance in maintaining his rule over Belgium; one reason he did not send his army to Belgium was the fact that it found more immediate employment in putting down rebellion in Warsaw. The authenticity of Polish nationality is less open to question than Belgian and the Poles had a long separate history. It was the nature of their management of their state, in combination with the covetousness of their neighbors, that resulted in the eighteenth-century partitions of Poland and the destruction of the Polish state. After 1815 Tsar Alexander I had become constitutional king of the greater portion of Poland. Here again, the nature of his rule, and that of his successor even more, gave rise to sufficient opposition to induce the rising in Warsaw contemporary with that in Brussels. The outcome in Poland was different, for the Poles were put down. They were harshly treated, all trace of Polishness was suppressed, and Poland was made in effect another Russian province, while emigration and Siberian exile decimated the leadership of the Polish national movement.

In the short run repression was successful, but after three decades had passed there was another rising in Warsaw. Another tsar ruled at the time, one indeed whose domestic reforms were to earn him the title of "Liberator," but the Polish rising of 1863 met the same fate as that of 1830. Romantic hopes and illusions, centering on the possibility of assistance from the West, were in both cases frustrated, mere sympathy being of little avail against Russian bayonets. For the remainder of the nineteenth century the Poles continued to exist under the alien rule of Russia, Prussia, and Austria; not a few became reconciled to their fate and even found high employment in the service of the states to which they formally belonged, but many also did not who kept alive the flame of

Polish patriotism and the consciousness of distinctness. Though prospects were long dim, the improbable collapse of the three empires among whom they were shared, unexpected by-product of the First World War, found Polish nationalism a very live reality, ready for resurrection. But that story is better left to later consideration.

Mid-Europe

By far the most notable achievement that can be credited to the force of nationalism in nineteenth-century Europe is the redrawing of the European map from the Baltic to Sicily. It may at first appear that the effect was one of integration, which indeed to a degree it was, yet not so in the reckoning and from the larger standpoint of Europe as a whole.

This was Metternich's own domain, consisting of three parts: the German Confederation, the Habsburg domain proper, and the Italian peninsula. It is significant that the parts overlapped, for a section of the empire of Austria, modern Austria and Bohemia, belonged in the Confederation, while another, the Lombardo-Venetian kingdom, was Italian. Such arrangements, largely alien to our later practice of sharp territorial separation of jurisdiction, must be seen as an expression of the deliberate refusal to acknowledge the nation as the proper foundation of the state. Metternich, quite rightly from his point of view, wanted it so. The emperor of Austria was by right President of the German Confederation, while Austria, in one form or another, was the paramount power among Italian states that, using more recent parlance, may well be called satellites. Thus Metternich's domain was perfect ground for the clash between irreconcilable principles, and the unfolding of that clash is enlightening.

If Italy was at this time merely a geographic expression, the memory of Italy as one had never wholly died. But it was definitely the impact of the French presence in Italy, especially Napoleonic arrangements, that opened up new prospects. The old order might be ostensibly restored in Italy after 1815; things could never again be the same. It is among the liberals of the day that we find the twin interests in constitution and union. These liberals were but a relatively small group in the society of the Italian states, the bulk of whose peasant population remained largely passive throughout the whole process of unification. This was important for the future of united Italy, yet leadership of change always resides in the educated and literate, especially in an economically backward milieu. In Italy also, the following of the liberal leaders steadily increased with the passage of time.

The Austrian paramountcy in Italy was a useful asset to Italian nationalism, for it supplied the concrete butt of opposition. The section under direct Austrian rule, Lombardo-Venetia, was the most progressive and best-administered section of Italy. It was also one of the chief foci of the national movement, where, more than anywhere, Austrian repression supplied martyrs to the national cause. How to achieve the desired result gave rise to much discussion. The peculiar nature of the papal office, with the Pope also among the Italian rulers, led some to envisage a federation, of which he would be head. Others saw better hope in a Piedmontese leadership, for in the kingdom of Sardinia, because of its location, the Austrian and French influences neutralized each other, making Sardinia the one authentically independent Italian state. There was also the more radical Mazzinian solution that, making a *tabula rasa* of all existing regimes, would establish a unitary republic in their stead.

For several decades all the discussion, some actual risings, and filibustering raids, produced nothing but failure, though all the while the educative effect of the agitation spread and the desire for unification overtook the initially greater hope for constitutions in the individual states of Italy. While he lasted, Metternich steadfastly fought the trend, the promoters of which his vigilant police watched and ferreted out. On occasion he would also use his armies when liberals had extracted a constitution, as in Naples in 1820, or ten years later when disturbances occurred in the central section of the peninsula. Yet all the while the agitation went on and made additional recruits for the cause of unification. Much of the agitation was literary in character, and the roster is long of names of that period that have found a permanent place in the history of Italian literature, but the line between literature and politics remained thin.

Thus the situation continued until, in 1846, the advent of a new Pope gave rise to a misunderstanding. Pius IX was never primarily a political man, but his lenient disposition caused him to open his reign with some concessions and reforms that made him the focus of both liberal and unitary hopes. The honeymoon was short and the events of 1848 soon made the Pope draw back. While a republic was established in Rome, Pius returned from his exile in Gaeta convinced of the danger of liberal agitation and for the rest of his long reign, another thirty years, remained the stanch defender of established ways, the conservative figure that history shows him.

One reason for the Pope's withdrawal in 1848 was the fact of war. Sardinia had declared war on Austria and for a time received the assistance, rather symbolic than effective to be sure, of contingents from other parts of Italy. The explosion of 1848, if the first instance of it was Italian, in Sicily, was far more than an Italian event; nearly all continental Europe was involved, much of the impulse of it came from the revolution in Paris, and it shook the entire Habsburg domain.

In the Germanic world a situation comparable to the Italian one had existed since the settlement of Vienna. The roots of German unitary nationalism, like those of the Italian, were initially and primarily cultural and may be associated with the Romantic movement, of which the German world was a prime home. But here also the impact of the French presence served, as in Italy, to give the movement a concrete starting point. The 1813 war of liberation and Fichte's *Addresses* have been mentioned. Also, the first half of the century was the heyday of German scholarship, and one aspect of that scholarship was the historical, than which none is better calculated to implant the national consciousness.

Thus the ground was prepared for the great upsurge, and in 1848 a rash of constitutions, or promises of constitutions, broke out in the Germanic world. Even in Vienna this was so, and Metternich, for once misjudging, at last gave up and went away. But the effects in his domain, Germanic proper and Habsburg, were now of contrary nature, though equally detrimental to the Habsburg position. For while in Frankfurt there assembled a Parliament in which the German people were represented,[1] in the empire of Austria, Hungarians, Czechs, and other Slavs asserted a centrifugal tendency. The overlapping of the German Confederation and of the empire of Austria at once created a dilemma in Frankfurt. To make a German Germany—allowing for the Bohemian exception—would have necessitated the disruption of the empire of Austria. To include the totality of the latter would create a state—Mitteleuropa—in which the largest single element

[1] One of the difficulties which appeared very early in the Frankfurt Parliament arose from the fact that in it were represented non-Germanic elements as well as the totality of the Germanic people. This situation arose from the fact that Bohemia, for example, was part of the German Confederation. Hungary, on the other hand, while under the Habsburg crown, was not in the Confederation, hence had no representation at Frankfurt.

would have been Germanic, but which would also contain a great deal else. The dilemma was made worse by the age-old rivalry between the ruling houses of Austria and of Prussia, Habsburgs and Hohenzollerns. The answer to this complex situation was "little Germany"—*klein-Deutschland*—the German lands that is, exclusive of those that directly belonged to the Habsburgs, the crown of which was offered by the Frankfurt Parliament to the Prussian king.

But by the time the offer was made to him, in March 1849, King William had recovered from his fright; also he recoiled from a possible conflict with Austria. The offer of the "crown from the gutter," he consequently declined. His fear of Austria was warranted, for in that state also the collapse of 1848 was by way of being retrieved, and Schwarzenberg, Metternich's worthy successor, able and ruthless, was re-establishing firm control; Metternich had yielded too soon and too easily. A resumption of war by Sardinia led to a mere repetition of defeat, and the loyal armed forces of Austria restored the former order, first in Prague, then in Vienna itself. For a while longer the Hungarians were obdurate in their resistance, but the combination of Austrian force, the skill that turned Croatians against them, plus the assistance of a Russian army, eventually disposed of them as well.

Thus it appeared in 1849 that the explosion of 1848 had been no more than a flare-up. Sardinia was defeated, and the French did for the Pope in Rome a comparable service to that rendered by the Russians in Hungary; Frankfurt disbanded into impotence and the old order had survived in the whole of Central Europe. Yet in a sense Metternich had been right. For if 1848 was, in the immediate, a failure, it was a warning and a measure of the progress that the liberal and the nationalistic forces had made. It took a little more than ten years for the latter to register almost complete success in the

95177

EMORY AND HENRY LIBRARY

Italian case, another ten beyond that for even greater success in the German.

The events of 1848–49 in Italy had, from the national point of view, discredited the Pope as well as the republican tendency. Sardinia, though defeated, emerged as a liberal state—King Victor Emmanuel had resisted the Austrian demand that he withdraw the constitution granted by his predecessor—and this same situation brought Cavour to the fore. With skill and deftness Cavour guided Italian destinies to the appointed end of union. The details of his diplomacy need not be considered here. Posing vis-à-vis Europe as the enlightened defender of order, he aroused much sympathy; but most of all he contrived to enlist the asset of French power that made war with Austria a plausible undertaking instead of a quixotic adventure. Cavour did not believe that *"Italia farà da sè* [Italy will manage alone]." His calculations proved right, shrewder than those of the French emperor. The latter's awkward handling of the situation, once war was under way, is, in the present context, of minor importance. With the defeat of Austria in 1859, the whole Italian structure irretrievably collapsed; a far more solid one took its place when the kingdom of Italy was proclaimed in 1861.[2] It was far more solid and durable for the simple reason that, allowing for its shortcomings and weaknesses, united Italy was founded in the last resort on the fact of Italian nationality. Here was indeed an outstanding success of the nationalistic force.

These Italian events had understandably elicited close attention and interest in Germany, where the *National Verein* came into existence in the year 1859 and where there was no relaxation in, among other things, the output of nationally-

[2] The Italy that emerged in 1861 was still incomplete, lacking on the one hand Papal Rome and on the other Venice that Austria still held.

minded historians. But things were quiescent in Germany until the counterpart of Piedmontese Cavour appeared upon the
Prussian scene in the shape of Prussian Bismarck. The two
men have often been compared and there is not a little
similarity between their accomplishments and their methods.
Practicers of *Realpolitik* that both were, their merit lies in
their accurate understanding of the possible, in their sound
judgment of situations and men, in their ability to use the
proper tool at the right time for the desired purpose. To be
sure, there were also significant differences.

In the space of less than ten years, from his assumption of
the Minister Presidency of Prussia in 1862 to the ceremony
at Versailles, in 1871, where the German Empire was proclaimed, Bismarck made Germany. Unlike Cavour, Bismarck
commanded large resources, and Prussia *farà da sè* was in his
case appropriate; no outside help was needed, merely neutral
non-interference, which his diplomacy secured. Starting with
the appropriately involved quarrel that grew around the disposition of the Danish-ruled duchies of Schleswig and
Holstein, he maneuvered Austria into a dispute and a quick
war. Once he had settled the ancient Habsburg-Hohenzollern
feud through the eviction of Austria from other than the
Habsburg lands themselves, he went on to deal with France,
who, he correctly judged, would not idly allow the formation
of a united Germany. The combination of his diplomatic skill
and of his adequate military preparations procured him the
desired result. As in the case of Italy his work was lasting for
the reason that it, too, was founded on the similar solid basis
of German nationality.

By 1871 the map of Central Europe had been thoroughly
remade, and in considerable measure simplified. For the
people of Italy and of Germany, nationalism was an integrating
force. However, some observations should be made about this

outcome as well as about the manner in which it had been brought about. The very making of Italy, the whole Risorgimento, had in large measure been an anti-Austrian operation. In 1866 Italy had again been at war with Austria and the result of half a century of struggle was the implanting of a deep-rooted tradition. The fact that Italy did poorly in the war of 1866, though she ultimately shared in the fruits of the Prussian victory, had the consequence of leaving an *irredenta*, and the slogan *Trento e Trieste* remained a rallying cry of Italian nationalism thereafter. It will be pointed out that within less than two decades, by 1882, Italy was joined to Austria in formal alliance. But the Triple Alliance, an arrangement born of power relationships and *Realpolitik*, papered over rather than really solved the nationalistic antagonism toward the Habsburg state. This factor ever remained a source of weakness in the alliance which in the test did not survive. The next European conflict would find Italy enlisted among the enemies of Austria.[3]

More serious than the Austro-Italian difference was that between Germany and France, and it provides the best illustration of the divisive influence of nationalism. That the German Empire should be born in the great palace of the French kings, symbol of past French grandeur even to those who would not have a king in France, was the gesture best calculated to humble national pride. It was perhaps of doubtful taste and rather less than wise, but the cession of Alsace

[3] Cavour and Bismarck were practicers of *Realpolitik*, meaning that they were primarily concerned with the promotion of the interest of the state and that they dealt with power. Nationalism, on the other hand, is largely an emotional force, in some respects idealistic. The two are fundamentally divergent approaches, but in a world of states the success of the latter depends upon the effective operation of the former. Thereby an element of ambiguity is introduced into the national state, with consequences that have been confusing in the operation of a world that has increasingly tended to become a world of such entities.

and a part of Lorraine was a more concrete and lasting injury
than the memory of a gesture that the passage of time might
soften and eventually erase. The case of Alsace has few parallels, for it is that relatively rare instance of an authentic
shift in national allegiance. Alsace had become French by
sentiment, as her representatives asserted in Bordeaux and
later continued to assert in the Reichstag in Berlin. Here is an
instance of a clash between two irreconcilable views of what
ultimately constitutes the proper test of nationality. On the
one hand, there is what may be called the French, or the
democratic—which, incidentally, is of necessity also the
American—view that nationality is a matter of personal choice:
he is French (or whatever else) who feels and asserts himself
such; on the other hand, there is the Germanic view that
would base nationality on some presumably more objective
criterion such as blood, or race. The weakness of this latter
criterion is patent, yet this fact is irrelevant, for men's beliefs
are the most potent and final determinants of their actions.
But what is most important here is that in either case the
supreme value of nationality is asserted. In this light, even
the view of Treitschke, who insisted that the people of Alsace
were German, and should be reminded of this, by force if
necessary, becomes understandable. No better instance could
be cited of the aberration that nationalism can be. For near
half a century the issue of Alsace did much to prevent any
normalization of Franco-German relations, and the mourning
garb that clad the statue of Strasbourg in the Place de la
Concorde was an apt symbol and reminder of a hopeless state
of affairs.

Thus we can see that, if the formation of Italy and of
Germany constituted a simplification of the map of mid-
Europe, the emergence of larger unified areas than had been
hitherto in existence was also a powerful contribution to the

disunity of Europe. The rest of mid-Europe consisted of the Habsburg domain proper, the Empire of Austria. The Prussian success in the war of 1866 induced a reorganization of the structure of that empire that was another clear instance of nationalistic success. The hyphenated Dual Monarchy that was Austria-Hungary was the result of the *Ausgleich* of 1867; the Hungarians largely secured that for which they had fought in 1848. The new arrangement might establish the possibility of diverse nationalities avoiding total separation and living together in peace on the basis of parity of position. But the *Ausgleich* was a mere halfway measure, for German Austrians in Austria and Hungarians in Hungary were minorities in their respective states. There were a number of other nationalities in the empire. Whether or not it could have survived on the basis of a larger reorganization, an extension of the initial dual pattern, we shall never know. The fact is that the nationalities that had secured recognition, the Magyars especially, refused to grant others the status which they had insisted upon for themselves. From the time of the *Ausgleich* to the end, the central problem of the Dual Monarchy was no less than that of survival; no better illustration can be given of the vitality of the nationalistic virus.

The Balkan Peoples

Nevertheless the Dual Monarchy still existed when war broke out in 1914. The Ottoman Empire also existed, but the nineteenth-century story of the European section of it may be summed up in one word—eviction. The Turks had conquered the Balkans during the fourteenth and fifteenth centuries, but they did little to absorb or assimilate their new subjects, apart from the toll of young recruits for their Janissary Corps they forcibly exacted. The Balkan peoples also for the most part remained Christian, a capital fact in preserving their separate identity from the Muslim Turks, particularly in view of the place of Islam in the Turkish state. The Balkan peoples fell to a low estate, especially as their masters declined and the quality of their administration deteriorated. As usual in the case of subject European peoples, the first sign of national revival took a cultural shape, of which the eighteenth-century Greek literary renascence is an illustration.

Low as they may have sunk, especially in Greece proper, the Greeks had certain special assets, among them the memory of ancient days, comparable to that of the Italians. In addition, they had the more tangible assets of commerce, shipping, and the Patriarchate of the Orthodox Church, customarily drawn from the wealthy Phanariote community of Constantinople. It was appropriate, therefore, that the Greeks should be the first to rise in rebellion, during the second decade of the century.[4] The struggle was harsh and prolonged but eventually successful for the Greeks. In 1830 the powers sanctioned the emergence of a sovereign Greek state. It is worth mentioning here the value to the Greek cause of the romantic philhellenic movement—Europe, we must remember, is Greek in an important segment of her culture—that manifested itself in much of Europe. For the English-speaking world in particular the case of Byron's death in Missolonghi is the most appropriate symbol of what happened; but there were others as well.

Thereafter the story continued in essentially uniform fashion, always intimately meshed, to be sure, with that of the politics of the powers. During the fifties, as an aftermath of the

[4] Strictly speaking, the Principality of Serbia had achieved a measure of autonomy as early as 1804. But she still remained linked to the Ottoman Empire and did not achieve full independence until 1878. Greece, on the other hand, immediately emerged as a fully sovereign state, which warrants considering the Greek case as the initiation of the process of emancipation of the Balkan peoples from Turkish control.

Paris Congress that ended the Crimean War, Rumania became autonomous, and gradually the Serbs had been asserting growing independence. The last vestiges of links of these states to the Porte were severed in 1878, when in Berlin another European congress, following another war in which the Turks had fared ill, settled afresh the Eastern Question. At Berlin also a little Bulgaria was born. For the next three decades matters remained fairly quiescent, but finally, in 1912, a Balkan alliance and war succeeded in evicting the Turks, save from the Straits themselves, where, for that matter, the population is prevalently Turkish.

The Balkan peoples in their struggles were sometimes helped, at other times hindered, by the powers, whose inability to agree about the fate of the Sick Man of Europe was the main cause of his delayed demise, but the sum total of a century of conflicts was the 1913 map of the Balkans, the lines of which followed reasonably well those of ethnic divisions. Another element in the story must be mentioned. The Balkan peoples had in common their religion and the desire to be rid of Turkish rule. But the alliance of 1912 between Greeks, Serbs, and Bulgarians was very difficult to contrive for the reason that in proportion to the extent to which these peoples were successful in achieving their common desire, their energies became diverted into internecine national differences. The last of the Balkan Wars in 1913 was one that pitted Bulgaria against her allies of the preceding year. Nationalism in the Balkans was no less a divisive force than in the rest of Europe.

To complete the roster of this record of the divisive national force, mention should be made of the fact that even the Scandinavian union of Sweden and Norway, arranged at Vienna in 1815, was finally dissolved in 1904. Again it was a

simple case of the separate assertion of the Norwegian nationality. This particular episode was contrived in unusually
civilized fashion and is one of the rare instances where the
successful assertion of separateness did not leave in its train
bitterness and recrimination. Separation it was, nevertheless.

Nor was the United Kingdom immune to the pervading
climate of the sacredness of self-determination. The Irish
people had long been held in subjection by those of the larger
neighboring island, but, like their counterparts in the Balkans,
began to agitate for the removal of their grievances. In moderate fashion at first, seeking no more than the redressing of
punitive discrimination and disability, the agitation grew in
the content of its demands that niggardly concessions had the
usual effect of abetting instead of assuaging. The case of Ireland is one of separateness within separateness, for the north-
eastern section of the island had in the course of time largely
been settled by immigration from Great Britain. The Ulster
minority was highly conscious of differences, religious and
others, fearful of submersion in the larger Irish Catholic
population, and by 1914 the British Government found itself
confronted with a seemingly insoluble dilemma and a threat
of civil war.

The nineteenth century is often seen as a period of peace.
Certainly it was such in contrast with our own century, yet
the period that covers the span of the Second French Empire
was one during which, on four separate occasions some of the
major powers were involved in conflict among themselves.
Save in the first of these, the Crimean affair, the issue was
fundamentally connected with a problem of nationality. In
all these cases France was very concerned, and in two of them
was a prime participant, although her involvement grew out
of considerations of her own position and power. The third

Napoleon, like the first, was intimately associated with the final making of Italy and of Germany, though not exactly in the manner that he would have preferred. Yet, curiously enough, Napoleon III was an authentic nationalist—his sympathies went to those, whoever they might be, who sought to affirm the right of self-determination. Whatever velleities he may have felt of a Europe successfully organized in peace on the basis of the universal application of that principle were destined to be sadly frustrated.

The Franco-Prussian War of 1870 is a landmark in the development of European nationalism. For the manner in which Germany was made by Bismarck, through the stamp of success that it put on his blood-and-iron methods, had the effect of abetting the intransigent, aggressive aspect of that force. The military tradition fitted only too well into the old practice of the Prussian state, a tradition thus transferred to the new German Empire, which the ineffectual forty-eighters had been unable to create by methods milder than the ruthless ones of Bismarck. That same conflict had an exacerbating effect across the Rhine, where modern nationalism may be said to have been invented. The Third Republic nurtured its grievance; the Boulanger episode is significant of a state of feeling, and the first decade of the twentieth century was to witness in France the *réveil national*. Much of Europe was in fact affected at that time by an intensification of the nationalistic consciousness, which contributed not a little to the breakdown of 1914.

Yet for nearly half a century after the Franco-Prussian War, apart from peripheral Balkan disturbances that caused no breach among the major powers, Europe contrived to stay at peace. For this fortunate passage there are various reasons, but among them not the least important is to be found in economic conditions.

III. The Contradictory Effects of Economics

The one central and all-important fact in the economic life of nineteenth-century Europe is the spread of industry over much of that continent. The novelty of industry must be emphasized, and the problems that it brought in its train were, like their basic cause, quite novel. The phenomenon of which the history books did not begin to take formal notice until late in the century, under the label Industrial Revolution, began generally in the latter third of the eighteenth century, roughly contemporary with the political upheaval in France. Its locale at first was England. By the time the powers assembled in Vienna believed they had successfully dealt with the political revolution, there was little of industry outside England, and even there it was far from having reached the scale of large enterprise. It is enlightening to compare the settlement of Vienna with twentieth-century treaties, that of Versailles for example. Much of the Treaty of Versailles is taken up with economic provisions of which the Vienna settlement was largely innocent, for the simple reason that there was no cause for it to be otherwise. A society which is still overwhelmingly agrarian is not involved in the multiplicity of intricate and delicate relationships that constitute so large a part of the concern of our day.

The story of the spread of industry in Europe is familiar and will not be dwelt upon. From its initial English home industry first appeared across the Channel, in Belgium and northern France, and the attempt to prevent the export out of England of technical processes and knowledge was neither very successful nor long pursued. By mid-century the development of the new activity in France was substantial; it had reached beyond the Rhine, and when the showdown with Germany took place the two countries were roughly on a par in industrial standing. The eastward and southeastward spread continued, until by the time of the First World War even still overwhelmingly agricultural Russia had begun to be penetrated by industry. She had the longest railway mileage of any European country, though, considering her dimensions, this meant very low density, and her foreign trade was of the same dimensions as that of little Belgium. By 1914 the distinction was valid between "inner" Europe, the Europe of steel and steam, and "outer," essentially agricultural, Europe. The former was roughly confined within the boundaries of a line that would run from Glasgow, through Stockholm, Danzig, Trieste, Barcelona, and back to the starting point. Inner Europe still contained much agricultural activity; the economic life of a country like France, for example, was about equally divided between agriculture and industry. Also, while industry was spreading on the Continent its dimensions were growing in Britain, though by the end of the century the British position of primacy was no longer unchallenged. We wish at this point to examine some of the consequences of this novel condition for Europe as a whole, especially from the standpoint of its impact on greater unity or further separation. These consequences were diverse.

Free Trade and the Social Question

The economic theory which prevailed at the time when industry made its appearance is that which generally is labeled mercantilistic. One characteristic of that view was a highly nationalistic and restrictive approach; it was considered to be the proper function of the state to enhance its wealth and the well-being of its members through the device of minute supervision and regulation of the whole of the economic activity of the nation. Protection, navigation acts, colonial monopoly, the work of Colbert and of Frederick of Prussia, are typical manifestations of this approach, generally accepted by all. The belief long prevailed in the fixity of the totality of wealth; competition for it through the attainment of a favorable balance of trade, leading to an accumulation of specie, was a corollary of the larger view. Everyone is familiar with the economic causes of the American Revolution.

But it was also highly significant that that event, putting an end to the British monopolistic position in the colonial trade, was followed by an increase instead of by a diminution of Anglo-American exchanges. It was appropriate that the date of the Declaration of Independence should be the same as that of the publication of the *Wealth of Nations*. Adam Smith's treatise questioned the validity of the restrictive practice; he and the contemporary Physiocrats thought that the freer way of *laissez faire* would be more advantageous. It was appropriate also that this novel alternative view of the most profitable practice in trade should come out of the initial home of the industrial revolution.

The disturbances that grew out of the French Revolution were hardly conducive to expanded exchanges; the economic war that was the Continental System has been mentioned. It is of interest that, while it went on, England made the most of the opportunity to break into the Spanish colonial monopoly that was offered by happenings in Spain and by the revolt of Spain's American colonies; while on his side Napoleon did his utmost to secure for French manufactures the European market out of which he was seeking to keep British goods. By the time the struggle came to an end a contrary interest had, to a point, developed between England and the Continent. If the Continent had need of England's production, and if the British were especially anxious to obtain unimpeded outlets for their accumulated output, the view that came to prevail on the Continent was, on the whole, that protection was needed from British competition.

It should not be inferred from what has just been said that British sentiment was unanimous. The agricultural interest was at this time still substantial in England and wedded to protection. Corn Laws were enacted in 1819. Nevertheless, especially in retrospect, the trend that favored the new rising industry is clear. Once the intense political contest that resulted in the passage of the Great Reform Bill in 1832 had been resolved the economic question became the greater object of contention. The Reform Bill itself, for that matter, if it was primarily a political act, was not devoid of economic content, giving as it did greater recognition to the new force whose strength resided in industrial wealth and in the growing cities that were so fast to alter the landscape of Britain. Increasingly, the *laissez faire* doctrine was taking clearer shape and gaining more adherents. One aspect of it in particular became the focus of attention—free trade. In simplest form the theory possesses much attraction that a century of development has not succeeded in destroying, despite much else of contrary orientation: let each concentrate on producing that which he is best qualified to produce, considering all the attendant circumstances, from the location of resources, to climate, quality of land, and human skills; let, in addition, all exchange the products of their skills in wholly unimpeded fashion. This will bring about the economic millennium whereby the greatest amount of the best goods will be available at the cheapest price to the largest number.

Attractive as the prospect may be in the long term, it would, in the immediate, necessitate readjustments, some of which might be drastic and harsh. The battle was prolonged and hard-fought, and the outcome of it, the abolition of the Corn Laws in 1846, is a landmark in the story of Britain. By espousing free trade without reservations the British people took the major decision to destroy agriculture in Britain; circumstances dictated that they were best qualified to produce manufactured goods, while cheaper grain than their own could be obtained from others. The decision was an outstanding success. Cheaper corn meant, among other things, by repercussion cheaper labor costs, hence cheaper goods that confirmed the British capacity to compete; Britain had no difficulty in procuring all the food that she needed in exchange for her manufactures and thus she became the workshop of the world. Under the new dispensation she prospered, until, with the passing of time, free trade became enshrined as a doctrine that took on some of the attributes of moral good rather than being merely the expression of a special interest.

But this is only part of the story. For if there is no denying that in the final reckoning the standard of living of the British people as a whole, the working mass included, followed a rising trend, the adjustment was not wholly automatic. It was but another aspect of the liberal doctrine in economics, of which free trade is one facet, that competition should operate unfettered in all aspects of economic activity. The market, the law of supply and demand, is the great regulator of price, automatic controller of the equilibrium that will insure the best for the most. Labor is in this view but another commodity, subject to the same law of supply and demand. Such an outlook, quite similar to that of the Malthusian view, many would now regard as barbaric, but the logical consistency of it must be granted. There is no denying that the ethos of capitalism, the ultimate sanction of profit, is the antithesis of the medieval concept of fair price based on effort and need.

It was also logically consistent that conditions in the factories of early nineteenth-century England should be harsh, although their individual owners were not necessarily hard men and sometimes actually deeply imbued with the Christian ethic of charity. But it could hardly be expected that the immediate victims of the system should derive adequate satisfaction from the contemplation of economic law and the prospect of the ultimate millennium. There were Luddite riots in England and the response of the laboring man was often ugly. The coming of industry in England had the effect of sharpening the class cleavage among those engaged in the new form of economic activity: the owners, the capitalists, the bourgeois, reaping the wealth of profit on the one hand; the depressed workers on the other. It was entirely fitting that Marx should obtain the chief support for his thesis of the inevitable class struggle from an analysis of nineteenth-century conditions in the factories of England. That Marxism in the end should have gained but little following in England does not concern us at this point, and of the Marxist view in general more will be said in later pages.

If the discussion so far has mainly focused on England it is for the simple reason that the developments under review took place first and on the largest scale in that country. No other country to this day has so exclusively diverted its activity into industry in the proportion that England has. But if England had a position of primacy in time of development, the same development of industry could, and did, happen elsewhere. And it is significant that industrial activity in all its aspects, be they setting of prices, rates of profit, financial connotations, labor problems, is not confined to national boundaries.

The free-trade view is par excellence international, and the English exponents of it took a world view rather than a national one, even if they did not grant sufficient weight to the peculiar advantage that accrued to Britain from the fact of priority in time of development. There were advocates of free trade in other European lands, but the agitation failed to accomplish that which its exponents expected. If the benefits of the uniformizing reforms of the French Revolution on the economy of France were never threatened in France, across the Rhine the German states were masters in their individual houses; but it was very shortly after the settlement of Vienna that some of them, mainly under Prussian prodding, began to join in customs unions. The movement, once launched, proved irreversible and within less than two decades the German *Zollverein* had come into existence. The political significance of this development was enormous, as we shall presently see, but for the moment it will suffice to observe that the benefits of free trade within the German union were not extended beyond its limited Germanic bounds. Vis-à-vis the outside, the *Zollverein* retained instead a protectionist attitude, as did France generally.

In France there was a period of hesitation, albeit a passing one. It was during the Second Empire that the advocacy of free trade reached its greatest success in that country. But the Cobden-Chevalier treaty concluded with Britain in 1860 was rather a temporary deviation than the herald of a new orientation. The French agricultural interests were desirous of retaining for themselves the French market, a desire that was shared by the French manufacturing interests; either might perceive the benefits for itself of free trade in the opposite sector, but the final outcome was agreement on protection for both. The Third Republic adopted on the whole a protectionist policy. And a similar situation developed in Germany, which the phrase "marriage of steel and rye" most adequately sums up.

In Italy, likewise, political union brought to the former states the common benefits of a larger free-trade area, but these benefits stopped at the new national boundary.

Thus it appears that the benefits of free trade were, during the nineteenth century, extended to larger areas in Europe

—the national states—but failed to extend across their borders. The vigor and intensity of nationalistic feeling in fact transferred itself to the economic domain, with the consequence that the expanding activity of industry became, at least to a point, a divisive rather than the integrating factor that it might have been. The validity of one aspect of the problem must also be granted, best associated with the need for protecting infant industries that could otherwise never strike firm roots in face of the competition of older establishments. The argument has been familiar in the American milieu, and while its nineteenth-century point, especially vis-à-vis Britain, may be conceded, the record has shown that the infant's desire for protection has often been maintained by the full-grown man, sometimes become a giant well able to look after himself. Traditions, especially such comfortable ones as seem to make profit assured, are understandably highly resistant to modification.

This turn of events was a disappointment to British free traders, whose reaction was in the last resort not very different from that of others. The spread of industry had the inevitable effect on Britain of making competition keener, the sharpest challenge of all eventually coming from Germany where, among European states, industrial development was greatest and fastest once political union had been realized. During the penultimate decade of the century some in Britain began to question the validity of continued devotion to free trade in face of the failure of the rest of the world to emulate the British example. Free trade in the abstract they still believed in, but reality must be faced, and why should benefits that Britain granted others remain unilateral? Their solution was the advocacy of free trade in the domain within British control, the Empire, but protection of that from the rest. The British Empire was indeed vast at this time, yet one can see in this a version of the same attitude that produced

the German *Zollverein,* then made it as a whole protectionist. It was entirely consistent and fitting that those who thought
in such terms—the group of Liberal Unionists clustered around
Joseph Chamberlain, a typical product of the new British industrial class—should secede from the Liberal Party, oppose
any concessions in Ireland, and advocate imperial expansion.

There is one other aspect of the situation that deserves
mention, one that is especially clear in the Anglo-German
relationship. The attitude that has just been indicated in Britain was most of all a response to German competition. However, it so turned out that the volume of direct Anglo-German
exchanges was very great, with the result that Germany was
at once Britain's sharpest rival and best customer. The outcome could be greater freedom of exchanges as well as re-
striction of them. Owing to the strength of the implanted traditions of free trade in England, free trade was not abandoned,
being merely questioned before the First World War. But
the dilemma continued after the war for Britain, if anything
in sharpened form and with important consequences.

The Second Industrial Revolution

Yet the picture of the divisive effects of economic development is not wholly unqualified. The period of roughly the
second half of the century is sometimes spoken of as that of
the second industrial revolution, a usage warranted by, among
other things, the phenomenon of the growing size of enterprise. This was the time during which business graduated into
the giant stage. As a concomitant to this growth the role
of banking and finance assumed a correspondingly larger share
and importance, and the effects of it again were divergent,
simultaneously promoting the extension of international links
while serving also as an adjunct to national policy.

This was the time when various forms of combination, mergers, trusts, and cartels began to flourish. They first appeared at the national level. Germany was the home par excellence of cartels, encouraged sometimes by the state, while in the English-speaking world, more permeated with devotion to free enterprise and competition, the tendency was rather to curb such combinations in restraint of trade. But whatever the difference in national outlook and practice, in one way or another business grew large. This growth showed not only the desire for profit inseparable from the capitalist practice, but also a response to technical conditions, complexity of man-ufacturing processes, and advantages in the form of reduced unit costs that flow from mass production. This tendency to combination, or at least mutually agreed regulations, did not remain confined within the national framework, but instead business became in some of its activities increasingly inter-national.

There was simultaneously an enormous expansion of the volume and value of international exchanges. The forging of the myriad links of international trade and the growing dependence of each upon his connections with all, made it increasingly desirable to preserve international order and peace. There is an apt saying in French, *L'argent n'a pas d'odeur*, which might in this context be translated as the internationalistic tendency of capitalism. Certainly this tend-ency was clearly manifested in the case of finance.

It is a fundamental law of the nature of capital that it will seek the most advantageous employment. Just as the market is the great regulator of economic activity in general, so the search for profit is the motivating drive that will direct the use of capital. At least this was the case in the heyday of free enterprise that was the world of pre-1914. At that time the influence of direction by the state was minimal, certainly by contrast with our day, and the view was generally accepted that the best government is that which governs least. Europe

produced a large accumulation of capital, a substantial proportion of which sought fields for investment, beyond the
range of near domestic opportunity, to the far corners of the
earth. American and Argentine railways were in considerable
measure built by British capital, while French capital filled a
similar function in Russia. Examples could be multiplied *ad
infinitum*.

The case of French capital well illustrates the concomitants
and implications of this type of activity. France is a rich
country and the relatively moderate tempo of French industrial growth made all the more available supplies of French
capital for use abroad. Russia, an undeveloped country, was
in need of foreign capital. She had secured much of it in
the German market. But toward the end of the eighties
some difficulties intruded between the two countries, with the
result that the Russians turned to the Parisian market instead.
From 1887 on, a steady flow of French capital, which by
1914 had reached the impressive total of some 12 billion francs,
found its way to Russia. To equate this financial connection
with the political act that was the Franco-Russian alliance
would be to take a simplist view, for, in the Franco-Russian
relationship, political and economic-financial factors are
closely intermingled and the political deserves priority of importance. Nevertheless, the fact is significant that the alliance
came into existence a few years after the flow of French loans
had begun. Thus we see the importance of financial power and
transactions in national policies and international relations.
French capital was also used for armament in Russia and
some of the Russian railway building, at French urging, was
guided by strategic considerations. It was during the eighties
and nineties also that the poor state of Franco-Italian relations coincided with what may be described as the substitution
of French by German capital in Italy.

Yet, on balance, the stress must be on the fact that the

growing multiplicity and intricacy of economic and financial relations was regarded as an integrating factor of peace rather than the opposite. The trader and the banker tend to prefer stable and smooth conditions that are best suited to the prosperity of their endeavors. Later on, after the First World War, much was written about merchants of death, those who drew profit from war. No doubt such existed, and instances occur where the munitions makers especially were found to have encouraged conflict and to have, with the consistent catholicity of the profit motive approach, dealt impartially with opposing belligerents. But, especially where the great European powers were concerned, the portrayal of the banker and the munitions maker as abettors of division and conflict is a misleading distortion.

Europe Overseas

Much has also been written on the issue of whether the trader follows the flag or whether the reverse is the case. Without entering that unrewarding controversy, this may be an appropriate place to look at the significance of imperial activity, again primarily from the standpoint of its divisive or cohesive effects.

Imperialism, in the broad sense of the tendency of the more advanced and the stronger to encroach upon the less advanced and the weaker, is an ancient activity, probably destined to thrive until the world is one. Imperialism may also be regarded as one of the classical means by which the ways of one culture are transferred to another. In comparison with others, European imperialism is young, even if one trace its development to the sixteenth-century beginnings of European expansion. The phenomenon is complex but it may be granted that by far the most powerful component in the imperial drive is economic motivation.

Europe's imperial activity had led to many conflicts, such as the great Anglo-French contest that reached its climax with the virtual elimination of France from empire in the eighteenth century. What happened in 1815 has been mentioned; it fitted well into Britain's by then well-established imperial tradition and primacy. Nevertheless, despite the fact that the Napoleonic wars resulted in imperial accretions for Britain, the memory of the successful American bid for independence contributed to the popularity of the view that empire-building was a self-defeating enterprise. The simile of growing children who eventually abandon the family fold to establish their own independent existence was commonly used to explain that colonies were in the course of time fated to reach maturity, then independence.

The coming of industry itself worked against vigorous imperial activity during the earlier part of the nineteenth century. For with it came, especially in Britain, the emphasis on free trade, in addition to which it is natural that industry should first concern itself with the nearer home market. The tendency therefore was to reverse the former emphasis on the monopolistic position of colonial trade; in the Far East Britain was rather concerned with the opening of the Chinese market than with the securing of exclusive control of territory in that country. What imperial activity there was in this period was mainly in the hands of three peoples, the British, the French and the Russians.

The special nature of the Russian case, the drive to the Pacific, has been mentioned, but the pressure in Central Asia on the back door of India also asserted itself. The French in 1830 began to lay the bases of their North African establishment even though they were not sure until some years had passed that it was worth their while to remain in North Africa at all. In China they followed the British. The French also established claims to some Pacific islands, as did the

British; one of the reasons the British came to be established in New Zealand, for example, was to prevent French settlement there. It was hardly a case of vigorous activity and competition, despite some minor incidents; it was rather, for both, one of carrying on a tradition. There was still much room in the world which the powers had not an overly strong desire to appropriate.

The second Napoleon in France, a restless and imaginative man, though one inclined to deficient steadiness of purpose and to the pursuit of too many hares at one time, showed some interest in imperial expansion. The beginnings of later French Indochina date from his time, and the Suez Canal was built while he ruled France. The Suez Canal Company was a private business undertaking that did not politically implicate the French state. It was, however, essentially a French undertaking and, because of its enormous significance for world trade, may properly be placed under the imperial label. It is significant that, despite the overwhelmingly important position of Britain in world trade at that time, it was not Britain that built the Canal. Palmerston was not pleased, but, apart from minimizing its significance, was content with a policy of pinpricks while the Canal was being built. But the most ambitious imperial enterprise that Napoleon III undertook was his ill-fated Mexican adventure. It is of interest that it began as a joint Anglo-Franco-Spanish affair to enforce the collection of Mexican debts, though the French proceeded alone to set up Maximilian as emperor of a presumably dependent Mexico. It was hardly a reasonable undertaking and understandably caused American displeasure, though America was momentarily neutralized by her own Civil War.

However, the doings of Bismarck across the nearer Rhine were more important for Napoleon III than American annoyance. The Mexican Empire collapsed when the support of

French bayonets was withdrawn. It was not many years before the Second French Empire itself met a similar fate.
The almost simultaneous making of Germany and of Italy
had naturally absorbed all the energies of the Central European world; that situation alone, even if there had been no
other factors, would explain why there was no energy or room
left for the cultivation of imperial interests on the part of
Germany, Italy, or Austria. But after 1870 the picture rapidly changes. The new Austria-Hungary continued to remain
too preoccupied with her domestic problems to develop the
luxury of extra-European interests. Such imperial tendencies
as she entertained, and they may fairly be described by that
name, remained confined to the nearer Balkans, which for
that matter were closely connected with those same domestic
problems, that of her disparate nationalities most of all. It was
otherwise with Germany and with Italy, especially with the
former.

This situation roughly coincided in time with another. The
relatively minimal incentive to imperial expansion that characterized the first part of the century because of the youth of
the industrial process, changed into a vigorous force with
the coming of the second industrial revolution. The driving
force of European growth, of which Germany is the best
illustration, was very great in the second part of the century;
not surprisingly, competition became increasingly sharp.

It was Disraeli who presided over the fortunes of Britain
during part of the seventies. It was he who, in 1875, in
brilliant and picturesque fashion, if perhaps straining constitutional propriety, in part at least retrieved the British error
in allowing the Suez Canal to be a French enterprise. The
episode of his snapping up the Khedive's bloc of shares is
well known. It was the following year that he induced Queen
Victoria to assume the imperial title of India. The gesture did
little to alter the reality of the British position in India,

but it was the most fitting symbolic assertion of belief in the validity and desirability of empire. Disraeli himself was a convinced believer in empire, and it was wholly appropriate that two years later he should threaten war to contain Russian ambitions toward the Straits. Not the least interesting aspect of that episode is the sharp turn of British opinion that accompanied it: full of sympathy for persecuted Balkan Christians at first, and correspondingly incensed against the unspeakable Turk, the perpetrator of Gladstone's *Bulgarian Horrors*, who deserved nothing but eviction from Europe, British opinion became violently pro-Turkish once it appeared that the desirable act of eviction might be effected by the Russians.

Disraeli was followed by Gladstone, a little Englander by predilection, whose bent was markedly against empire. Yet it was Gladstone who, in 1882, was responsible for initiating the long "temporary" occupation of Egypt.[1] Differing from his predecessor, Gladstone took the step with reluctance and qualms, but the fact that he did take it is all the more significant, for it furnishes conclusive evidence of the momentum that the imperial drive had acquired by this time.

The French felt frustrated in Egypt, although they themselves had renounced the opportunity to join in the British action. For Egypt had become the particular focus of their Near Eastern interest: from the first Napoleon's picturesque expedition, through Mehemet Ali, to the Suez Canal, a continuing tradition had taken root. The French abstained in 1882 as the result of a domestic situation, but they themselves, the year before, had taken rather more definite action by

[1] Britain remained in effective control, though formally in "temporary" occupation, of Egypt until her status was regularized with the establishment of her protectorate in 1914. She subsequently had to contend with the force of Egyptian nationalism, but not until 1955 did she wholly relinquish her hold of that country.

establishing their own protectorate over Tunisia. The case of French imperialism is in some ways exceptional, for it fits rather poorly the primarily economic explanation of that activity. France was unusually self-contained, suffering from a deficiency instead of a surplus of population, and French capital did relatively little to exploit the French colonies, going to such places as Russia instead. This makes it all the more remarkable that the generally pacific Third Republic should have built an empire, second in dimensions to the British alone. Yet this was done, though it was in large measure for psychological reasons: empire and prestige in some degree compensated for the humiliation of the Franco-Prussian War. At all events the French imperial drive operated with vigor, even if on a shoestring at times.

Using established positions, North Africa, some equatorial holdings, and small Somaliland as operating bases, the French began to shape a vast scheme, which, centering on the Sahara and Lake Chad, would make almost the entirety of Africa north of the Equator into an enormous French preserve. The concrete symbol of such dreams took the form of the expedition that Captain Marchand was to lead from the west coast, across the Nile, to the Red Sea. But the British imperial tradition had even greater continuity and force than the French. The British dream in Africa took the shape of a vision of which the Cape to Cairo railway scheme is the best expression. These visions overlapped and might well be expected to lead to rivalry if not open clash: the tradition of Anglo-French imperial rivalry had old and deep-rooted precedents into which the late nineteenth-century situation could insert itself to a nicety.

The rivalry did indeed develop, and not in Africa alone. It was in 1893 that the two powers met in Southeast Asia where the equilibrium of their forces was largely responsible for the independent survival of Siam instead of her partition. In

Africa it was the French among others—the Germans joined
them in this—who blocked the purchase of a strip of the Belgian Congo that could have served to establish territorial continuity of British holdings. But when finally Captain Marchand appeared on the Nile at Fashoda in 1898, he was met
by Kitchener, who asserted a British claim to the whole Nile.
The situation was dramatic: the two handfuls of men represented the extreme tentacles of movements, the roots of which
were respectively in London and in Paris, the whole power
of which stood, in the last resort, behind them. Had there
developed an open clash our history books should doubtless
now explain how such an episode was a most natural, perhaps
even inevitable, outcome in the light of the centuries-old background of Anglo-French imperial relations.

But the clash was avoided, essentially by the French reasonableness in yielding on this particular occasion, and the
Fashoda crisis with its aftermath furnishes one of the most
enlightening examples of the complex repercussions of imperial activity on intra-European relations. Feeling was strong,
especially in France, after Fashoda, but the British, having
had their way on the Nile, were also willing to be reasonable. Within less than a year an agreed line of demarcation
of spheres of influences in the Sudan was drawn. This, to a
point, was prelude to the much larger accomplishment of
1904, when the possibility of composition of Anglo-French
imperial rivalry, not in Africa only but in the whole wide
world, was established—as it turned out nearly for good.
There were other elements that went into the making of the
Entente Cordiale besides the adjustment of differences in an
activity pursued in rivalry and reasonableness, but these may
better be left for later consideration. The emphasis at this
point is on the balance between rivalry and agreement, born
of a substantial area of common outlook.

The British and the French, if they were properly in a sense the most outstanding contestants in the imperial domain, were not the only ones by this time. Once Germany was made, Bismarck took the position that his creation was a satisfied power whose proper role remained confined to Europe. This he genuinely meant, but the very forces that unification had released, and the development of which he himself encouraged, economic growth most of all, could not long be contained in their initial mold. Though Bismarck had at first no interest in empire, he could not resist the development of German colonialism even while he was still himself in office. The French occupation of Tunis in 1881, and the British of Egypt the following year may be regarded as the opening guns of the colonial race which very soon assumed very large proportions. Africa was largely unpre-empted, much of it still unknown during the preceding decade, but all manner of claims began to be staked out in the eighties. The dangers of unregulated competition were clearly visible to all who shared in common the desire to promote their individual interests while avoiding some violent clash. This is the background of the colonial congress that gathered in Berlin. In addition to dealing with the specific matter of the Congo, and establishing its international status, the congress went on to formulate certain rules, the purpose of which was to introduce a measure of order into the chaos of imperial competition. It too was expression of a measure at least of common ground and agreement among the powers.

This did not prevent certain clashes. The Anglo-French conflict is perfect illustration, and there was friction between the Germans and the British as well, for Germany, too, had grandiose ambitions of an order comparable to the British and French. Her existing possessions might serve as bases for the coalescence of a vast Central African domain. The telegram that the German emperor sent to President Kruger of Transvaal was a gratuitous gesture that served the purpose of irritating the British while doing little to assist the Boers. They did, however, enjoy well nigh universal sympathy when the British proceeded to their final subjugation at the turn of the century. But the Boer War did not result in significant international complications, while at the same time the powers were able to co-operate in China in putting down the Boxer Rebellion. The European forces that went to Peking were made up of various national contingents jointly under a German commander. Here was a concrete manifestation of European unity of a sort.

The Russians had no stake in Africa, Asia providing ample scope for their imperial ambitions. The growing tension that developed between themselves and the British in Asia has been mentioned: from Peking to Constantinople these two interests came into ever closer contact. But in this case, as in the Anglo-French, the outcome was accommodation rather than open conflict. The Anglo-Russian agreement of 1907 is of the same nature as that which was the basis of the Entente Cordiale of 1904: Tibet, Afghanistan, and Persia furnished the bases of agreement, just as Morocco and Egypt had in the Anglo-French situation.

But it was out of Africa that some further and also very sharp crises developed. Morocco was an independent country, albeit one that was backward and maladministered, to the extent that one might fairly question whether or not it properly deserved the name of state by the norm of European conditions. In the context of pre-1914 imperial activity, Moroccan independence was doomed. Also, in the context of existing establishments as they had grown to be by the close of the century, Morocco properly "belonged" to France. All had an equal right to trade in Morocco, however—a situation sanctioned by the international act of Madrid of 1880—and all had potentially equal claims to possession. The French did the proper thing in securing the consent of others who had significant interests in Morocco, in each case for what may be considered an adequate price: Libya for Italy, Egypt for Britain, the Mediterranean section of Morocco for Spain. There was but one exception—Germany. The Germans, too, agreed that Morocco would one day be French, an outcome to which they had no objection. But they wished to secure a price for their consent, and quite naturally the best obtainable price. Yet in the end, despite two major crises over the issue, in this case also the fundamental understanding of common ground prevailed, for in 1911 the quid pro quo of German consent in exchange for the price of part of the French Congo was reached. The establishment of the French protectorate over Morocco in 1912 led to no further complications.

From the brief foregoing sketch of some of the manifestations of Europe's imperial activity it will appear that there was a common approach to the problem, a willingness by all to acknowledge the legitimate rights and ambitions of all. Agreement on the definition of "legitimate" might not always be easy to reach, and the play for power ever remained in the background; yet in the last resort agreement was always reached because of similarity of understanding over the nature of the process.[2] This imperial activity may be viewed in a somewhat different light, for it also provided an outlet for the huge reservoir of European energies and, by furnishing such an outlet, contributed to the lessening of intra-European tensions, to the preservation of peace and thus to the belief in the reality of an orderly European community.

[2] The clash of Russian and Japanese imperial ambitions that resulted in open conflict in 1904 may be regarded as an exception. The war was unnecessary, and while its outcome inevitably resulted in a Russian setback in the Far East, its settlement amounted to a compromise of equally "legitimate" interests.

IV. The Impact of Ideas

Yet this is only part of the tale; another side is illustrated by the aftermath of the Moroccan crisis. The imperial agreements between Britain on the one hand, and France and Russia on the other, in 1904 and 1907 respectively, were not passing accidents without a morrow. They led instead to increasingly close co-operation and to the ever closer links of the Entente, Cordiale at first, then Triple. It was otherwise in the case of Germany and Morocco. The crises that arose out of that land grew above all out of Franco-German difference. In the first of these crises, in 1905, Delcassé, the French Foreign Minister, finally had to resign, an outcome that may fairly be credited to the intransigent position taken by the German Chancellor, Bülow. Bülow had undoubtedly achieved a major victory over Delcassé, even if his subsequent use of it was unwise. There was in France much anti-imperialist feeling, and even more against a war with Germany over Morocco—which is precisely why Delcassé was forced to resign. But, especially in view of the manner in which Bülow sought to push his advantage, resentment also developed in France, directed toward Germany, at what many regarded as saber-rattling tactics and unwarranted foreign interference in domestic affairs.

The second Moroccan crisis, in 1911, where the Franco-German relationship is concerned, is in some ways surprisingly reminiscent of the earlier. Agreement was reached, to be sure, and the fact that it was equally criticized in Germany and in France may be taken as evidence that it was basically not unfair in its terms; but it left an aftermath of bitterness, especially on the French side, though German tactics had succeeded in conveying the impression of aggressive intent to more than just the French alone.

Thus we find a conjunction between imperial activity and national feeling. For all that there were many in all Europe who criticized and opposed imperial activity for a variety of reasons, those who promoted it were generally not apologetic, and Kipling adequately expressed the dominant view which took pride in the white man's accomplishments in carrying his burden, that became *mission civilisatrice* in the French version. It will be noted, in the Franco-German case again that Morocco had been assuming a larger role than Alsace in the relations between the two countries. Not that Alsace was forgotten, but the passing of two generations while a *de facto* situation persisted had undoubtedly taken much of the sting out of the 1871 feeling. But this was also the time of the *réveil national* and it is precisely on the eve of 1914 that the Alsatian issue seemed to take on new life, aided besides by local and border incidents.

The state was consciously abetting the national consciousness and urging it into aggressive channels. Pride in the contemplation of imperial accomplishment was one aspect of this, most sharply illustrated by the large patches of the same color, most prominently the British red, scattered over the world's map. The school—compulsory elementary education was the common practice—was the most suitable instrument for implanting the cult of nationality in the malleable minds of the young, and it is an enlightening exercise to peruse the history textbooks that were used in pre-1914 Europe. They were well-calculated to convey the view of overwhelming national superiority in each case. In this respect there is little to choose among different nations. Thus the gentle, in fact praiseworthy, love of native heath became deflected into the intransigent worship of idolatrous abstractions.

The British knew that they were a superior race, and to rule lesser breeds—not unkindly or harshly, and with a minimum of coercion—was as much an obligation as a right. Precisely where the lesser breeds began might of course be debated; some would have said across the Channel. That the French were the quintessence of civilization was to the French so obvious a fact that to explain it was unnecessary. Of German primacy and power, German accomplishments were clear evidence that others were only too slow in acknowledging. The Russians may have been backward in material development, but theirs was the only road to salvation; it was the mission of Holy Russia, wherein the Third Rome was located, to lead the world on the right path. And as to the Italians, could there be any question that they had given Europe her civilization; had not Gioberti demonstrated the civil and moral primacy that was theirs?

One particular form of these vagaries deserves passing mention. Houston Stewart Chamberlain was of British origin, but it was both appropriate and consistent that he should gain German citizenship, for had he not given adequate proof, in his *Foundations of the Nineteenth Century*, that the highest manifestation of mankind was to be found among the Teutonic peoples? The concept of race is loose, but this did not prevent its being seized upon with uncritical enthusiasm, and the Nordic myth prospered. If Greek achievements were not to be decried, they could be easily explained as due to the influx of blond invaders from the north. Even before Chamberlain, French Gobineau had expounded the myth of Teutonic superiority; he had little difficulty in equating it with French, through the sleight of hand of explaining the Germanic origins of the French aristocracy, whereas the Teutons had either moved away from Germany, or there been bastardized by alien admixture, such as the Slavic. These might be no more than harmless vagaries, even endowed with a measure of charm, so long as they remained the lucubrations of literary people who might debate *ad infinitum* and *ad absurdum* the relative merits of diverse cultures. Competition among different cultures might even have a wholesome stimulating effect. But notions of racial superiority could also be used as adjuncts to the armory of power, though not until our day did one witness the frightfulness that they would be capable of producing when adopted with humorless consistency as bases for the actual policy of a great state fallen into the hands of uncultured barbarians. At all events the nationalization of culture is a typical nineteenth-century phenomenon that contributed little but divisive effects.

This is not to say that boundaries were closed to cultural interaction, which, on the contrary was both frequent and free. The impact on the Western countries of the discovery of Russian and of Scandinavian literature was as great as it was fruitful, and the work of the scientific community was truly international. Also at the upper levels of society, especially among the heirs of the ancient aristocracies, one can almost speak of a *de facto* if informal international. But here we must point to a development that parallels the reversal, from universalistic to national, that took place in the French Revolution. For the whole trend of the nineteenth century, in the broad sense democratic, giving the common man more education, and giving him ever more recognition in the direction of the affairs of the state, was detrimental to the influence of the former ruling aristocratic class so characteristic of the eighteenth century. The change, though not sudden, was rapid, and far from complete by 1914; also, the intensity of it varied much, the opposite extremes to be found in France and in Russia. But taking Europe as a whole, the stress is on the magnitude of the contrast between 1789 and 1914, be it in the structure of society or in the cultural climate.

The eighteenth-century legacy of interest in man and society in the large, including the assumption of the common humanity of man, did not suddenly vanish, but under the impact of nineteenth-century developments, perhaps the economic most of all, went through an evolution.

Socialism, Utopian and "Scientific"

Adam Smith, the Physiocrats, Malthus, and many others may be seen as forerunners of change. It was during the period of the Restoration that the variety of socialism usually called Utopian flourished. This may be seen as a combination of the eighteenth-century approach with the impact of the new contribution that the coming of industry was making. This is very clearly the case in such a work as the last that St. Simon wrote, the title of which was, revealingly, *The New Christianity*. St. Simon died in 1825 and Fourier in the next decade; it was entirely fitting that Fourier was an engineer by profession, more broadly what we should nowadays call a technocrat. The ideas of such men, which found much response in English Robert Owen, were focused on the construction of an ideal society compatible with the newer technical developments, although their thought to a degree showing a reaction against some of the less attractive aspects of technological development. Social planning was stressed by these men, who in divergent fashion emphasized at once the individual and the state. The concrete schemes to which their thinking gave rise, ideal communities, phalansteries, American New Harmony, are sufficiently known. None of them in the end succeeded, for they were indeed Utopian, resting on a deficient understanding of the fundamental traits of human nature; but the emergence of this type of thought is none the less significant, and the evolution is gradual from it to that other variety of socialism that dubbed itself scientific. It is of interest to note the titles of two contemporaneous books:

Cabet's *Voyage to Icaria* appeared in 1840; it was preceded by a year by Louis Blanc's *Organization of Labor*. The difference in wording is telling. It was also appropriate reflection of conditions that Utopian Socialism should thrive in Britain and in France, especially in the latter; but in any event, though induced by local circumstances, there was no trace of consciously national, let alone nationalistic, content in Utopian Socialist thought.

Such is indeed not the case of Mazzini. He was well steeped in the background of eighteenth-century thought, though much of it he found uncongenial and consequently rejected; his was fundamentally a religious temperament, for all that the Church of Rome elicited from him mainly contempt. But of the possibilities of association he had the greatest hopes. Mazzini was a thoroughgoing nationalist, and to think of him in connection with the making of Italy, if entirely warranted, is also far too narrow; he founded, to be sure, Young Italy, but his interest in the other "young" movements of Europe was no less. Taking the fact of nationality as both fundamental and good, he envisaged a Europe—Europe for him was the whole world—joined in a happy union of freely associated peoples. Good Italian patriot that he was, he understandably assigned to his Italy, where Rome had been the center of political, then religious, world unity, a role of leadership among nations. But there is nothing in his thought of petty nationalistic pride, certainly no aggressive inclination, and one must grant the nobility and attractiveness of the ideal of a Europe united in the diversity of her varied peoples. Although Mazzini's thought contained much vague messianic cloudiness, and his actions were ill-contrived and ineffectual, this was nevertheless nationalism at its best. Utopian though it was, it represents a far from negligible strand in the evolution of Europe.

The Utopian socialism that he knew in his youth Mazzini found attractive—it, too, laid stress on voluntary association —but the later "scientific" version was to him highly uncongenial. The Chartist movement in England was a form of association, but the collapse of it in the 1840s was final. The social problem raised by the conditions of the growing working class employed in the factories was not thereby resolved. Free enterprise, economic liberalism, the free play of the market, wherein labor was but another commodity, had an answer; it, too, was, in its way, Utopian in character, placing in some distant future the attainment of the perfect economic equilibrium that would insure the greatest good of the greatest number. Out of it, too, as out of Mazzini's nationalism, some highly desirable products grew, of which Mill's *Essay on Liberty* (1859), is one of the noblest expressions, one certainly not confined by national boundaries.

But the more immediately pressing issue was that raised by the urban industrial proletariat whose numbers, especially in Britain—this was the age of mushroom cities—were fast growing. It should not be surprising that, in view of the accomplishments of the scientific endeavor, scientific in the narrow sense of the measurable and the mechanical, the hope should have arisen of extending the scientific approach to the social domain. Thus was born that misnomer, social science. The desire to uncover the laws of human evolution, of history, was hardly new; the interpretation of history as the unfolding of some divine plan was a possible answer, but this could hardly be called scientific. Mankind was emerging from the metaphysical into the scientific stage, as Comte, who dubbed his philosophy Positive, put it; the emphasis was now to be on fact, concrete data, statistics. It is out of this mid-nineteenth-century climate that scientific socialism was born. Karl Marx was a typical bourgeois intellectual in his background and preparation; if, like Malthus, he drew his intellectual sustenance from the observation of surrounding conditions, like Comte he went far beyond the immediate. The essence of the Marxist view is familiar and there is no necessity to delve into the dreary Teutonic heaviness of *Das Kapital*. For purposes of the present discussion, it may suffice to retain the simple central fact that Marx believed he had discovered in the economic condition the key to historic development, past, present, and future.

It is a reasonably safe generalization that any such attempt is wrong—the human mind is too limited. Yet the endeavor is too fascinating not to be forever pursued, and it is also true that the ordering of a vast segment of reality opens up new horizons and, when the work of a superior mind, offers much of significance and high value. There is no need to dwell on the subsequent importance of Marx. European society had reached the industrial stage, wherein labor—industrial labor, that is, for the peasantry was to Marx an encumbrance by him unwisely neglected—the ultimate creator of all wealth, would come into its own, its present role being that of wresting control from its capitalist exploiters. These too had played a role, and a useful one in their time, but their function was superseded and they must join the scrap heap of history. "Workers of the world unite, you have nothing to lose but your chains," could be a stirring slogan, and the necessity of the class struggle was the reality of which the proletariat must be made aware. It is of interest that the *Communist Manifesto* was issued in the month that preceded the outbreak of revolution in Paris, in January 1848, although there is no causal connection between the two events. Louis Blanc, who for a time was a member of the French provisional government, was a socialist to be sure, but the proletariat was neither sufficiently large nor sufficiently conscious of its historic role to play a decisive part at this time. The *Manifesto* was a prelude and a preview, a mere brief pamphlet, that long antedated the weightier documented analysis of *Das Kapital.*

It is only natural, inevitable one may say, that such ideas should arise among intellectuals, who appropriately were, in the early stages, the chief propagandizers of the Marxist doctrine. The inner humanitarian motivation that drove many of them—were they not in themselves the clearest denial of the determining power of economic motivation?—does not alter the fact of their attachment to the concrete and the material, the presumably scientific view. Even a materialistic outlook, one that spoke of religion as the opiate of the people, can become an ideal, and ideals have ever proved potent forces of change, sometimes dangerously so, when they become too doctrinaire.

At any rate the Marxist gospel prospered, if somewhat slowly at first. From our present standpoint, its universalistic aspect, as with the French Revolution at first, is perhaps the most significant. The workers of the world, waging the struggle of class, had no stake in the state, which for that matter was but a tool of the entrenched capitalist class. As with Mazzini, self-determination was indeed acceptable, but conflicts among nations were mere manifestations of capitalist competition; so was imperial rivalry, which later Lenin dubbed "the highest stage of capitalism," the universal villain. Quite consistently, Marxism was anti-nationalistic, anti-militaristic, and anti-imperialistic; it behooved the workers to unite and form an association that would deny the validity of all national lines of division, the meaning of which would evaporate in the Utopia of the universal society. The dream is old, no stranger to Christianity, for example, and it is certainly not devoid of nobility.

Thus was the workers' International born. The initial version of it, the First International Workingmen's Association, the First International for short, was organized in 1864, with headquarters suitably situated in London. The First International itself fell on evil days; the episode of the 1871 Paris Commune, which elicited Marx's enthusiasm, was on the whole a setback, and some of his supporters—Bakunin is the best single instance—were drawn into anarchism, hardly a suitable base for close-knit associational organization. Anarchism found its most fertile ground in the Latin countries, a situation variously accounted for by temperamental proclivity or by the prevalence of the Catholic religion, perhaps diverse aspects of a more fundamental tendency. At any rate, within just over ten years the International collapsed.

But the organizational failure did not prevent the spread of the Marxist interpretation, which caused Bismarck sufficient concern to induce him to abandon the *Kulturkampf*, the unrewarding struggle with the Roman Church, in order to concentrate his efforts on the social question. Kark Marx himself died in 1883, his great work not all published, but in 1889 there was organized in Paris the Second International Workingmen's Association—the Second International—whose purpose it was to co-ordinate the activity of the various national socialist[1] parties. It is of interest to mention, in passing, that for its war song it adopted the French *Marseillaise*, an illustration perhaps of continuity in filiation. In 1889, after all, France was, among major European states, the only republic, a word replete in many minds with radical connotations.

The very success of the socialist doctrine became a source of division within the movement itself. For in a parliamentary democracy, with the franchise nearing universality, was it not

[1] Twentieth-century happenings, specifically the Russian Revolution, have introduced a measure of terminological confusion. Socialists and Communists are now often bitter enemies. They are both, however, of Marxist derivation, and, before 1917, the term socialist includes all, having superseded the adjective in Marx's original *Communist Manifesto*.

possible for socialists to obtain a parliamentary majority which would, in peaceful fashion, give them control of the state and enable them to enact whatever legislation might be needed for the institution of the ideal society? Such a view, essentially that of the English Chartists, was naturally more tenable in the democratic states, but even in them there were those who insisted on the inevitability of violence at some point in the process of change of control. The discussion between reformists and revolutionaries filled the debates of socialist congresses, but the movement contrived to avoid formal fission before 1914. By that time socialist parties had become well organized in various countries, and there was a reasonably close correlation between the degree of their strength and that of industrial development. There are two important qualifications. In Russia, because of economic backwardness in combination with curbs on political freedom, socialism was confined to underground operation largely directed from abroad by exiles. In most industrialized Britain, for reasons which may best be summed up as the political evolution of Britain in the course of her history, socialism made little impression as a mass movement; even a Labour Party had barely begun to exist before the First World War.

But of the International great hopes and fears were held, according to one's political predilections. In any case there was no denying that it was a powerful movement and some even thought—again, hoped or feared—that the union that joined socialist workers regardless of national frontiers might be sufficient to prevent the governments from resorting to war. At the worst, if guns were put into socialists' hands, there could be no assurance that they would be turned against the national instead of against the class enemy. At the very last moment, in July 1914, the murder of the French socialist leader Jaurès, which prevented him from meeting his German counterparts in Brussels, was for that very reason held by some to have been a calamity of the first magnitude. Confronted with the fact of war, international socialism collapsed, socialists with hardly any exceptions giving first priority to their respective national allegiances. But before this had happened, international socialism must be seen as the force that, more than any single other, could indeed make Europe one. It was in its own way, after all, one more expression of the common culture of Europe, especially significant because its field of operation was the political and social.

The same can hardly be said of the common Christian heritage. The days of the wars of religion were long past, and while much prejudice continued to exist, *de facto* universal tolerance was increasingly the order of the day. The Christian churches might have every reason to concern themselves with the social question and in the last analysis the classless society ought even to have been attractive to them. Pope Leo XIII was indeed concerned with these matters, as his pronouncements show, just as he was concerned with the larger problem of accommodation of the Roman Church with the whole modern world. But just as the Vatican Council of 1870 had essentially turned the face of the Church against the newer tendencies, be it in politics or thought, so likewise, at the beginning of the present century, modernism was condemned. The effect was, broadly speaking, to dissociate the Church of Rome from the concept of change and to foster the view that it was on the whole conservative, not to say retrograde. This was not least the case in supposedly Catholic countries, where anti-clericalism thrived; the contest between the Third Republic and the Church is well known.

The looser and more flexible Protestant milieu could encompass a wider range of opinion, from the strictly fundamentalist and literal to that which with ease accommodated itself to any novelty, or any form of "progress." As to the

Eastern Church, subservient to the state in large measure, it was definitely a force of conservation. In any case, and in whatever form, the common fact of Christianity had by this time little effective significance in terms of any European unity. It is hardly any exaggeration to say that the active thought of Europe, a very living force indeed, and one that operated above and across national boundaries, operated essentially outside the Christian churches. The climate of that thought was overwhelmingly secular; the challenge of optimistic materialism was inadequately met by the Christian religion. Europe, as it has been put, was becoming de-Christianized, though the process had only gone a partial distance among the masses of her peoples.

V. The Actual Record

In the sketch that has been drawn so far, an attempt has been made to analyze some of the dominant forces that were at work in nineteenth-century Europe, with a view to appraising their cohesive or divisive effects. In addition to what has been said, to the specific illustrations given of the influences of nationalism or economics, for example, it will be useful to cast an over-all glance at the manner in which Europe as a whole operated during this same period.

The fundamental fact was that of a community of sovereign states, and something has been said of the nature of the European state system, whose functioning was regulated by the great device of the balance of power. The disturbance induced by the French Revolution, the injection of a novel ideology, plus Napoleon's performance, had given the system a severe jolt, and the primary concern of the statesmen gathered in Vienna had been the re-establishment of the *status quo ante*, be it in terms of domestic systems of governance

within the individual units of Europe or in terms of equilibrium among them. Restoration and legitimacy were properly
the slogans of Vienna in 1815.

But the magnitude of the disturbance of and challenge to
the old order had also had the effect of emphasizing the consciousness of common interest in preserving the order of Europe. The more limited Quadruple Alliance, the tsar's looser
Holy Alliance, have been mentioned, and Metternich in any
case was much attached to the Concert of Europe. Perhaps it
might be put this way: what is the real meaning of that
phrase? or alternatively, would a concept so loose and so
vague, deprived of formal institutional organs, be capable of
showing any effectiveness; would it tend to dissolve into impotence in the face of the rivalries of states; or would it possibly, in the face of changing circumstances, new ideas and
ways, evolve into a more concrete reality, the seed perhaps
of European integration? This is what we wish to look at.
There are those who see in the nineteenth-century Concert
of Europe and in the Holy Alliance precursors of the twentieth-century League of Nations.

One preliminary observation should be made. It is essential
to bear in mind the interaction and clash of two factors that
mesh and cut across each other: the influence of ideologies
on the one hand, the facts of power on the other. For all that
the leaders at Vienna largely spoke the same language, that
they agreed that government was the proper appanage of
the qualified, a measure of division existed among them
which had old roots and in a sense still obtains. In broad
terms, Britain and France were the liberal states in which
some of the people had at least some say in their governance,
whereas the three main states of the center and east, Russia, Austria, and Prussia embodied the conservative, autocratic principle. The fact of these ideological affinities meant
much to Metternich, as it did later to Bismarck, but on the

whole was not sufficient to heal over the rifts of contending
interests. The coming together of Britain and France at the
beginning of our century was more a matter of power relationships than of ideological affinity.

The difference is considerable between the merely negative condition that is the avoidance of conflict and the
achievement of unity, though the former is at least a necessary precondition of the latter; whether or not Europe could
live at peace is therefore an important matter. From this
standpoint the whole nineteenth century falls into three distinct segments: before 1853 and after 1871 there are no wars
that involve the major powers with each other, but between
those two dates several such conflicts take place.

The Concert of Europe

The tsar and Metternich were at one—the Prussian king
meekly following—in their concern for what went on in other
states, and it had been provided that the powers would meet
whenever an issue might arise that was of general concern to
Europe. This was the nearest thing to a formal organization
achieved by the Concert of Europe. Within three years of
Vienna the powers met, at Aix-la-Chapelle. The issue at the
time was France, who had fulfilled her obligations under the
second Treaty of Paris and seemed stable within. Accordingly, she was given what may best be described as a certificate of good behavior, the foreign occupation was terminated,
her indemnity liquidated, and, most important of all, she was
admitted as a member in good standing of the community
of Europe.

But the decade of the twenties produced a different type
of problem. In Naples and in Spain liberals succeeded in ex-
tracting from their rulers that magic talisman of early nineteenth-century liberalism that was a constitution. Such an

event, especially in Naples, might easily have repercussions in the whole Italian peninsula. Since most of Italy was at the time a preserve of Austrian influence, Metternich was properly concerned and the powers met to consider. The outcome of their deliberations was Austrian intervention in Naples, where there was little difficulty in restoring King Ferdinand to his "proper" position. On the way, the Austrians performed a similar service in Piedmont. The implications of this action were highly important, for the Austrian intervention was more than the defense of a limited Austrian interest, though it was that as well. That intervention represented the joint action of Europe, moved to assert a common interest that justified intrusion in what was not regarded as the purely domestic affairs of a state. Wherever one's sympathies may lie on the ideological score, joint action, or at least the joint underwriting of action, as a measure of unity is of the highest significance.

The Spanish case was in many respects similar to the Neapolitan and the outcome was also similar. The tsar was quite willing to lend the use of his army for the restoration of order in Spain, but, apart from the fact that the prospect of Russian forces marching across Europe commanded little enthusiasm in any quarters, the logic of geography indicated the French as the suitable agents of Europe. Accordingly, a French army restored King Ferdinand in his "proper" position on the throne of Spain. But it is very significant that the French had been hesitant about the desirability of the undertaking, and that the British, at the Congress of Verona where the matter was adjudicated, expressed very strong opposition. The episode has been sometimes regarded as the breakdown of the Concert of Europe. This is unwarranted, though in the case of the transatlantic possessions of Spain, currently in revolt, British opposition succeeded in preventing the extension of any European assistance—the tsar was willing again—to maintain the legitimacy of the Spanish position across the ocean. Commercial interest played a part in the British position, as it did in the American assertion of the Monroe Doctrine for which the episode was occasion.

That the Concert of Europe was not defunct is well established by what happened in 1830. The independence of Belgium has been mentioned. In this case also, another tsar was willing to respond to the appeal of the legitimate Dutch king for assistance in putting down rebellious subjects, though the Austrians and the Prussians, in geographically closer proximity, seemed less anxious to perform a similar service. There was understandable ideological sympathy in Paris for the Brussels rebels, and the new king of the French—not king of France, be it noted—let it be known that the Belgians would receive French assistance if others intervened, though he himself wisely eschewed any acquisitive designs. That was all that was needed in Britain, largely indifferent otherwise to the plight of the Dutch king. Once Talleyrand had convincingly conveyed in London the authenticity of French intentions, an Anglo-French front was created, in the face of which the other powers acquiesced. Meeting jointly in London they gave Belgium her certificate of birth, which even the Dutch king eventually acknowledged; the powers in addition agreed to the perpetual neutralization of Belgium.

This was essentially accomplished in December, one month after another certificate of birth had been issued, also in London, to Greece. The Greek revolt, or the war of Greek independence, fills most of the decade of the twenties. It, too, has been mentioned, but something may be added regarding the behavior of the powers in that case. For them the Greek problem was but a limited aspect of the much larger issue that was the Eastern Question, the fate of the entire domain of the decadent Turk. Of the great powers of the day, four —Russia, Austria, France, and Britain—had definite interests in the problem. Metternich, consistently stressing legitimacy of rule, would have let the Greek rising spend itself "beyond the pale of civilization"; the Sultan may not have been Christian, he was undoubtedly legitimate. The tsars, first Alexander then Nicholas, were torn between that view of things, sympathy for coreligionaries, and the possibility of advantage for Russia. After some years, partly under the prodding of the wave of philhellenic sentiment, the powers, Austria excepted, met in London where they agreed on joint mediation between the Porte and the Greeks. Accident in large part— Navarino was not intended—precipitated hostilities with the Turks, whose defeat insured the independence of Greece. The powers made jointly the decisions that set the boundaries of Greece, her fully sovereign status, and gave her Bavarian Otto for king. This episode, too, must be regarded as a case of the successful operation of the Concert of Europe. Thus, in the year 1830, Belgium and Greece furnished at once examples of the divisive effects of the nationalistic force—there were in Europe two new states—and occasions for the manifestation of the common purpose of Europe.

THE POWERS AND THE EASTERN QUESTION

The Eastern Question was, in fact, one issue, the unfolding of which provides an excellent illustration of the extent to which the Concert of Europe functioned or failed to function, as well as of the manner in which it operated. Anticipating certain other developments, to which we shall return presently, this may be a good place at which to follow the further evolution of the Concert. The condition of the Sick Man of Europe made the prospect of his demise an ever-present possibility, one which internal conditions alone might suffice to bring about. But the disposition of his still vast inheritance raised the acute problem of adjusting the competing interests of the powers. Partition schemes ever recurred in the chancelleries

of Europe, but also failed to produce other than agreement on
the impossibility to agree. The schemes were consequently
abandoned, and as the powers also were at one in their preference for the preservation of peace, they repeatedly adopted
the solution of guaranteeing the integrity of the Ottoman
state, or what remained of it after an accident such as the
Greek revolt had caused some losses.

This sensible consensus, if it may be described as one of
the large, permanent policies of the powers of Europe, was
not however automatically implemented, but furnished instead much occupation to her diplomats. Thus, the desire of
Mehemet Ali of Egypt to create his own state in that land and
even use it as the basis for imperial expansion brought tensions
to an acute point. For in the thirties Mehemet Ali was
France's protégé, whereas Britain and Russia on the whole
supported the Sultan. In the first clash between him and his
Egyptian vassal, in 1832, when the Turks were defeated, it
was the promised assistance of Russian power that, for a price,
rescued the Sultan. A renewed clash in 1839 served to bring
out mainly Anglo-French rivalry. Palmerston's success in
bringing a union of all Europe save France, in the 1840 Treaty
of London, raised the international temperature of Europe.
There were in France visions of a revived anti-Napoleonic
coalition and talk of war on the Rhine. It was a passing fever,
however, for once peaceful Louis-Philippe had got rid of
the (at the time) bellicose Thiers and Mehemet Ali's ambitions had been checked, the powers in 1841 could agree on a
Convention of the Straits.

During the following decade, it was Russia, or perhaps better an Anglo-Russian misunderstanding, that caused a major
disruption of the European Concert. War broke out in which
Britain and France joined the Turks against Russia. The Russians were eventually defeated on their home ground, in the
Crimea, and for this naturally had to pay some price. But

what is of interest in the case of the Crimean War is the extent to which diplomatic contact was maintained among the belligerents, conveniently in neutral Vienna, and perhaps even more, the atmosphere of the Congress of Paris where the issue was settled in 1856. It was still largely a case of a gathering of men who spoke the common language of the diplomacy of Europe, and the French emperor—his wife conveniently giving birth to a son for the occasion—graciously entertained the Congress, where the Russians appeared not at all under a cloud of moral guilt. The powers agreed to certain rearrangements in the East, and having jointly guaranteed the integrity of the Ottoman Empire made the additional gesture of granting it admission to the Concert of Europe, a fairly empty gesture to be sure. Being gathered in Congress, they used the occasion to deal with other matters of common concern: they took note of the fact that there was such a thing as an Italian question, and they endeavored to define and extend the domain of international law, particularly in the matter of the rights of belligerents and of neutrals at sea.

For two decades the Eastern situation was largely quiescent, but in the middle seventies, out of domestic Ottoman disturbances, which in turn were occasion for some Austro-Russian diplomatic mishandling, war again broke out between the tsar and the Sultan. Although the Russians were eventually militarily successful, they had broken the rules of the game by their unilateral action in altering conditions that were the common concern of the powers. To the terms they imposed on the Turks—a far-reaching rearrangement in the Balkans—they found others, the British in particular, objecting. The choice was theirs of whether to accept once more the test of force with Britain, or else consent to a European revision of the Treaty of San Stefano. Wisely, they chose the latter course and, in 1878, the powers met in Berlin. What they did there was very similar to what had been done in Paris; the guide of their decisions was the maintenance of the balance of power, by allocating comparable gains, all at the expense of the Turks to be sure, then again reasserting their support of the integrity of the (reduced) Ottoman domain. The Concert of Europe, in the last resort, had successfully asserted the validity of its purpose, of which Britain this time had been the chief upholder, though it is worth noting the difference between the climate of 1878 Berlin and that of 1856 Paris. Whereas on the earlier occasion Franco-Russian relations were amicable and thereafter improved, from Berlin the Russians went away disgruntled, the point of their resentment being directed not least against the "honest broker" Bismarck.

For the next thirty years relatively little happened in the Near East that affected the collectivity of European powers as a whole. A Serbo-Bulgarian explosion in 1885 did to a point disturb the harmony of the relations among the three Eastern empires, but in the nineties Russia and Austria, by mutual consent, "put the Balkans on ice." A Greco-Turkish outbreak in 1897 was the source of only minor friction over Cretan arrangements, and not until 1908 did the annexation of Bosnia-Herzegovina by Austria seriously shake the Concert of the Powers. However, the accent was not this time on Eastern affairs, and for that reason the 1908 crisis will be considered in another context.

In 1911 Italy declared war on Turkey for the purpose of acquiring Libya. Though, as mentioned before, in the context of the imperial activity of the day, the Tripolitan War was a minor and not an unreasonable action, it proved highly unpopular with all. This was because of the fear that it might raise, in acute form, the perennial issue of the fate of the Ottoman Empire. The fear was amply justified by the outbreak of war in the Balkans in 1912, where Serbs, Bulgars, and Greeks, momentarily putting aside their differences, joined in aggressive war against the Turk. The Balkan Wars of 1912–13 may in fact be seen as the last instance of the successful operation of the Concert of Europe, yet even that success was dearly bought. For what happened was this. The Balkan allies waged a successful war, following which they might have implemented their previously made plans for the division of the Balkans. But, essentially for reasons of balance of power—the small Balkan states were clients of the larger European ones—these arrangements were not acceptable to all, especially not to Austria. Thus the ambassadors of the powers, gathered in London, proceeded to revise the settlement, for which they substituted another. The powers in the end had their way, although at the cost of much difficulty: there was another Balkan war, that pitted Bulgaria against her former allies, and Serbia would not yield until the Albanian coast was blockaded and Austria faced her with an ultimatum. The ultimate outcome was an exacerbation of intra-Balkan, as well as Austro-Serbian, differences that boded ill for the future.

Yet in the last resort the great powers of Europe had once more shown their ability to agree among themselves, and once they had done this, to enforce their joint will. In their common ground of acceptance of common responsibility for preserving the order of Europe, meaning the peace among themselves, they had been driven to flout the desires of the lesser powers. The fact of the recognition of power is therefore paramount. It is also worth mentioning that the initial Balkan alliance, in the spring of 1912, was essentially a success of Russian diplomacy, albeit somewhat irresponsible in its operation. It is precisely that element of irresponsibility that brought remonstrances from Russia's ally, France, when Poincaré, the French Prime Minister, was informed of what had been passing. Thereupon Russia consented to join the other powers in putting pressure on the Balkan states not to implement their aggressive plans. When that was done, it was too late.

Finally, it might also be mentioned that, from about 1890, Germany began to develop her own interest in the Near East. Her intrusion did not take the form of territorial ambitions but was confined to the economic domain: trade, and most of all that famous scheme that was the Berlin-Baghdad railway. The other powers were concerned, for a variety of individual reasons, and negotiations that centered on railway construction in Anatolia lasted over many years. However, it proved possible in this case also to reach an amicable allotment of shares of influence and of investment. The last of a series of such agreements was made in May 1914. Thus the record of the Eastern Question during the whole nineteenth century points up the possibility of agreement, despite occasional breakdowns, and therefore may be viewed as a manifestation of the successful operation of the Concert of Europe. But it must also be emphasized that there were two levels of power, the great and the small, and that the latter in the last resort had no voice in court. This frank acknowledgment of the fact of power was doubtless realistic, but it is also undeniable that, especially in view of the increasing potency of the nationalistic force, new stresses and tensions were being introduced.

The Mid-Century Readjustment

For the climate of Europe at the opening of our century was quite other from what it had been fifty or a hundred years before, and we must now go back to pick up some of the other threads in our story.

In 1830 and shortly thereafter, the French had made their revolution, the Belgians gained their independence, Italian risings been put down, the Polish insurrection crushed, and the great Reform Bill become the law of England. For nearly twenty years the European scene as a whole was essentially quiescent while Britain launched on the free-trade experiment and developed her factories, the July Monarchy in France followed the bourgeois king's advice of *Enrichissez-vous*, industry pushed across the Rhine, and Metternich controlled with firmness the politics of Central Europe. Despite the 1840 duel between Palmerston and Thiers and some acrimony over Spanish affairs, even Anglo-French relations were on the whole amicable, adequately symbolized by the visits that Queen Victoria and Louis-Philippe exchanged, to the point that the phrase "first Entente Cordiale" has been used to characterize these relations. Save in connection with the Near Eastern situation, there was little work for the Concert of Europe to do.

But there was discontent under the surface, simmering from the Channel to the borders of Russia, and dissatisfied, if momentarily impotent, liberalism was its bearer. A variety of conditions, not least among them economic bad times, precipitated the Parisian explosion of February 1848, that gave birth to the Second French Republic. Events in Paris had, appropriately, Europe-wide repercussions, and something has been said of the events of those two years that seemed for a moment to threaten the entire political structure of Europe. To a considerable extent the eyes of liberals everywhere were turned toward Paris, but one remarkable thing about the mid-century revolutions is that, to a surprising degree, they remained confined to their separate milieus. The failure of the French revolution to come to the assistance of others is the most significant fact, and the summation that by this failure "France saved the peace but killed the revolution" has justification. The initial surge of radicalism in France was mastered by June, but already in March the provisional government had proclaimed its non-interventionist intentions, to which in the event France adhered.

What the result might otherwise have been makes for interesting, if idle, speculation. There was considerable common ground among the 1848 liberals throughout Europe. Certainly the failure of the German liberals in Frankfurt to unite Germany at this time can fairly be regarded as a major turning point in the German development, one which opened up the possibility, subsequently realized, of Bismarck's blood-and-iron methods. The consequences of that deflection of the course of German events are perhaps incalculable; the variety of nationalism that in the end made Germany has been explained, and it is one of the most significant things about the 1848 revolutions that the use of national differences played a large role in their failure. After that the prospects were definitely dimmer of a Mazzinian Europe united in the co-operation of diverse liberal nationalisms.

The Second French Republic soon became the Second Empire, the span of which coincides with the nineteenth-century interval during which the Concert of Europe broke down. The extent to which the Congress of Paris served to display how much in common the belligerents had does not alter the fact that three major European powers had been involved in war. Thereafter three other major conflicts ensued: the Franco-Austrian, out of which Italy was born, the Austro-Prussian, which destroyed the German Confederation, and the Franco-Prussian, from which united Germany emerged. Napoleon III's France was directly involved in two of those wars and very much concerned with the other, yet, save in the first, she was not the prime mover of events, that role falling instead to Germany, or rather to Bismarck. There is irony in the fact that Napoleon III was not primarily a military man, or one bent on pursuing a policy of aggression. For nationalism everywhere, even in Germany to a point, he felt sympathy,

and his repeated suggestion of European congresses to deal
with this and that question, if not entirely divorced from the
possibility of gaining some French advantage, inserts itself
well into the concept of an orderly Europe. The shortcomings
of French policy under his direction stem from the fact that,
not devoid of intelligence, charm, and imagination as he was,
Napoleon III lacked steadiness of purpose.[1]

The Balance of Power

The very opposite was certainly the case with Bismarck.
Once he had made Germany, the state of European relationships embarked on a different course and it is not unfair
to say, taking a broad view of the subsequent events, that
the affairs of Europe were dominated by the German problem.
Had things in our own century turned out otherwise than
they did, our history books in all likelihood would be using
the rubric "German century," as they refer to earlier Spanish
or French. This is not likely ever to be the case, and one
way to put it perhaps is that the German misfortune is to
have been born too late. Yet, in a sense, the German century
it has been, for after 1871 Germany has been more than any
other single nation the center of European, even of world,
affairs. Of the second half of the nineteenth century, the period from the Franco-Prussian War to the war of 1914 something more must be said.

THE "REIGN" OF BISMARCK

It was for Europe a period of peace, in the sense at least
that no open conflict took place among the major powers.
For the first twenty years of it Bismarck was Chancellor of

[1] Of the important readjustments that remade the map of Central
Europe during the fifties and sixties no more need be said at this point
since they have been dealt with in an earlier section, mainly as manifestations of the force of nationalism.

Germany, molding the shape of his creation and, more than any other single individual, dominating as well the international relations of Europe. He must be credited for the preservation of peace in his time, for to that end he authentically labored. Bismarck, if hardly an attractive figure in personal terms—he was crude, limited, and boorish—was nonetheless a reasonable and a rational man as well as a statesman of the first rank. He wished primarily two things, twin aspects of his view of what Germany ought to be: at home an orderly state, modern, industrialized, and progressive, but essentially based on a conservative social structure; vis-à-vis the outside, primacy of position in Europe. But he had no aggressive designs; in Bismarck's view Germany was a satisfied power, and peace was the most adequate condition to maintain that satisfactory state of affairs.

Thus his domestic and foreign policies are related. By the alliance of the Three Emperors, the union of Germany, Russia, and Austria, he set great store, for it would serve a double purpose. These were the three great conservative powers of Europe, defenders of the proper social order. The *Dreikaiserbund* was but a refurbished version of the earlier Metternichian design, although, unlike Metternich, Bismarck in his time was a modern man who certainly did not reject, at least where technical aspects were concerned, the new ways of the world. In addition, the tripartite connection would furnish the only sensible solution of the Austro-Russian rivalry in the Balkans. For dealing with that apple of discord, Bismarck had a simple, rational solution: the equally legitimate interests of either should be acknowledged by the other; in concrete and practical terms, the Balkans should be divided in two—the eastern half Russia's preserve, the western Austria's. As he put it himself, in Bulgaria he was Russian, just as in France he was Republican; as far as he himself was concerned, the whole Near Eastern question was not worth the bones of a

Pomeranian grenadier. This, to repeat, was rational, though rationality is always easier to practice when one's own interest is not directly involved. Twice the arrangement broke down and the *Dreikaiserbund* was disrupted. But Bismarck never abandoned the attempt to keep Russia and Austria in the German camp, separately if not together. If driven to an unwelcome choice, he would opt for the second country; this he did in 1879, and thereafter the Austrian alliance became the one fixed point, the cornerstone, of German foreign policy. Within two years, however, his persistence succeeded in reviving the Three Emperors' League, and when that broke down once again, unable to drive the Austro-Russian team in harmony, he resorted to that juggling act, skillful no doubt but fragile, that was the simultaneous existence of the alliance with Austria and the Reinsurance Treaty with Russia.

Bismarck would have liked to bring Britain as well into his camp, and he did entertain the prospect of an alliance with her. But the secure and self-confident Britain of his day preferred to adhere to the tradition of splendid isolation. Bismarck did not insist, but for that matter the tradition of satisfactory Anglo-Prussian relations, despite some British criticism of the terms of the Treaty of Frankfurt, extended to the Anglo-German. Britain came close to underwriting the Bismarckian system by her exchanges with Italy, the Mediterranean Agreements of 1887, in the making of which Bismarck had a hand. He was careful not to challenge the British position of naval supremacy, and the beginnings of German imperialism did not, in his time, reach sufficient dimensions to constitute a challenge to the British position in the imperial domain.

The Mediterranean Agreements of 1887 involved Britain with Italy. Bismarck never had much esteem for the power of that country, but from 1882 she too was in his camp through the Triple Alliance that she made with the two Central Powers. One of the most important reasons for entering into that arrangement was, from Bismarck's point of view, to prevent the possibility of a Franco-Italian connection. With France after 1871, despite occasional threatening talk, Bismarck had no quarrel, and would in fact have been quite willing to establish good relations. But French feeling that never reconciled itself to the territorial loss of 1871 was beyond his control. The alternative was to keep France isolated, for of France alone he had no fear; the isolation of France is but another aspect of his other connections. France was aware of this, but, while he lasted, was unable to break out of her isolation.

This then was the Bismarckian system,[2] the guiding line of which was the preservation of peace on the basis of the status quo. Bismarck, no starry-eyed lover of peace in the abstract, was not a lover of war, which he regarded merely as a tool to be used when none other was available. His system was devoid of any aggressive intent, but Berlin was, more than any other capital, the active center that guided the international life of Europe, a fact clearly revealed by the network of lines that connected it with Vienna, St. Petersburg, and Rome. One may speak to a point of a condition of German dominance, one resting on diplomacy, however, rather than on force, and in the last resort upon the willing consent of the other participants in the system. The system can hardly be called one of a balance of power, though Bismarck was keenly sensitive to the factor of equilibrium between, say, Austria and Russia, or between the latter and Britain.

Nor could this system be equated with any sort of European unity unless one see in it a preliminary step to a more clearly asserted German hegemony. Such an intention, however, may

[2] There were in addition, some minor connections, the Austro-Serbian alliance and the one of Rumania with both Germany and Austria-Hungary, that may be regarded as rounding out the Bismarckian system.

not properly be charged to Bismarck. But this is precisely where trouble began. For Bismarck could not be everlasting, and it is one of the nicer posers of history to speculate on what might have been the fate of Germany and of Europe had Bismarck himself, or another Bismarck, presided over the destinies of the Germany that Bismarck himself had created and molded. Just because Germany was so successful and powerful and because she was growing so fast, unusual skill would have been needed to make possible in peace the adjustments of inevitable frictions to which the very fact of her growth gave rise.

WILHELMINE GERMANY

Once the old emperor had died in 1888, Bismarck was not retained for long by his grandson, William II, fated to be the last German Kaiser. Bismarck himself, to repeat, had no aggressive intent toward others; Napoleonic visions of hegemony or union were not the sort of dreams he entertained. The new young emperor, an unbalanced romantic, was in contrast given to dreams, though he also did not plan deliberate conquest. But power has a way of feeding upon itself, and in the very fact of German growth the possibility of aggression was implied. This is what others came to fear, and in the last analysis what counts in determining the actions of individuals or nations vis-à-vis other individuals or nations is not so much an objective reality as the subjective image that is formed of that reality.

After 1890, when Bismarck was dismissed, Wilhelmine Germany was unwisely guided, and her new emperor was the most appropriate, as well as the most unfortunate, embodiment of the more undesirable traits of that too-successful Germany. Bismarck's dismissal coincided with the necessity of a decision in the matter of relations with Russia. Some irritations had developed that in the long record of friendship might pass away and be adjusted. Instead, they were magnified and allowed to grow into the seeds of ever sharper difference. There were indeed solid reasons for the German decision not to renew Bismarck's Reinsurance Treaty with Russia, but the changed attitude of Germany could not but constitute in Russian eyes a less than friendly gesture, and one sure to change past trust into present and future suspicion.

It is significant, if not surprising, that in this new climate of Europe the persistent, but hitherto sterile, French efforts to escape isolation should at last bear fruit. France had been of necessity the greatest objector to the Bismarckian system, aimed indeed in part at herself. The Franco-Russian alliance was in a sense an unnatural association because of the divergent interests of the two states. In so far as they had a common focus of enmity, that focus was Britain, but the points of contact and friction of British interest with Russian and French lay, in the main, in diverse regions of the world. The cement of the Franco-Russian alliance was the fact of the common suspicion of German intent, and the cement at first could be judged none too solid. The Russo-German connection could easily have been resumed, and there were ever those in both Germany and in Russia who hoped that it might be.

The alliance was an unwelcome surprise to Germany; had not the possibility of the war on two fronts been Bismarck's great nightmare? But this diplomatic setback did little to moderate the drift of German behavior, irrevocably set on the *neue Kurs*. Germany would loudly proclaim her right to a place under the sun; no one could in fairness deny her this right, but the question of what place would be proper was raised. For Germany this meant empire; hence, her future lay on the water. This in turn meant a navy, the program for which was finally launched in 1898, thanks to the combined efforts of Emperor William and Admiral von Tirpitz, though there were those in Germany who had qualms.

No one in Britain claimed an exclusive monopoly of empire, but empire to Britain was a vital matter, as was the condition of naval supremacy. One is reminded of the quip, where Germany is concerned, that her lease of Kiao-Chow was for the purpose of establishing a coaling station for the needs of a nonexistent navy which it therefore became necessary to create. That Britain should evince concern at Germany's new plans was both legitimate and inevitable. Yet this need not necessarily mean conflict or clash. The British reaction to the new conditions was to reconsider the merits of their own deliberate isolation. The conclusion was the desirability of lightening commitments, and in view of both current circumstances and past background it was wholly natural that Britain should look first to the possibility of some understanding with Germany. Precisely what understanding was a flexible matter, and Britain might go the length of a defensive alliance, though not of a commitment to neutrality whatever might take place on the Continent.

But the arrogance of Wilhelmine Germany blinded her to the possible advantages of moderation. Bülow's advice to the Kaiser was definitely inept. His assertion that Germany was *arbiter mundi,* and hence could hold the bid high, was a gross misunderstanding of British power and of British psychology. For three years Joseph Chamberlain, believer in the peculiar virtues of Anglo-Saxondom, tried to achieve some understanding, but his advances failed in face of the too-high German price the British would not pay. Britain was after all, at this time, still first among the powers. The consequences of this failure are comparable to those of the 1890 breakdown of the wire to St. Petersburg, and the fact of failure in itself created a new situation. It was in 1904 that the Entente Cordiale was formed. Among the reasons for it must be seen the lesser British fear of French power—remember Fashoda; the skill of a supple and moderate French diplomacy which, unlike the German, did not misinterpret British willingness to liquidate differences into British weakness; but perhaps most of all Germany herself, the prime architect of the earlier Franco-Russian connection as she was now of the Anglo-French.

The impossibility of such connections had been a cardinal guiding principle of German foreign policy, rudely proved mistaken by this time. Bülow, the German Chancellor, was properly concerned. Only one more connection—one which also was not supposed to be feasible according to the German book—was needed, and it, too, was made. The 1907 agreement between Britain and Russia completed the circle of the Triple Entente. It must be stressed that both these agreements, the Anglo-French and the Anglo-Russian, were negative in nature. They were compositions of imperial differences, not even neutrality pacts or defensive alliances, let alone offensive arrangements, of which none were made in this period.

The French would have preferred an alliance or at least closer ties. But the French ambassador in London, the able Paul Cambon, while ever pressing the point, did so with patience and tact, eschewing unwelcome insistence. The British contention that the validity of basic community of interest and intent was greater than that of formal paper commitments proved right in the event. The Anglo-French connection was destined to grow increasingly close, and Cambon's best assistant in London was Germany again. Something has been said of the crisis of 1905 that grew out of Morocco, of the fundamentally not unreasonable German intent, and of the mistaken handling of the situation by Bülow. There is more to the episode. For Bülow was rather less interested in Morocco itself than in testing the precise nature of the Entente agreement. He suspected, with justice as it turned out, that there was more to it, in the form of concrete

plans for Moroccan partition, than had been publicly revealed
by its makers. His tactics only too successfully conveyed
to the French the intended picture of German intransigence.
But the British were equally convinced, with the consequence
that, within a year of its formation, the Entente Cordiale had
involved Britain into supporting France to a far greater extent than had been her original intention when she had
agreed to the Egyptian-Moroccan *quid pro quo*. The Anglo-
French military conversations began in 1906. But lest one
be misunderstood, it must be stressed that these conversations, and the military plans which came to be formulated as
a consequence of them, were not tantamount to an alliance,
or even to any sort of British commitment, as Grey kept reit-
erating to Cambon. They did nevertheless reflect a situation
and a state of mind, and Grey's interpretation was no doubt
to a point an attempted evasion.

By 1905, and even more by 1907, Germany began to show
an understandable concern over the fact of her encirclement,
the much touted *Einkreisung*. But at this point it is relevant
to ask why, and there is only one answer to the question—
Germany herself, by the impression she had conveyed of
herself, had brought about the encirclement. It was little
use to explain that Germany had no more deliberate and
conscious plan of aggression than the Triple Entente had;
the fear that was a compelling fact in the making of plans,
decisions and policies was real. A vicious circle had developed, the breaking of which was not impossible, but in any
event did not occur.

Looked at somewhat differently, the decade and a half
that followed Bismarck's passing from office witnessed the
transformation from a situation in which power was overwhelmingly concentrated in one locus, to another where a
more even balance prevailed. The dominance of Germany

under Bismarck's guidance was not unduly oppressive to
others, and certainly it was intended to insure the orderly
functioning of Europe in peace. One must be skeptical of
the prospect that the continuance of such a situation, coupled
with continued German growth, was likely to constitute a
possible foundation for the integration of Europe. The French,
understandably, never became reconciled to the Bismarckian
system and were ever on the alert for opportunities to escape
from their isolation. In any case the new course adopted by
Wilhelmine Germany, a more hesitant direction that found
expression in a mode of operation that increasingly conveyed
to others the image of aggressive intent, made the continuation
of German dominance, or even leadership, impossible. The
concrete manner in which the transformation took place has
been explained; it finally took the shape of the division of
Europe into two rival camps. Europe may thus be said to
have reacted in instinctive fashion to this, the latest threat
to her liberties, the continued independent existence of all.
As German power grew, the circle of those who coalesced
against its real or imagined threat became larger. Nothing
better expresses the new drift than the shifting position of
Italy. Since 1882 a member of the Triple Alliance, she did
not abandon that association, but the "interpretation" she
gave to the French of her position in the association, the
1902 exchange of letters between her foreign minister and
the French ambassador in Rome, is perfect measure of the
ambiguity of her position. It is a broad indication in turn
of the changing drift of the relationships of European powers.

Conclusion: The Closing of an Age

What took place during the first decade of the twentieth
century may therefore be regarded as a return to the classical
situation of equilibrium among the powers of Europe. By

1907 Europe was split into two camps. But one must guard against the wisdom of hindsight; it is indeed the proper function of historical analysis to explain how and why that which did happen happened, but this should not be equated with any sense of inevitability. The bipolarization of power that the existence of rival combinations expressed did not necessarily mean that a clash between them must occur or that European relationships were irrevocably frozen. There was still much fluidity in these relationships; for example, there was nothing fated about the course of the Anglo-German naval race, and some agreement on ratios of power could have been contrived. The British kept striving for this end, and there were those in Germany who worked to the same purpose. The Russo-German relationship, even the Austro-Russian, were not inevitably set on collision course, and even in Morocco there was for a time an authentic attempt to find a viable Franco-German accommodation.

None of this, as we know, succeeded, and it is useful to pause at this point in order to examine the crisis that occurred in 1908, the year after the Triple Entente combination was born. That episode is highly instructive, especially as it was in effect a preview of the crisis of 1914. The basic elements in it were two: the domestic problem of the nationalities of Austria-Hungary, especially as Austro-Serbian relations impinged upon it; the perennial Russian drive toward the Straits. Out of these two conditions, an Austro-Russian understanding of sorts was contrived by the foreign ministers of the two countries, Aehrenthal and Izvolsky respectively, in September 1908. The understanding was loose, and trouble was precipitated by the unilateral Austrian action that decreed the formal annexation of Bosnia-Herzegovina in October. The substance of the change was very small indeed, but in narrow legal terms the action was undoubtedly a violation of the international agreement that was the Treaty of Berlin of 1878. Izvolsky, though not blameless, was understandably annoyed and, like Germany in the case of Morocco in 1905, resorted to the demand for an international conference as the only agency empowered to sanction a modification. The Austrian refusal is what made the crisis European, bringing into play the network of existing connections. The crisis was prolonged and the fact that Austria in the end had her way was due to two things: on the one hand, the French and the British refused to give Russia sufficient support; on the other, the determined endorsement that she received from Germany.

This was Bülow's last major international success, a Pyrrhic one perhaps; if he took pride in it, his later measured judgment was to advise his successor not to attempt the same methods again. The outcome was a clear success for the Central Powers combination,[3] and Russia was dissatisfied with her own associates, but for that very reason the need was also felt to close ranks for the future. Ironically, yet appropriately in a way, what grew out of an Austro-Russian agreement was an exacerbation of Russo-German relations; the anti-German focus of the Franco-Russian alliance was now felt by Russia, as much as, if not more than by France, in contrast with the situation when the alliance was initially made. The German behavior was not so much due to deliberate aggressive intent as to a combination of rashness and fear, fear of the tightening encirclement, which Germany wished to test and if possible break; but the manner that she chose was best calculated to convey aggressive intent. The distinction between the imagined and real has been mentioned; to repeat, it is the image that counts in motivating action.

[3] It should be pointed out that Italy, though a member of the Triple Alliance, was not called upon for support by Austria. Italy took in fact an unfavorable view of the annexation and the following year entered into an understanding with Russia which further loosened her bonds with her formal allies.

Europe had for some time been an armed camp, and much has been written since about the danger of arms, a danger of which the world was aware before 1914. It was in fact, as early as 1899 that, at the call of the tsar, a conference met at The Hague for the purpose of dealing with armaments. The result was disappointingly meager: a permanent court of arbitration was created, some conventions were signed for the pacific settlement of disputes, and some agreements reached for a limited humanizing of war. Even less came out of the second conference of The Hague of 1907—an American initiative this time. It is again significant that in these meetings Germany contrived to bring upon herself the onus of obstruction. This was clumsiness on her part, for basically her position was not at all unique. What one must see in these abortive attempts is the premature beginning of a common awareness of the desirability of dealing with a danger in potential, an awareness much sharpened since. Before 1914 the simple fact is that Europe was not ready to consider disarmament. Europe had long been at peace, and the prevalent view, honored again in our time, was that of the old Roman maxim, *si vis pacem para bellum*. We call it now balance of terror, a phrase not used in earlier days, but the argument was not unfamiliar in 1914 that precisely because all had so many so powerful weapons, they would not be unleashed, for that would mean the end of civilization. It was inconceivable that the great civilized powers of Europe would commit collective suicide.

It has been pointed out, in retrospect, that the succession of crises, evidence of accumulated tensions, was at some point bound to result in open clash. Crises there were, no doubt, and in the last decade they recurred with increasing frequency; from that which arose in Morocco, to the annexation of Bosnia, to Morocco again, then to the Balkan wars, the intervening respites were brief. Yet from this very state of affairs comfort could also be derived: was not the fact that all these clashes were in the end resolved in accommodation proof that the civilized powers of Europe were capable of resolving their differences in peaceful fashion and that the crude test of force was one that had been superseded? Prophets of gloom there were, who proved right in the reckoning, but the dominant tone of Europe on the eve of Armageddon was one of optimistic confidence in unlimited progress.

What, in this climate, was the significance of any unity in Europe? In a sense there was none, and this was more than any earlier time the age of superheated, extravagant nationalisms, some of the aberrations of which have been rehearsed. There were no prospects of political unity, only of further fragmentation, in this age. The Sick Man had not died, though the national force had virtually evicted him from Europe; many foresaw his proximate final demise, and the prediction had been made that on his passing his place in the sickbed would be taken by the Danubian Monarchy. What unity there was existed at the level of the heritage of the past, though even it was being increasingly superseded by the stress on the more recent aspects of diverse national cultures. Christianity was no longer the great reality it had once been, but the Marxist creed and the socialist movement were making rapid progress that stood above frontiers. Might not the two find common ground in some way? Christian socialism was not altogether unknown before 1914. And was not international trade, which created a multitude of links binding nations together, a great contributor at least to universal peace?

We know what happened and how disunity was to assert itself in catastrophic fashion. Yet just because it was so catastrophic, the seeds that had existed of other possibilities than those of competing disunion were to assert themselves after the holocaust. The roots of diversity were very strong in Europe and had on the whole been growing stronger. They are still far from dead. The next thirty years were to be for Europe an uneasy and painful passage during which the main conflict was that between the old, struggling for survival, and the new striving to be born. It is, not surprisingly, a confused passage yet one that has no lack of fascination: the record of that contest is what will be examined in the next section of this book.

Part Three

THE BREAKDOWN OF THE CONCERT OF EUROPE AND THE SEARCH FOR AN ALTERNATIVE

I. The Meaning of the First World War

Twenty years ago a book appeared in Italy, since made available in English, the title of which is *The Origins of the War of 1914*.[1] It is a scholarly treatise, consisting of three heavy tomes, the first of which is devoted to a review of the relations among European states during the period from 1871 to 1914; the other two volumes concern themselves with little more than one month, July 1914. There have been other works with a similar distribution of attention and a whole library has grown around the issue of precisely what happened during that fated month, and most of all of how and why it did happen. All of which indicates a proper recognition of the significance of the first great conflict of the twentieth century.

On the twenty-eighth of June the heir to the Habsburg crown, Archduke Franz Ferdinand, together with his wife were shot in the Bosnian capital of Sarajevo by some young local enthusiastic hotheads. The deed created the proper amount of sensation abroad, but there was at first little reason to expect from it major international consequences. Balkan terrorism was hardly an unfamiliar ingredient of European

[1] Albertini, Luigi, *The Origins of the War of 1914* (Oxford, 1953–7).

politics. Yet the result, within five weeks, was that all the great powers of Europe, save one, Italy, and two secondary ones, Serbia and Belgium, were embarked in a conflict that was irrevocably to change the face and course of Europe, and of much beyond Europe as well./

This is not the place to rehearse in detail the events of that month, a thing which has been done many times. Certain facts alone are relevant to our discussion. The power and importance of the nationalistic force have been stressed, and the deed perpetrated in Sarajevo is but an illustration of it. There were some Bosnians who wanted emancipation from what was undoubtedly alien control; that Franz Ferdinand, who was supposedly favorable to concessions to the Slavs of the Monarchy, should have been their target merely shows the degree of intransigence nationalism had reached. It may be pointed out that, at this time, the complete destruction of the Habsburg state was the improbable vision of but a very few, yet it was in the end the more intransigent extremists who were to be proved right. Their irresponsible willingness to bring down the house of Europe in order to achieve their limited desire was also correct calculation and judgment, in so far as it may have entered their plans.

At this point we must bear in mind the whole antecedent background of Austro-Serbian relations: the 1908 Bosnian crisis and the recent Balkan Wars, and the Austrian ultimatums to Serbia, which explain the Austrian reaction, or that, at least, of those in charge of her affairs. Little Serbia by her very nature—ethnic affinity with the South Slavs—and her independent existence constituted a threat to the existence of Austria. That she must be destroyed, or at least taught a lasting lesson, was a conclusion based on rational thinking. There was also levity in the conduct of the operation by the Austrian minister, Berchtold, who was determined to proceed regardless of larger consequences. For, by contrast with 1908, in large measure *because* of what happened in 1908, Russia was set this time on an unyielding course.

At this point the play of larger relationships, the network of existing alliances, entered the situation. Also acting with levity, Germany underwrote Austria's action, thereby reversing the Bismarckian purpose, surrendering to Austria control of her own policy, instead of the reverse. Some of France's leaders happened to be in St. Petersburg at this very time, and she also had come to the conclusion that force and determination alone were the language that Germany understood, that what we now call appeasement was a mistake. In contrast with 1908, partly again because of 1908, France gave Russia support. When an irresistible force approaches an immovable obstacle a collision ensues. Thus war came to Europe. The first formal declaration of war that involved major powers with each other, on August 1, was, revealingly, that of Germany against Russia.

Germany was well prepared for war, yet this was not what she had deliberately sought. The closing days of July were a time of intense distress for her Chancellor, the far from belligerent Bethmann-Hollweg, but all avenues of salvation seemed closed. If it was to be war, the military scheme long since worked out for this particular eventuality, the famous Schlieffen Plan, must go into effect. It was regrettable that this involved the violation of Belgian neutrality by one of the guarantors of it, Germany. But necessity, as was said, is the higher law, and also, is not history written by the victors? In the orderly, relatively law-abiding world of 1914, the cost of such callousness was to prove very high. Yet in the immediate sense the attack upon Belgium was secondary, for even if it clinched the British intervention it did not cause it, that decision having been made independently, on the basis of an assessment of the balance of forces.

Europe and the German Problem

What emerges from this brief recounting is this: out of a Balkan situation in which Austria was the prime mover, within a month a different state of affairs had emerged where Germany was at the center of events. And this was both appropriately and symbolically confirmed by the fact that within another month the first significant encounter had been fought out in northern France. The significance of the Battle of the Marne is very great, comparable to that of the 1940 Battle of Britain. In a sense both were negative results, yet they contained in seed the ultimate outcome, the defeat of the German bid for the control of Europe.

Perhaps some clarification is needed. We are not here asserting a calculated German plan of aggression, but something in a sense more insidious and more difficult to deal with, for it was basically inherent in the nature of things. The central fact is that of German growth and of the rate of that growth that made adjustment of it and to it very difficult, in the reckoning impossible. There had been in Germany much talk about the rightful German place in the sun; out of this grew the vicious circle of suspicions, that German actions led by a clumsy diplomacy did much to confirm, and in the end the inability to find agreement between Germany and others on what that proper place should be. Therefore, it is quite correct to view the First World War as an episode in some respects of the same kind as the Napoleonic bid of a hundred years earlier.

Such a bid for hegemony has so far never succeeded in Europe; the story of the war, in brief, is that of another defeat of the attempt. Here again the purpose is not to tell the story of the war, but merely to extract from it certain relevant observations. To repeat, in 1914 there was not a clear and conscious German plan for uniting Europe under German dominance; yet there is no denying that German victory would have gone a long way toward achieving that end. Such plans in Germany were rather formulated in the course of the war and perusal of them is not less instructive because of the fact that ultimate defeat made their implementation of merely academic and historic interest.[2]

The German bid was not a senseless dream. Despite the early setback of the Marne, the advantage of geographic position and better preparation long told in favor of the Central Powers. On the strength of paper calculations, manpower and the whole totality of resources, the Allies' were no doubt the greater, but much of this was potential that time alone could transform into actual power. This was well known to all and was the reason why on the German side it was felt, and quite rightly, that victory could only be procured if rapidly achieved, while on the other side the best that could be hoped for was the avoidance of immediate defeat, a holding operation that would allow the eventual mobilization of these greater resources. Hence the significance of the Marne, which made possible the implementation of such a strategy.

The First World War failed to produce on either side one of those great military leaders, men of imagination, who for a time at least carry all before them. Instead, the record was one of much fumbling, much quiet competence and undramatic organizational skill, and the total story of the war may well be summed up as that of the greater weight eventually crushing the smaller. The story has been told many times.

[2] What would have been the shape of Europe in the event of a German victory may be gathered from the memoirs of some of her war leaders, such as Bethmann-Hollweg and Ludendorff, and even better from the documentary collection gathered by the investigating commission set up by the Reichstag after the war.

But this summation of the war does not mean that its conclusion came about without some unexpected things having occurred, some of which affected all the belligerents in similar manner, while others had divergent effects.

One of the beliefs widely held in 1914 was that if, by some chance, war should break out, for technical, if for no other reasons, it could not be of long duration. The power of the guns of August was thought to be so great that their users were confidently expected to be home by Christmas. But the initial German failure did not cause Germany to abandon hope, nor were the guns as powerful as thought, and both sides therefore settled to the long slogging match for an indefinite duration, seeking on the one hand to translate ever more of their respective potentials into concrete engines of war and looking abroad on the other for additional assistance among the initially noncommitted.

The first of these aspects of the war had enormous consequences that may best be summed up as the acceleration of the previously existing trends of change, economic, social, and political, a judgment that seems warranted despite the fact that in some of their forms the new trends seemed a reversal of the old. The task of mobilizing resources could mean one thing alone, a vast increase everywhere of the activity and powers of the state. What other agency could implement such programs as the selective organization of manpower, the allotment of economic resources, food rationing, the distribution of shipping, and the financing of so vast an operation? These, to be sure, were viewed as temporary measures, enforced by an emergency on societies which for the most part were believers in the greater merits of free enterprise and the minimal powers of government. But if the war was indeed an emergency, it can be seen, especially in retrospect, that although it did not by itself create many of the developments inherent in a modern industrial society, it did give them a great boost. The termination of hostilities was not to make possible the undoing of much that the war had induced and a simple return to the "normal," free days of pre-1914. It was precisely the failure to understand this at the time that created much of the postwar confusion and fumbling. This, to repeat, affected all, although in varying degrees, but we are in a sense anticipating our story.

The Classical War

The other aspect of the matter was the extension of the war, from the initial European circle of belligerents until it truly became a world war. It is worthy of note that the Central Powers were able to recruit only two additional adherents, the Ottoman Empire in 1914 and Bulgaria the following year, and that the whole of their war remained to a remarkable degree in German hands; truly it was a German war, an expression of the German bid for power. The other side collected an enormous roster, much of which to be sure had but little significance. Also, it must be emphasized that, for all its world-wide repercussions, the First World War remained an overwhelmingly European affair, certainly so where the battlefields were concerned.

In its initial stages the war had been one of wide and rapid movements that within a month brought the Germans to the gates of Paris. But after the retreat from the Marne an equilibrium of forces was reached. There followed the race to the sea, and soon there was established from the North Sea to the Swiss border the solid continuous front that was to remain in existence, with but relatively minor alterations, for the next four years. The war became a war of siege, the well-known trench warfare, with all its heroism and horrors. This was the state of affairs in the West. In the East a similar situation developed, once the initial Russian thrust in Prussia and in Galicia had been brought to a halt.

There matters stood for more than two years, which may be said to have been characterized by a series of limited but inconclusive successes for the Central Powers. While extensive slaughter occurred in the West, the Eastern front was pushed eastward, bringing most of Poland under Austro-German control. The Turkish participation induced the Allies to make an abortive attempt to break through the Straits and extended the war into the Middle East, also in inconclusive fashion. That of Bulgaria brought about the temporary destruction of Serbia and the establishment of a quiescent Balkan front. Rumania's intervention in 1916 proved a miscalculation and brought about her downfall. Meantime the German imperial positions were gradually overrun, mainly by British or imperial British forces, with some participation by the French, and in the Far East by the Japanese. The Italian intervention in 1915 failed to achieve significant results merely creating an additional front.

This phase of the war was characterized by much diplomatic activity; it was the classical diplomacy of power. The diplomacy of the Central Powers was relatively simple because of their small numbers and because of the German preponderance; in any case final defeat deprived it of the possibility of implementation. The diplomacy in the Allied camp was far more intricate and the results of much of it came to be written into the postwar settlements. The details of that activity need not detain us and it will suffice to say that, because it was based in considerable measure on the application of the principle of nationality, it looked to various rearrangements in Europe, though not to the destruction of Germany. Allied plans did, however, provide for the complete destruction of the Ottoman Empire, the Russians to achieve their secular ambition at the Straits, the Arabs to be liberated from the Turks under varying degrees of British and French tutelage; and even Turkey proper to be divided into spheres of influence. The German colonies were to be shared among the victors.

This, to repeat, may be seen as illustration of the classical operation of power, though the influence of the principle of nationality is not to be ignored. It was a simple fact that Alsace-Lorraine was under German rule and that Austria-Hungary contained an Italian *irredenta* as well as many other peoples in addition to the dominant Germans and Magyars. The Polish problem was an awkward one for all. But in any event the principle of nationality applied to prewar Europe could not be but a source of increasing division.)

The Intrusion of Ideologies

Before the war broke out, one of the arguments that had been used against its likelihood was the existence of large numbers of adherents to the Marxist faith. As has been pointed out, socialism was by its very nature international, and even often anti-national. Could one be sure of the direction of the aim of guns placed in the hands of the workers? The talk of socialist congresses justified this apprehension, and the socialist behavior during the July crisis was keenly watched by the governments; it has been mentioned that the murder of the French socialist leader Jaurès on July 31, 1914 was regarded by some as a major calamity. These fears—or hopes—turned out to have been unjustified, for in one fashion or another the various national sections of the International all found it possible to accept the defensive view of the war —the Germans vis-à-vis the reactionary government of the tsar, the French with similar views in regard to the militarism of Prussia that dominated the government of the Kaiser. The result was that the national component, or emotion, overrode in all cases what international velleities there were among socialists. The Second International was in effect destroyed and the setback to the socialist movement correspondingly great.

But only for a time and to a point. As the war drearily went on, making ever greater demands on the masses, it was largely among socialists that questioning was voiced of its purpose, validity, and aims. The highly popular work of the French writer Barbusse, *Le Feu,* was motivated by more than sheer revulsion against seemingly senseless slaughter. Even before its appearance, in 1917, socialists from various quarters had met in neutral Switzerland, at Kienthal in 1915, and at Zimmerwald the following year. Italian socialists, Italy being neutral at first, had adhered to the classical socialist view of the conflict as a clash of rival capitalisms; they had opposed their country's intervention. They were at best lukewarm in the Italian war effort; however, they did not sabotage it. On the whole, until 1917, socialism did not create appreciable difficulties for the governments.

But in 1917 change came in a wholly unexpected quarter. Of the impact of the war upon Russia it will suffice to say that it soon began to appear that the Russian state, essentially because of its economic as well as political backwardness, was incapable of sustaining the effort of a major twentieth-century war. The Anglo-French failure to open the Straits meant in addition that Russia was to be largely left to her own resources, deprived of appreciable aid from her better-equipped Western allies. Some of the happenings at the Russian court are a tax on the imagination; they were reflection of the incompetence of the Tsarist régime, and the sum total of this state of affairs can best be summed up in the one word, breakdown. Revolution ensued, as it had twelve years earlier. At first it was dedicated to domestic reform while continuing the war; but the provisional régime that followed the abdication of the tsar proved incapable of introducing change. For that matter revolution in the midst of war is ever a risky operation. Thus the March revolution was followed by another one in October that was an altogether different affair.

The Bolshevik seizure of power was perhaps more a coup than an authentic revolution; on the whole, the Russian people were overwhelmingly innocent of Marxism, but the slogan "land, peace, and bread" offered a concrete reality they understood. At any rate Bolshevism was master of Russia and has contrived to remain so to this day. Lenin and his initial followers were hard and ruthless men, but they were also dedicated believers. The unexpected accident of circumstances gave them a base of operation—the most unlikely, to be sure, by the teachings of the prophet himself—yet one that could be made to serve the wider revolutionary purpose. With total consistency, the Bolsheviks proceeded to terminate the war where Russia was concerned and appealed to all, ex-foe or friend, to follow their example and turn the war of nations into the war of classes, thereby raising the curtain for the dawn of the millennium.

This may seem fantasy, and in a sense it was. Yet no more important event has occurred in our century than the October Revolution. The Marxist gospel was familiar fare to much of the masses of non-Russian Europe. This fact, in combination with the growing weariness induced in all by the unending slaughter, might be expected to evoke considerable response to the appeals issued by the third Rome, Moscow, whither the Russian government betook itself. The additional tool of publicity given by the Bolsheviks to the network of secret agreements that their former allies had contrived was at best highly awkward and well calculated to support the contention that the peoples were tools of their capitalist masters.

There was indeed response to the Bolshevik appeal—and corresponding worry by the governments—but it was insufficient at the time to halt or change the course of the conflict, which continued in the absence of Russia. But in any event the Russian Revolution had the effect of introducing a novel element into both the internal functioning of states and their mutual relations. There is no need to explain the universal character of its appeal; it is wholly comparable to that which the French Revolution had brought into effective existence. In some respects the Russian Revolution could be seen as no more than the continuation or completion of the French. The success of Communism in the various states of Europe would at the very least have gone a long way toward their union; it would, among other things, furnish an answer to the very different German bid for control under German dominance.

But because the Russian appeal failed at this time, the German bid had to be resisted. Needless to say, in terms of power, the Russian defection—which was all that the revolution in Russia effected as far as the war was concerned—constituted a victory of the first magnitude for Germany and a corresponding setback for the Allies. That was in fact the reason why the Germans had provided facilities for the transportation of Lenin from Switzerland to Russia, and, in the immediate sense, their calculation was proved right. It might have fared ill with the Allies as a consequence had not the initial revolution in Russia virtually coincided in time with another equally important development, a more important one in its immediate effects. To put it most succinctly, in 1917 the United States took the place of Russia in the war; for the Allies it was a most profitable substitution.

The details and the specific reasons—divergencies in regard to the issue of the freedom of the seas and submarine warfare—of the American intervention in the First World War are not our concern here. In retrospect and broad perspective it does not seem unfair to see that intervention as deriving from a certain view of the national interest. For all that the issues of the conflict in Europe seemed largely alien to America, she could hardly remain unaffected by its outcome, and long before 1917 Colonel House had expressed his views of the consequences of victory by either side. Also, broadly speaking again, it may be said that the United States was adopting a policy similar to the traditional British—opposition to the emergence of too great a power on the continent of Europe, especially a strong military power. Put another way, what happened in 1917 was the formal consecration of the coming of age of America as a full member of the community of states. There is no prospect of the consequences of this event being spent in any foreseeable future.

In the last analysis, the reasons for the magnitude of these consequences may be summed up as the fact of American power. For in 1917 America ranked first in the whole world in terms of power, even though much of this power was still largely potential and had yet to be translated into concrete instruments of war. The German actions which had brought about the American intervention were a miscalculation of the same kind and order of magnitude as those which had ranged Britain against her. At any rate, the mere knowledge that the virtually unlimited reservoir of American resources was now enlisted in the Allied cause provided it with a vital and much needed boost. In simplest form the American intervention insured ultimate victory for the Allies.

This situation, the fact of American power, also made it inevitable that the American voice should carry very great weight in the future, as indeed was to be the case. This overwhelmingly important condition, and the manner in which it took effect, necessitates certain observations. The operation was not a simple one, but was instead accompanied by much ambiguity and confusion, gave rise to many unexpected problems and stresses, and in any case was vital to the future course and shape of European events.

Apart from sheer power, there was also the highly significant fact that the American position was different from any other. The American President was highly conscious of this condition, too conscious perhaps. President Wilson refused to acknowledge for his country the parity of allied status, insisting on that of "associated power" instead. Even if one allow the common purpose of preventing the establishment of a German hegemony in Europe, the United States shared none of the concrete interests of the European belligerents, interests best expressed in their plans for effecting territorial changes in Europe and in the imperial domain. These plans had found expression in the already mentioned network of agreements, all of which were secret. To be sure the United States did not share the Bolshevik views of the class struggle and world revolution, but on the issue of the wickedness of secret diplomacy and agreements the two certainly did agree in 1917. For that matter, even within the just indicated divergence, there was also common ground in so far as the change instituted in Russia had for its ultimate purpose the creation of the ideal society. As a consequence the revolution in Russia was not at first regarded as inevitably and irrevocably inimical to American purposes, and a development with which accommodation was necessarily impossible. We thus come to a situation where, for a time at least, the new Russian régime and the older American were to a point competing rivals for the attention of the masses of the whole world. The relationship between these rivals seemed not inevitably unfriendly. Or, as it has been put, at the close of the war Lenin and Wilson stood as the pole

stars toward whom the gaze of much of mankind was hopefully directed.

This state of things clearly puts stress on the ideological
aspect of the situation and it is but a little exaggeration to say
that the combined effect of the events of 1917, in America
and in Russia, was to shift the stress of the war from the
aspect of power to that of ideology. The difference was only
of degree to be sure, yet the degree of change was great.
America had the advantage that the ideology it endorsed
had the backing of enormous concrete power, the opposite
being the case of Russia at the time. Perhaps this is the place
to recall the Napoleonic dictum that a revolution is an idea
that has found bayonets.

Thus, in easily understandable fashion, America eventually
assumed the role of chief exponent of the aims of the Allied
cause. This fitted nicely the necessities of the day. It became
increasingly desirable, especially as the war was prolonged and
the end of the carnage not perceptible, to maintain the
allegiance of the masses. A result more easily accomplished
by stressing moral values; the response to these is more ready
than to the intricate, obscure, and often little-known concrete
objectives of power. The stress on the defensive aspect of
the struggle on the part of all the initial belligerents has
been mentioned. To take a specific illustration, the French
might be well-nigh unanimous on the score of the desirability
of undoing the wrong of 1870, but they might well have
second thoughts on the price to be paid for that purpose; the
mutinies in the French Army in 1917 were quite a serious
matter. Similar considerations apply to the Italian *irredenta,*
and the roster of such illustrations could be easily extended.
But stress on the one hand on the necessity of resisting the
designs of the aggressor, combined on the other with emphasis
on the bright promise of the future, was another matter again.

Lloyd George's electoral slogan in 1918, "A world fit for heroes to live in," bears recalling.

This type of activity has been much criticized, and indeed with some justice. The fact that the word "propaganda" has acquired pejorative connotations is the result of the abuses to which it has been put; the word is neutral in content and to propagandize for truth used to be called enlightenment, still a commendable activity.

But to come back to the war and the United States. It is a fortunate aspect—though it has also led to limitations in understanding—of American history that the American people assume they only engage in successful wars. Doubts of the outcome never entered the American consciousness during the First World War, and plans for the future could therefore be contrived in confident expectation of their eventual implementation. Such plans were accordingly made, and they were made with much care, great competence, and a high degree of dispassionateness; they were not the result, as a legend would have it, of the incompetent lucubrations of an innocent abroad. Familiar as they are, they deserve at this point more than passing attention.

The American program for the peace and the future was steeped in the American tradition and experience, which by this time reached into the fairly distant origins of America. Not many states in the twentieth century can boast the record of unbroken duration in their constitutional ordering that the United States can. The democratic concept quite easily derives from the eighteenth-century premise of the fundamental goodness of man. Therefore "to make the world safe for democracy" was appropriately the American slogan of the war; once this ideal was translated into concrete practice, justice would everywhere prevail and there would be no cause for quarrels among nations, or states. The other result of the war, which was to be a war to end all wars, would also be accomplished. Incidentally, within the state, the institution of the democratic practice would render meaningless the Marxist concept of class struggle. Democracy may well be described as successful in the United States where Marxist views have had but mediocre success.

This may seem rather vague and to a point naïve. To a degree it is. Yet the power of ideas is great, which is why this background has been sketched. In addition, the leaders of America and the President himself, had been practitioners at home of practical politics, hardly a naïve art, and they fully realized that in the end the peace must deal with concrete matters such as frontiers, economic, and other arrangements. This is where specific competence came into play, which eventually found expression in the famous Fourteen Points, the program presented by the President to the Congress on January 8, 1918. It is a historic document.

A perusal of the Fourteen Points reveals two kinds of things, concretizations of the broad general background outlined. The influence of the French Revolution has been explained—it gave modern nationalism its start by placing the source of sovereignty in the people. The case indeed is difficult to counter for it rests in the last resort on the simple notion of justice. Once the fact is granted that such a thing as, say, a Polish people exists, it would take some moral and intellectual contortions to proceed to contend that such a people should be ruled by Germans or Russians. At least such a position has become uncongenial to the twentieth-century way of thinking. The Polish instance can be extended to all. Thus, the majority of the Fourteen Points is concerned with the assertion of the validity of the principle of self-determination in the Polish and in a number of other cases. Rather than being an innovation, the American plan endorsed and gave the sanction of good to the well-established trend that nationalism had become in the nineteenth century.

The rest of the American program consisted of broader and looser principles: the condemnation of secret diplomacy (open covenants, openly arrived at), freedom of the seas (not precisely defined), and finally, most important of all and Wilson's very own,[3] the last of the Fourteen Points asserted the desirability of establishing an association of nations for the purpose of avoiding a recurrence of the current catastrophe. A world consisting of democratic states would unite in establishing the rule of law among equal sovereign states, extrapolating at the international level the condition of order under law that had come to prevail within the community which is the individual state.

It has been said, and quite correctly, that Wilson knew little and cared rather less about the details of specific European disputes. To him the matter was simple and best summed up in the revealing phrase that he used in addressing the American delegation on board the *George Washington* on its way to the peace congress: "Tell me what's right and I'll fight for it." Of competent advice there was no dearth; his experts would tell him precisely where predominantly Polish or Italian inhabited lands were; he would then fight for the frontier of justice. Granting the simple loftiness and the apparent reasonableness of the ideal, this admittedly was a somewhat simple view of the history of European peoples.

Who will publicly advocate sin? The American program received widespread endorsement, more authentically at the level of the peoples, more guardedly on the part of their governors. Under the fairest of applications the principle of nationality could not but redound to the detriment of the

[3] The idea of introducing some rule of law in the relations among states has old roots. It was taken up by various individuals and organizations in the United States, and in a sense Wilson himself may be said to have come to it late, though he made the idea his own.

Central Powers; the case of Russia was simplified by her withdrawal from the struggle and her independent endorsement of self-determination. So long as the leaders of Germany, meaning primarily her military leaders, thought victory still possible they evinced little interest in the American program. But once they had reached the conclusion that such an outcome was excluded, in August 1918, rational men that they were they drew the conclusion that the war should be ended. They also, at that point, discovered the possible uses of the civilian government of Germany and they willingly entrusted it with the task and saddled it with the responsibility of extricating the country from an awkward predicament.

Consequently, the German Government addressed to the American a request for the termination of hostilities on the basis of the American program. The Allies at this point were called upon to make a formal commitment to the same effect, and, after some argument, they did. From this point armistice negotiations proceeded that led to the final cessation of fighting on the Western Front on November 11, 1918.[4] The active phase of the war was terminated. Mention should be made of an ambiguity which arose at this point, one that was subsequently to have very regrettable consequences. When the armistice was concluded, the Germans were still in occupation of much enemy territory—they had been for four years—yet because Germany was defeated she was asked to yield her weapons and place herself at the mercy of the victors, in effect to surrender unconditionally. She had no choice in any case. But this had nothing to do with the commitment, freely made by these same victors, to a peace that in the simplest form can only be called one of justice for all,

---

[4] The German armistice put an end to the war. It was undoubtedly the most important such instrument, but had been preceded by similar armistices concluded with her allies, Bulgaria, the Ottoman Empire, and Austria-Hungary, during the preceding six weeks.

Germany included. These distinct, but inextricably related, aspects of the matter were and remained badly enmeshed.

From the conclusion of the final armistice to the formal beginning of the peace discussions in Paris, just over two months elapsed. To the world of the 1960s, living familiarly with the prospect of disaster and chaos, to which it has become inured, the climate of the autumn and winter of 1918–19 is difficult to describe. Yet some attempt must be made to re-create it. The weariness of war was universal in Europe as was the wish to believe that its recurrence could be insured against. In Europe this was perhaps the main emphasis. The New World had truly come to redress the balance and the shortcomings of the Old, and its physical impersonation in the form of the American President truly stood for a brief moment in the dangerously exalted position of Messiah of the New Order, a phrase which he himself was fond of using. He was fully aware of his position of power and of the hopes centered on him and his country, and he willingly accepted the role. He even thought, not wrongly for a moment, that he was more authentically representative of the hopes of mankind, in its various national guises, than the representatives, even if democratically elected, of the various national entities. The authentic enthusiasm of the reception given him by the masses of Europe bears witness to this—to the point that it worried the governments. To pave the way for the future had not a revolution taken place in Germany that sent the Kaiser and his minions away and made Germany a democracy? Had not Wilson proclaimed that he had no quarrel with the German people, but only with their masters, especially the Prussian military? And had not the Habsburg domain internally disintegrated, when in Vienna, Budapest, Prague, and Zagreb independent régimes proclaimed the separate existence of the separate national components of the defunct empire?

All this might seem full of promise and hope, automatically implementing much of the Wilsonian program, and leaving only the adjustment of some minor details of frontiers. Experts would supply facts and Wilson would fight for the right. But there was another face to the coin. On the desirability of justice all would agree with ease, but how would the French interpretation of it fit the German, or the German the Polish, or the Italian the Slav? The roster of specific instances is legion. Moreover, if all again would agree that war was an evil, four years of it had also exacerbated national feelings and the consciousness of difference to the point of white heat. The belief in German aggression, whatever the historical validity of it might be, was in 1918 largely an axiom among those Germany had fought, especially at the popular level. Is not the retribution for crime the implementation of justice? But the German people had got rid of their guilty masters —assuming that guilty they were; why should they, the innocents, be punished after having performed an act of virtue and atonement?

Finally, this, too, should be pointed out. Britain alone had been incapable of swaying the fortunes of the war; her traditional role of external balancer and savior of the liberties of Europe had fallen to the United States. The repetition of the situation when the bid for unity through conquest had failed was due to the intervention of what could not by any stretch of the imagination be called other than a non-European power, however much its roots might stem from the old Continent. The American view was founded on a world rather than a narrowly European order, and the Wilsonian association of nations was to be universal in scope. The more concrete reality in 1919 was, for Europe, the exacerbated consciousness of national diversity. The registration of the conditions that the war had produced must now be examined.

II. A Critique of the Peace

The war that had just ended is properly called a world war, for the effects of it were indeed universal. Nevertheless it was far more European than the subsequent conflict, both in terms of the locale of hostilities and in the intensity and importance of the specific issues with which its settlement had to concern itself; Europe for that matter is the main focus of attention in the present discussion.

While nearly the whole world was represented in Paris it was obvious that the elaboration of concrete terms of settlement could not be achieved through the adoption of some parliamentary process of discussion. That problem was resolved in simple fashion, basically through the recognition of the significance of power. What had been the directing agency of the war on the Allied side, the Supreme War Council, simply became the Supreme Council, the central directing agency of the peace, the court of last resort, in the making of decisions. Two things must be noted at this point. In contrast with the procedure adopted a century earlier at Vienna, in part precisely because of what had happened at Vienna, the enemy did not participate in the elaboration of the peace. In addition, because of the uncertain condition of Russia, that country, too, was excluded from the peace conference of Paris.[1] The consequence of this was that the task of shaping the settlements devolved overwhelmingly upon five powers,

[1] A German delegation was invited to Paris, but only after the Allies had agreed among themselves on the terms of the German peace. What observations were registered by the Germans had essentially no effect, and the German treaty was not really a negotiated instrument. The desirability of Russian participation in the peacemaking was also considered, but in part because of the chaotic condition of Russia no agreement could be reached on the basis of Russian representation.

the five great powers that were members of the victorious coalition. But of these five, one, Japan, had little interest in European issues; save where her limited Far Eastern interests were concerned Japan played a rather insignificant role in the peacemaking. Of the remaining four, Italy, partly for reasons of her own power, also played a secondary role in most matters, even to a lesser and smaller degree than she need have. Therefore the work of peacemaking was to an unusual degree the responsibility of three powers; in the last analysis, the role and power of the Big Three, three men, Wilson, Lloyd George, and Clemenceau, assumed inordinate importance. There is no room to go into consideration of their personalities and idiosyncrasies; this has been done in many places, but the significance of this aspect of the matter is obvious. Needless to say, these individuals, above all political leaders of democratic states, were not possessed of the technical competence required for the making of many decisions; they were accompanied by very large delegations, and it was inevitable that much should be turned over to the competence of technical *ad hoc* commissions. Much that went into the final settlements was indeed the result of the work of these commissions, work that was in the main of a high level of competence. The fact remains, however, and the importance of this must be stressed, that the locus of ultimate responsibility for decisions was in the hands of the Big Three.

The world of 1919 was a far more complex thing than that of 1815, and all of Europe had to be attended to. But, as the preceding pages have emphasized, the central issue of the war had been the German problem; as a consequence the attention of the Big Three was overwhelmingly focused on its solution. The awareness of the complexity of things was not lacking, and because the world was a world of states it was inevitable that high priority should go to the location of frontiers. Where Germany was concerned this was relatively simple. There was never any question of France's recovery of the loss of 1870, and once it had been made clear that France could obtain no more, the problem of Germany's western frontier was settled. The discussion was somewhat more difficult in the East, but here also agreement was reached which was essentially an application of the principle of nationality. This statement is true despite the loudness of German recriminations and of criticism in other quarters.[2]

It was more difficult elsewhere. The necessity of delimiting the boundaries of Central Europe was the inescapable consequence of the collapse of Austria-Hungary. The reason for the greater difficulty in this region was in large part the simple fact of the long historic existence of the Habsburg empire where various nationalities had long coexisted and to some degree intermixed. This consideration applied to a certain extent to the western reaches of the tsar's former domain as well. Clear lines of demarcation did not exist, but bands of territory instead, in which two or more ethnic groups cohabited in varying proportions. But frontiers must be sharply drawn lines, and since no one suggested in 1919 that recourse should be had to the crude and barbaric device of shifting populations in order to make them fit the frontiers, it was inevitable that many people should in the end find themselves on the wrong side of boundaries. There were still further complications, results of the vagaries of history. Should,

[2] The delimitation of the frontier with Poland gave rise to much discussion. If Poland was to be reconstituted it was inevitable that some of her territory would have to come from Germany, though precisely how much might be debated. Population statistics were largely used—the German census of 1910—and Danzig, Poland's port but a German city, was placed under League supervision. Also, Memel was seized by Lithuania, Denmark recovered the Danish portion of Schleswig, and the Saar, like Danzig, was also placed under League supervision, though only for fifteen years, after which time a plebiscite returned it to Germany.

for example, the new Czechoslovakia retain the historic boundaries of the kingdom of Bohemia, or should the German infiltration, which had made the Sudetenland Germanic, cause a modification of those boundaries? Nor is it surprising that, in 1919, importance should be given to strategic considerations, of which Czechoslovakia again furnishes a good illustration. It was felt that a strictly ethnic line between Germans and Czechs would make that country militarily indefensible. It is perhaps not irrelevant to recall at this point what happened in that region in 1938 and immediately thereafter.

Rather less importance was attached, in 1919, to economic considerations, of which something more will have to be said. A prime illustration of what in many respects is an ultimate absurdity was the virtual exclusion of Russia from the Baltic. The Paris Congress did not deal with Soviet frontiers which were later adjusted as a result of direct agreements between the Soviet Union and her various neighbors. The Bolsheviks accepted the principle of self-determination, and since there are such people as Finns, who are indeed not Russian, Finland, and other states, were able to emerge in independence. Yet Pilsudski's observation, highly improbable sounding in 1915, may be recalled that the independence of Poland would occur as a consequence of a Russian defeat at German hands followed by a German defeat by the Western Allies. This unlikely sequence was what had happened, and it is difficult to conceive that not only Poland, but also the small Baltic states, minute entities that stood between enormous Russia and the sea, could have emerged into independent existence had it not been for the unexpected succession of events that took place in that part of the world, Russian revolution and defeat followed by similar occurrences in Germany.

Yet, to repeat, there *are* Lithuanians and Latvians, as well as Poles, Finns, and Estonians. The outcome around the Baltic may be seen as self-determination with a vengeance, and it has justly been remarked that the political map of Europe after the First World War was the nearest approximation to its ethnic divisions ever achieved. The map could have been drawn somewhat better, though not a very great deal and the continued existence of minorities in Europe was rather the result of the history of that continent than of any negligent callousness of revengeful disposition. This is worth emphasizing, and illustrations could be multiplied that bring out the extent to which efforts were made to find solutions that were at once reasonable and fair. It would take us too far afield—and astray—to attempt a listing and a discussion of all the controversial issues that were the legacy of the peace, but, by way of illustration, the case of Danzig may be mentioned, especially in view of the fact that it may be regarded as the particular point where the Second World War began.

Once it had been decided that a Polish state should be restored to independent existence, it was wholly reasonable to give it free access to the sea; the reverse would in fact have been an absurdity, and already in the Fourteen Points secure Polish access to the sea had been mentioned. But Poland's port was Danzig, an unquestionably German city. The first decision was to give Danzig to Poland on the not unreasonable plea that the economic life of a country of some 30,000,000 could not be jeopardized for the sake of a strict application of the principle of nationality to 1 per cent of that number. There were second thoughts, however, and in the end a compromise was effected between the divergent desirabilities; Danzig was made a free territory entrusted to the care of the League. Was not this as fair a compromise as could have been contrived in the circumstances? When war broke out again twenty years later, Danzig was not the cause but a convenient pretext. And we could also cite the innovations that were the minority treaties. The new countries of mid-Europe that contained substantial ethnic minorities were made to accept this interference with their sovereign prerogative that was the right of intrusion granted to the world organization in order to protect the rights of those minorities.

That peace was not insured for long is undeniable, but to lay the responsibility for this outcome at the door of the arrangements that were made in 1919 is a different matter. If the principle of nationality is accepted—and how deny it? —and associated in turn with that of democracy, what else could have been done? It was authentically believed after the war that a world made safe for democracy would be one that insured the greatest possibility of lasting order and peace. One may indeed be driven to question the validity of the democratic principle itself, but that is a different matter, and who, either then or now, would dare advocate such a position who is active in politics? The issue in a case like Danzig was not so much the fate of 300,000 Germans, as it was the future relations of Germany and Poland. It may be worth calling attention to what happened in the eastern section of Germany after another war, and it would be rash to claim that present arrangements provide a sounder and more stable basis of future order and peace in that part of the world.

The greater difficulty of the peace lay in another direction, and it is true indeed that what was done in the peace settlements failed to resolve the dislocations, most of all the economic ones, that had been the result of the war. In the world of 1914 a vast network of interrelations had come into gradual existence which were abruptly disrupted by the war. It was widely believed that normality would return upon the cessation of fighting and that, for example, the vast burden of financial obligations that were a legacy of the war could be dealt with in classical fashion. That this was economic na-

ïveté may be granted, but one must point to the length of
time it would take before Keynesian views,[3] in this and in
other respects, would gain widespread acceptance.

A word must be said about this. Two things must first be
pointed out: the astronomical cost of the war, and the widely
held belief in German aggression. It was a comforting prospect for the victors to believe that the implementation of
justice would result in making good the damage that they had
suffered, and this was especially true in the French case, since
France had been the battleground. It might also be pointed
out that, quite apart from moral guilt, even a pooling of resources by all for the purpose of general reconstruction would
have had the very similar effect of creating a large German
obligation to France. In any case, Germany could, and in fact
did, expect to be saddled with a large burden of debt. But,
diverging from the customary practice of imposing an indemnity upon the defeated—for the simple and incontrovertible
reason that he is defeated—the Treaty of Versailles stressed
the moral aspect of the matter. The result was the unprecedented step of the opening article of the reparation section
of the treaty—reparation, be it noted, not indemnity. The
famous article 231 is worth quoting:

> The Allied and Associated Governments affirm and Ger-
> many accepts the responsibility of Germany and her allies for
> causing all the loss and damage to which the Allied and
> Associated Governments and their nationals have been sub-
> jected as a consequence of the war imposed upon them by
> the aggression of Germany and her allies.

[3] Keynes was one of the early critics of the economic aspects of the
peace, and his indictment, *The Economic Consequences of the Peace*,
achieved justified fame, even though the manner of it was to a point
detrimental to his purpose. More broadly, the Keynesian views on the
score of the financial management of the economy have achieved well-
nigh universal acceptance.

The American share in the authorship of this clause may be appropriately recalled. This is the famous war-guilt clause, which had unexpected effects. For the German people did not agree with the interpretation that charged them with exclusive guilt. Besides, had not their recent democratic revolution purged them of whatever guilt might have been their rulers'? Here was clearly invitation to controversy which, needless to say, flourished. Moreover, if reparation was the consequence of moral guilt, the disproval of such guilt would eliminate the basis for reparation. One may feel that one is entering the domain of the absurd and the fantastic, and such a situation can only be understood in the vanished climate of hope and expectation that prevailed in 1919. It was in line with the same type of approach that the enemy was disarmed. This was another logical consequence of the belief in German aggression; Germany was in effect being put on probation, and it was the general expectation that, once she had worked her passage, others could proceed in turn to disarm. The inverted belief in the causal function of arms in encouraging war was widely held after the war.

But there was more to the peace. Apart from the awareness of its imperfections, the overriding concern of the American President was less with the details of the settlement, territorial or economic, than with the international organization that he hoped to create. The organization of peace is an ancient dream of mankind rather than a Wilsonian invention, but Wilson's dedication to its realization warrants crediting him with the fatherhood of the League of Nations. If it had not been for the power that America commanded, one may well doubt that there would have been a League in 1919. To make assurance doubly sure it was decided that the Covenant would be incorporated into the treaties of peace themselves. For the first time in history an attempt was made to formalize in law the organization of international order, and the subsequent failure of the attempt detracts not a whit from either the nobility or the significance of the effort. Here was something more substantial than the loose Concert of Europe.

The details of the Covenant will not be considered here. It will suffice to say that the logical contradiction between the subjection to law and the assertion of the attribute of sovereignty was not resolved, a weakness reflected in the ambiguities that survived in the Covenant and in the failure to define the precise powers of the League and to endow it with effective means of action. The future alone could decide what the organization would and could do and what it might become. We have the answer, but it is also significant that we have not been able so far to contrive anything but another very similar device.

What then was the result and nature of the attempted settlement of the war? The triumph of the principle of nationality is clear, reflecting a historic continuity rather than innovation. The same may be said to apply to the democratic principle, which, immediately after the war, took on the guise of universal panacea. The new Germany and all the new states could not at first conceive of any but parliamentary democratic systems for their future governance. The war, needless to say, had exacerbated national sentiments, and the nationalism of the newly created entities was also characterized by its virulence. The war therefore can hardly be said to have had, in Europe, other than divisive effects.

Yet it had also laid common ground. The revulsion from war was well-nigh and understandably shared by victors and defeated alike; the war to end all wars was a highly popular slogan and a hope that did not stop at frontiers. And if the fundamental goodness of man was a correct assumption—of which the democratic principle was expression in the political domain—there might be hope, after some time, that passions could subside and peaceful order prevail. This, to be sure, to a considerable extent would depend upon the fulfillment of other widely shared expectations, which may best be summed up as the realization of a greater degree of social justice within the individual states. Clearly one enters at this point the realm of social and economic issues.

In the immediate sense, to repeat, the war had emphasized difference and division in Europe and left behind a vast legacy of suspicion and bitterness. This condition hardly fostered any thought or talk of union, nor in fact was there any; and it is significant that the League was intended to be of universal, rather than mainly European, application. It was, for that matter, a device intended to create order in the whole international community rather than to submerge the separate identity of its members. The Europe of 1919 was a collection of problems, some of which were easy to perceive, but the nature of many was also hidden or very badly understood. Perhaps it might be put this way: shaken as it had been, the fundamental and traditional structure of Europe had survived; the German challenge, like others before it, had been successfully met, and the liberties of Europe—the separate existence of her members, more numerous now than before —had been saved, this time thanks to the intervention of an unquestionably non-European power, the United States.

Would Europe set out on a new course, or seek to return to her traditional grooves? History is a powerful force, and the past always a heavy mortgage on the future; yet history cannot be static, certainly not in a twentieth century characterized by rapid change. At any one point of time treaties are to a large extent the registration of the relationships and forces that exist at the time of their making; yet they are also in a sense the charter of the future—certainly the League was meant to be such. Treaties are not eternal, just as conditions are not static. In 1919 it was not known what use would be made of those that were the outcome of the war. We must now look at the record of the fumbling attempts that characterized the two decades properly called the Long Armistice, for the First World War turned out to be not so much a solution of old problems, as the creation of new ones, the opening chapter of a stage in the story of change quite as much as the closing of another. It was indeed unfinished business.

III. The Long Armistice: Continued Failure of the Forces of Cohesion

In a very real sense the significance of the First World War may be found in the defeat of the German bid for hegemonic control, even if one discounts as legend a conscious German plan designed to that effect before 1914. The fact of German power is sufficient, and there is little question that German victory would have had the result of establishing, if not complete German control, at least a crushingly dominant German position in Europe. The outcome in 1919, in the shape of the peace, was measure of the distance Europe had traveled in a century. One of the forces that had helped defeat Napoleon was that of national feeling; yet in 1815 that force was relatively weak, and the peoples could in large measure be ignored at Vienna. It was no longer so in Paris in 1919, for the nationalistic seed had prospered during the whole nineteenth century, and it had been sufficiently explained that the postwar settlement registered the greatest triumph of nationalism so far.

It was precisely because the war had been a peoples' war to an incomparably greater degree than the Napoleonic wars had been that the treatment of Germany after the First World War was so different from that of France in 1815. The peoples, through their representatives, were incapable of taking the detached, rational view of things that the rulers had taken a hundred years before; unlike the Germans at Versailles, Talleyrand was anything but an outcast at Vienna. But the 1919 situation created problems of another kind, and more difficult ones than those with which Europe had dealt a hundred years before. Germany was defeated, but the German problem was not necessarily solved; moreover, in deference to the unquestioned Germanness of Germany, apart from peripheral losses that self-determination largely justified, the bulk of Germany remained. The pre-1914 issue of the proper place of Germany under the sun remained, but with the difference that Germany must now begin by seeking first to recover some place of parity. Even if the German people had all become peace-loving democrats, the goal of German policy, under whatever domestic political dispensation, was set with inescapable simplicity: riddance of the onerous liabilities and discriminations with which the country was saddled. In addition, it may be pointed out that German national feeling was no less exacerbated than others; on the score of the iniquity of the *diktat* of Versailles consensus was well-nigh unanimous among the German people.

The fate of the Danubian Monarchy was far more drastic: it simply was no more. To a degree matters were simplified by this outcome, for if the issue of survival could be debated so long as Austria-Hungary existed, there was little prospect of reviving the corpse. The problem of Danubia bears no resemblance to the German problem; it was the problem of organizing the existence and the relationships of a collection of new entities, of the third or lower order of magnitude in dimensions of power. Democratic constitutions, intense consciousness of newly acquired and jealously guarded sovereignty, plus tariff barriers were not the best approach to the problems of Central and Eastern Europe as a whole.

There was finally the vast Soviet state, almost reduced in

Europe to the position Russia had occupied when Tsar Peter I launched his state upon its course of European imitation and expansion. Russia, besides, meant revolution and for the moment internal conditions that were chaotic. But, barring the unlikely permanence of chaos, Russia, Soviet or otherwise, would presumably recover and then have to find her proper place among states. Russia, like Germany, had a long distance to travel.

Thus, in a sense, the three great problems of Europe after the war may be said to have borne the names Germany, Danubia, and Russia, a fact which is a measure of the disorganizing impact of the war. Yet one could hardly wait in passive stance, and Europe must somehow organize herself and immediately function. Looking at things from a somewhat different angle, it might be said that the war signified the collapse of the state system of Europe which had functioned since the days of Westphalia with only the passing interruption of the French Revolution and Napoleon, which had been fairly easily put to rights. Ostensibly, Europe was still, as she had been, a collectivity of sovereign states, but the effects of the disruption which began in 1914 far exceeded those introduced by 1789. New solutions and approaches were needed, but the nearest thing was the League, the new world organization of universal rather than especially European outlook and intent. Furthermore, neither Russia nor Germany were initially members of the League. There could hardly be any question under the circumstances of any sort of union in Europe; nor was there any at a time when the accent was all on diversity and on a multitude of jarring differences. It would need another collapse before a sufficiently clean sweep could be made of the past. It may be put this way: great as its impact was, the First World War had insufficiently shaken the previously existing structure of Europe. How then did Europe proceed to organize herself and function?

The importance of the role of the United States in procuring the outcome of the war and in shaping the peace has been mentioned. The League of Nations and its Covenant, which Wilson had forced into the treaties of peace, was the special American contribution to the future. But the United States disowned its own child. The reasons for this strange reversal need not be examined here; enough to say that the decisive one was American jealousy of American sovereignty, any conceivable infringement of which would not be entertained. The American Senate in March 1920, finally declined to ratify the Treaty of Versailles, not because of its German provisions, but because of the terms of the Covenant which was part of the treaty. There was no remedy for this situation; the League must organize itself without America. Needless to say this was not an auspicious beginning. But there was more, for this rejection may be seen as the beginning of another great reversal, which culminated in the feeling that the American experiment in participation in the major affairs of the external world had been an error. With the Republican success in the presidential election of 1920 America embarked on that curious passage in her story, the attempt to return to the supposed purity of her uncontaminated past. As in the case of Europe, the experience of one war had been insufficient to break the hold of tradition, and it would take another to accomplish this result. American isolation and isolationism were not so much a theory as a historic tradition. Europe must then proceed without America and yet in a sense the American endeavor was futile, for America as well as for Europe. Actually the impact of American withdrawal was different—although not less—from what active and conscious participation would have been.

The Anglo-French Divergence

With the demise of Austria, and the at least temporary eclipse of Germany and Russia, Europe was left in a strangely unbalanced situation, where the victors had in their hands the power and the responsibility for the direction of all. The victors meant three powers, but to make matters even more extreme, one of them, Italy, because of her power and the impact and strain of the war upon her, embarked on a policy of retrenchment and played at first a very minor rule in the subsequent direction of Europe. The very fact of victory, for that matter, and the complete destruction of German power, had robbed Italy of the traditionally most valuable asset of her foreign policy, the balance of power.

Thus two were left, Britain and France, an unprecedented state of affairs. Britain and France no doubt were great powers, but what was especially significant was that for them the victory was ashes, despite the misleading appearance of their unfettered dominance and even despite the concrete gains, imperial positions for example, that they secured for a brief time. It was a fact known to all, and certainly to the French themselves, that French power had long been in relative decline. Clemenceau's judgment was wholly right that France had secured victory only because she had had the good fortune of being part of so powerful a coalition. From this he drew the logical conclusion that France ought to capitalize as much as possible on the fortunate conjuncture; she might thereby insure her safety for a generation. If he accomplished this result, Clemenceau thought he would have served his country well.

The relative British decline had been more recent and less evident. Yet the British had been aware of the diminution of the margin of their power even before the war; it was this common condition, more than any other reason, that had brought Britain and France together before and in 1914. The war itself had injured both countries very severely; the British hurt was less apparent, while the French one was more evident: casualties that were a true bloodletting, attaining biological proportions, and the physical destruction of the industrially most valuable part of France.

For Britain and for France the war had been a fundamentally defensive operation. Both were, as they had been for some time, satisfied powers, the "haves," whose main endeavor was to hold their own. In the uncertain, dislocated world that issued from the conflict their basic interest remained the same, the maintenance of their positions and possessions, opposition to violent change, peace and the status quo. The status quo might stand in need of some revision, but this should be effected, if at all, in orderly fashion. Acting in unison it is conceivable that they could have contrived to organize and lead Europe toward a new stability, using their adequate forces if necessary to repress advocates and forces of violent change, using that same superior force again to direct into orderly, peaceful channels, what change was warranted and inescapable. Even this is an optimistic view of what the future might have been; it was at least a possibility certainly worth pursuing.

The British view of things had the merit of being sympathetic to the concept of change. Even before the German treaty had been signed, mercurial Lloyd George, somewhat to the annoyance of his American and French colleagues, wanted to modify some of the terms of an agreement achieved with so much difficulty. However, against this desirable flexibility there was another, less fortunate, aspect of the British position. Instead of a clear realization that she and France were truly in a similar defensive position, the view of the war that became prevalent in Britain stressed the historic similarity between the last and earlier conflicts. Britain had fought the Kaiser for the same reason and to the same effect that she had fought Philip II and Napoleon.

The observation is apt at this point that "Britain has no permanent allies, she has only permanent interests." The British interest lay in the defense of the liberties of Europe, concretely translated into the preservation of the divisions of the Continent best guaranteed by the balance of power. German power had threatened to become excessive; it had been successfully resisted and set back. But German power was a necessary component of the balance of Europe; therefore it should not be unduly diminished lest the balance be tipped in another direction. In 1815 Britain, for precisely such a reason, had favored the preservation of French power lest Austrian or Russian power be insufficiently checked. On the continent of Europe in 1919 there was one effectively organized power, apart from the insufficient Italian; it was the French. In British eyes this was an uncongenial situation which ought therefore to be redressed. To translate this into saying that Britain turned anti-French and pro-German would be a crude oversimplification, for all that it was not very long before there developed in England a strong current of sentimental sympathy for Germany and her woes.[1]

This was the great British mistake, a well-nigh unpardonable misreading of history and of the facts of the day. The British interpretation may have seemed founded in both history and reason, plus a measure of presumed fairness, but

[1] The circumstances of the wartime alliance were insufficient to overcome effectively either of the two long-standing traditions of Anglo-French rivalry and Anglo-German affinity, either at the political level or even more at that of popular sentiment, where a distorted sense of fair play served to induce much sympathy for the defeated. The controversy on the origins of and responsibility for the war inserted itself to perfection into this situation. In this last respect a similar phenomenon occurred in the United States.

the central fallacy lay in the failure to perceive that France in 1919 was a very different France from that of 1815, especially where power was concerned. If the prospect of victory was pleasing to France, the war had also been a sobering experience. France in 1919 was overwhelmingly desirous of being allowed to cultivate her garden in peace. But France may not, as America could at least superficially, attempt isolation; she cannot help but have a policy for Europe.

The French view of things was vastly different from the British, and on the score of a correct appraisal of the reality of things far more sound. For France the war was not so much the recurrence of traditional experience in the successful achievement of purpose as it was another effective demonstration of German aggressiveness and German power. This power was momentarily broken, but the bases of it remained undestroyed; and it continued to be the great threat of the future which must be guarded against by all possible means. The terms of victory brought France little elation—in an apologetic fashion Clemenceau defended the Treaty of Versailles in parliament as the best that could be obtained in the face of allied wishes.

In the spring of 1919, when Clemenceau was compelled to yield certain demands for control of the Rhine, a limited but additional concrete guarantee of French security, his surrender had been obtained as the result of a compromise. The counterpart was an Anglo-American contribution in the form of a tripartite treaty which insured France of American and British assistance in the event of future German aggression. This arrangement had a great many merits: for one thing it gave satisfaction to the wholly legitimate French desire for security, but it accomplished this without doing violence to German national feeling, avoiding the creation of an Alsace-Lorraine in reverse; if Germany should abandon aggressive intent, the guarantee would never be called into play, while in the opposite case the prior knowledge of that guarantee would have served as the most effective deterrent. Finally, by creating in France a sense of security, it might assist the elimination of the disabilities with which Germany was saddled by the peace, hence facilitate her reintegration as a member in good standing of the European community. Unless or until this is done Europe cannot hope to function in order and peace, let alone in union. The American and British contribution was statesmanship of a high order.

Or at least it would have been had it corresponded to the real and the possible. To make a long story short it will suffice to say that the treaty of guarantee or reinsurance never even reached the floor of the American Senate for discussion, and consequently died the death of legislation pigeon-holed in committee. This was a very awkward situation, for one part of a *quid pro quo*—certain provisions of the Treaty of Versailles of prime concern to France—had been delivered, while the counterpart—the American guarantee—was refused. An escape clause furnished the British with a reason for withdrawing from the arrangement as well, a decision that may be described as more legally correct than politically wise.

Clearly, it would hardly be adequate satisfaction to suggest to the French that they should inform themselves of the operation of American constitutional processes. To the French, French security was important, which must therefore be sought by whatever other alternatives might be available. To be sure, the French obsession for security immediately after the war seemed unwarranted, if not a fraudulent pretext for an abuse of power. Of course there was in 1919 no effective German danger, nor could there be for some indefinite future. Also mention should be made of the view that advocated a policy of generous acceptance of Germany in the hope that it would be precisely this which would secure in Germany the lasting triumph of the forces of democracy and peace.

The prospect was not devoid of attraction, but in the context of the realities of power it cannot be regarded as either reasonable or fair. The first legitimate proper care of the foreign policy of any state is security, and the assumption on which a liberal and generous policy toward Germany would have rested was too uncertain for France to be expected to gamble her security upon it. It would have been otherwise if France had had, or felt that she had, adequate power to deal with the German danger unassisted. This points to the inescapable importance of considerations of power. Put in different form, Germany also must make a vital contribution to the security of France and to the general stability of Europe. Beyond Germany, the English-speaking peoples could also have contributed much. This is the precise point at which they may have missed their opportunity, some would say sought to dodge their responsibility.

The consequences of this state of affairs were very large for all. But recriminations are futile, and reality cannot be bent to suit wishes and hopes; the circumstances being what they were France would look to her own safety as best she could, in other quarters if possible. But the effect was also a regrettable distortion. Because Germany was *the* problem for France, the Franco-German relationship assumed undue importance in the affairs of Europe as a whole. France did indeed evolve a scheme for the organization of Europe; it was a scheme, however, in which the German focus had a distorting effect.

The Organization of Europe

The peace itself, more narrowly the German treaty, had given France certain solid assets: Germany was disarmed and liable to an enormous financial obligation, in which the French held a majority share. These terms must be enforced in literal and intransigent fashion since they would serve to maintain and prolong the impotence of Germany; the policy, if harsh, was logical. The tale of reparations is both long and dreary and will not here be rehearsed in detail. It reached a climax in the closing days of 1922 when the French chairman of the reparations commission submitted to that body two propositions: first, Germany was in default of her obligations; secondly, her default was intentional. The four members of the commission, British, Italian, and Belgian, in addition to the French, found unanimously in the affirmative on the first proposition. It was a matter of objective fact, though it is significant that the specific default was of insignificant dimensions. But on the second proposition, a matter of intent, it is also revealing that the British member cast a dissenting vote. The issue was in essence political and turned into a test of force and will between France and Germany; for the French proceeded to enforce the law by taking sanctions in the form of the famous episode known as the occupation of the Ruhr.

It is worth noting that in this operation the Belgians gave some assistance, the Italians little more than acquiescence, while the British expressed strong disapproval and condemnation. But the British view never took any other form than the verbal; in the face of French determination it was devoid of effect, save perhaps to a point in misleading German resistance. Here was therefore essentially an isolated Franco-German test of force; in the immediate and limited sense the French were successful since they broke the German will to resist. Passive resistance, the only weapon available to Germany at the time, was largely instrumental in producing the great inflation, the total collapse of the currency and much social and economic chaos. Poincaré's reported observation, "Let there be chaos," whether authentic or apocryphal, aptly describes a line of policy; it fell to Stresemann, a conservative and patriotic German, to implement the realistic necessity of a second surrender.

But the aftermath of the Ruhr is also revealing in another way. Apart from the fact that, in narrow economic terms, the French attempt to extract payment from Germany, was, in the last resort, an impossibility, the French did not push their advantage. To be sure, their own economic difficulties rendered them also vulnerable, and the outcome, the Dawes Plan, was largely an Anglo-American instrument. But, in addition, the French people repudiated Poincaré in the election of 1924. The French policy of which the Ruhr episode was a manifestation may be characterized as both mistaken and brutal, and the abandonment of it could be widely hailed; yet this abandonment may also be read as a failure of will. Irresolute confusion is never an adequate policy.

Meantime much else had happened, of a more purely political nature. Traditionally, France had looked to an eastern alliance in Europe as a counterweight to Central European power, be it Habsburg or Hohenzollern. The Turks, the Swedes, the Poles, had in part filled this role at one time and before 1914 the Russians. But there was no power in Russia after the war, while the ideology to which the Bolsheviks were dedicated made Soviet Russia the enemy of all, particularly the victors, France therefore in first place. France had a policy vis-à-vis the new Russia, which was at first that of intervention in order to destroy the new dispensation. This having failed, and especially after the Russo-Polish War had stabilized the situation in that quarter, French policy became that of the *cordon sanitaire* which was essentially the same policy adopted by America after another war, when it was called containment: the danger of political infection that Russia embodied must be prevented from spreading. The fact that the very large French investment in prewar Russia was

now lost naturally contributed to inimical French feeling, and
France became the prime exponent of the policy of quarantine
for Russia, far more than Britain, whose greater commercial
propensity inclined her toward some accommodation, or than
defeated Germany upon whom the Bolsheviks were inclined
to look with a degree of favor. The Bolsheviks thought that
Germany, for a time at least, might be suitable ground for
revolution, and Germany could be reliably counted in the
anti-French camp. However, as conditions achieved a measure
of stability in Europe, and hopes of revolution faded, Russia
increasingly turned inward, concentrating on the necessary
task of domestic reconstruction. Lenin's New Economic Policy
may be taken as the signal of change, and, after Lenin, once
the struggle for his succession had resulted in the elimination of the more world-revolution-minded Trotsky, Stalin, the
successful heir of Lenin, confirmed the stress on domestic
preoccupation. Bolshevik Russia seemingly could exist in a
capitalist world, while the vastness of her dimensions and
resources would make possible the successful construction
of "socialism in one country." World revolution was not abandoned but put off to some indefinite future, and meanwhile
a minor revision of prophecy would suffice. Russia for many
years was a relatively inactive factor in European affairs.[2]

New Poland, next door to Russia, fitted nicely into the
French policy of quarantine, while the traditional Polish enmity toward Russia created between herself and France an
authentic bond of interest. There was an even greater bond,
one to the west of Poland, where German feeling ran high
on the score of the "bleeding frontier." Nothing in this context

[2] Anti-capitalist and anti-imperialist as she was, Bolshevik Russia
nevertheless evinced sympathy for any opposition to the dominant
powers. Thus she furnished a measure of assistance and advice to the
revolution that established the régime of Chiang Kai-shek in China in
the twenties.

could have been more natural than the conclusion, in 1921, of a Franco-Polish alliance. Both states had the same common wish to preserve the benefits that they had derived from the war. The asset of French power was understandably welcome in Warsaw; Polish power was less, though by no means negligible, and the prospect of the asset of a number of Polish divisions was equally welcome in Paris where no one at this time raised the cry, "Why die for Danzig?" The Franco-Polish alliance seemed solid, though the fact that Poland by her very existence constituted a bond between her two far more powerful neighbors could not be ignored. But any such prospects obviously lay in some indefinite future.

There were others, besides Poland and France, who of necessity shared the desire to maintain the results of the war, generally speaking all those who were the beneficiaries of its outcome. The German action in 1914 had torn the guarantee of Belgian neutrality. That arrangement was not renewed after the war, and Belgium, too, welcomed the concrete asset of French protection. A Franco-Belgian alliance had antedated the Franco-Polish by a year.

In mid-Europe there were three states, Czechoslovakia, Yugoslavia, and Rumania, wholly or in substantial measure carved out of the former Habsburg domain, who wished above all to maintain their position and their territory. Thus was born the Little Entente in 1921. The focus of this combination was naturally directed against either Austrian or Hungarian revisionism, especially the latter, which was far the more vigorous. Because Czechoslovakia had as well a common border with Germany, a Franco-Czechoslovak connection was a natural development, though it did not come into formal existence until 1924. For the rest, France's main interest in Central Europe was in preventing the precedent of any alteration of the status quo. In 1925 and 1927 France concluded separate alliances with Rumania and Yugoslavia respectively, the former also fitting into the policy of Russian containment. A Polish-Rumanian link was also forged, but the Teschen dispute prevented the creation of a similar one between Czechoslovakia and Poland.

Thus came into existence what is sometimes described as the French security system, which in some respects may be compared to the Bismarckian network of relationships contrived by the German chancellor in his day. The two systems had in common the purpose of maintaining order and stability on the basis of the existing situation, both were essentially defensive in intent. But there were also some important differences. No doubt, on paper, the totality of forces that would result from the addition of those of France's allies to France's own was impressive, though the validity of this reckoning depended on the solidity of the main core, or keystone, of the system, France herself. Obsessed with the nightmare of her own security the French view was too defensive and negative, although this was concealed for a time by the absence of countervailing force elsewhere. The test would come, as it did, if and when such force would come into existence. How would France feel, or act, in the event it would be necessary for her to take the initiative of action in defense of one of her allies? The French system was effective, to put it in sharpest fashion, when there was no necessity for it. So long as Germany and Russia were impotent no one could effectively challenge or threaten the power of even France alone, let alone that of the French-centered coalition.

This to a point is to anticipate, for the lack of French aggressive will, or at least of positive determination, was not tested for well over another decade, and in fact the prevalent picture in the twenties, and much of the contemporary talk, was of French hegemony and militarism. If we ask the question how and why the French contrived to put themselves in what was fundamentally an unsound position, the answer is that there seemed to be little choice. The destruction of the three great empires of Europe had been the work of the war, and the position taken by the United States and Britain was to place France in this situation, an absurd one, indeed. France, the one effective power on the Continent, must adopt a policy for Europe. However, as mentioned before, twentieth-century France was not the France of Napoleon. For reasons of power alone, which were reflected in the psychology of her people, France could not control Europe for an indefinite time. The result was a false situation, false in the sense that it did not correspond to existing reality, and some of the French actions, born out of fear, were not solutions, but instead stored up additional tensions. The Ruhr episode is a good illustration.

For a brief time this did not appear to be the case and the Ruhr episode might even be thought to have had a clarifying effect, similar to the healthy process of the bursting of an abscess. The 1924 repudiation of Poincaré by the French was evidence of the deficiency of French aggressive will, but it also seemed to open the door to other possibilities. Two lines of development can be traced at this point.

In 1919 there were some who thought, or at least hoped, that the new institution of the League of Nations would succeed in its primary function of insuring universal peace and the security of all. This was a sanguine view; the deficiencies of the League, structural for one thing and the limitations of its membership for another, were too patent. There seemed little prospect of American participation, though that of Germany might come to pass—and in 1926 it did—making the League universal in Europe, except for the Soviet Union. But something also might be done to remedy the structural deficiencies. The central issue was simple in formulation: in order to have meaning the League must have power and from the beginning many—not least the French—had insisted on the definition and organization of such power, which to be sure, is not an easy thing. Thus from the very inception of the League a debate was initiated in Geneva, and its focus was precisely that issue, one limited but crucial aspect of which was the search for an effective definition of aggression.

There were many proposals and the details will not be examined here. The climate of the early twenties, the state of Franco-German relations in particular, was hardly conducive to the prosperity of the Genevan discussions. But the liquidation of the Ruhr difficulty and the elections in France and in Britain that brought men of the left to office, Herriot and MacDonald respectively, altered the prospect. It was possible to produce the Geneva Protocol,[8] a source of high hopes that received overwhelming endorsement. The prospect had to be abandoned, however, in the face of a governmental change in London that returned the Conservatives to power. But, for that very reason, the new British Government wished to make some alternative contribution; it gave encouragement to the German initiative which led to the Locarno agreements, finally concluded in October 1925.

Locarno was a high point and a very great contribution that seemed to initiate a new era for Europe. The essence of what was done at Locarno was to provide a solution for the Franco-German problem, and the importance of this for Europe as a whole cannot be overstressed. It was an ingenious solution that reconciled the French desire for security with the German wish for the recovery of place in the community of Europe. Britain and Italy were to be guarantors not of France, of Belgium, or of Germany, but of the frontiers between the

---

[8] This was an ingenious solution of the difficulty of producing a workable definition of aggression. The refusal to accept arbitration of a dispute, or to accept the verdict of arbitration, would constitute aggression.

first two and the last. As a consequence of Locarno, Germany received the following year the further stamp of rehabilitation implied in her membership in the League.

In German eyes Locarno was but a step on the lengthy pilgrimage to complete equality with others. Locarno was not a substitute for Versailles, whose provisions—reparations, disarmament—remained unaltered; in fact some were strengthened—the demilitarization of the Rhineland for example—by their reiteration on the basis of free German consent. This was Germany's contribution to the allaying of persisting French fears.

Much has been written on Locarno and on the ambiguities that it undoubtedly contained. If French security was insured, what inducement would France have to come to the assistance of Poland, for example? To be sure, the Franco-Polish alliance, like the Franco-Czech, was publicly reconfirmed as part of the Locarno arrangements, although Germany refused to undertake vis-à-vis Poland and Czechoslovakia commitments similar to those of the Rhineland Pact. The Poles were of two minds about Locarno, which undoubtedly raised for them certain doubts about the dependability of French purpose. The personality of Stresemann, chief German architect of Locarno, is highly controversial. Had he become truly reconciled, a Westerner in the context of Germany's diverse foreign orientations; or was he merely taking a first step on the road the end of which would be renewed aggression? Despite contemporary criticism of it, Locarno was widely acclaimed as the most significant contribution so far to the liquidation of the war and of its aftermath of rancor.

In the era newly opened the peaceful orientation prospered for a time, while French Briand and German Stresemann sang in unison their Genevan duet of concord. There was not a little surviving distrust and suspicion but a new climate was undoubtedly abroad in Europe, of which the widespread talk about "the spirit of Locarno" was the most suitable expression. No better illustration of it can be cited than Briand's stanch support of the German candidacy for League membership. Their final admission was the occasion for one of his memorable oratorical performances: "Away with rifles, machine guns and cannons. Make way for conciliation, arbitration and peace," was his conclusion to the tune of genuinely enthusiastic applause. Locarno was not a substitute for the League, or a cure of its deficiencies, but so large a contribution to the general stability of Europe as an authentic stabilization of the Franco-German relationship would clearly be an important contribution to the general purpose of the League.

These were the days when much stress was put on the desirability of disarmament and arms were considered in themselves one of the great producers of conflict. This is in contrast with the view prevalent before 1914—as it is again at present—that the equilibrium of forces is the best guarantee against their being brought into use. It was in 1926 that a Preparatory Commission for the study of the question was finally brought into existence under League auspices. The ultimate failure of the attempt must not blind one to the fact that this development was adequate expression of the climate of high hope of the day.

The same applies to the signature in 1928 of the Kellogg-Briand Pact, or Pact of Paris, which in retrospect may seem like little more than a meaningless, at best harmless, aberration. This was a declaration underwritten by virtually the whole world, including the United States and the Soviet Union, whereby war was renounced by all as an instrument of national policy. No implementing provisions were included in the Pact of Paris, which by itself added not a whit to anyone's security; it could not be taken as a contribution to the general purpose of peace, but must rather be understood as a symbol, an expression of the spirit of the time.

It is not surprising that, in such circumstances, Germany should achieve further successes along the path of total rehabilitation, a necessary preliminary to her possible authentic integration into a peaceful and orderly community of Europe. In 1929 another important step was taken in the matter of her financial obligations. The Dawes Plan of 1924 had not dealt with that obligation as such; it merely re-established order in the German financial structure and left unaltered the sum total of reparations previously established. Now that the various Allied debts to the United States had been funded and scaled down, the recipients of German payments were willing to take a similar step in her case. This was the purpose of the Young Plan in 1929. And, as an additional earnest of the changing position of Germany, the occupation of some of her territory was terminated in 1930, five years ahead of the time scheduled in the treaty of peace. This involved a measure of prevarication; the implied judgment that Germany had faithfully fulfilled her obligations was not wholly in concordance with the facts. But, as Briand had confided to Stresemann, he never troubled to look at the bulky dossier on the inadequacies of German disarmament. German breaches, to be sure, were not very significant, and Briand was willing to take a tolerant and a large view of things; and for this he was widely applauded.

European Union

In this promising state of affairs the idea could be planted that much more could be done. All Europe, and not just France and Germany alone, could put aside its quarrels, abandon the crude superseded activity that is the use of force, and take the next large step of uniting, not under the pressure of compulsion by any one of its members, but because of a freely consented-to decision. The idea, as pointed out on various previous occasions, is an ancient one; and the spirit of Locarno and of the Kellogg-Briand Pact might provide a favorable climate to its growth. For some time, there had been discussion, in unofficial fashion, of the idea of European union. In 1923 an Austrian, Count Coudenhove-Kalergi, published a small book, *Pan-Europa*, and founded the organization Pan-European Union, whose purpose was propagandizing for the idea. It is significant, in the light of what has been pointed out earlier about the eccentric positions and roles of Great Britain and Russia, that the Soviet Union, the United Kingdom, and the Irish Free State were left out of Pan-Europe. But another body, also private, that called itself European Co-operation, would have brought in the British Isles; this second organization had the endorsement of the French Foreign Minister, Briand.

The prospect of Pan-Europe can hardly be said to have fired the imagination of the peoples of Europe, although it was seriously discussed; Count Coudenhove-Kalergi served the function of keeping the idea alive and of carrying on educative propaganda. The climate of the late nineteen-twenties was suited to the prosperity of the concept of union. It was a time when economic conditions were favorable, the revulsion from war still very strong, and the view was gaining ground that what had happened in 1914 was a mistake that the civilized powers of Europe should never have allowed to happen. It might also be pointed out that there was the beginning of awareness that the European great powers might no longer enjoy the role of primacy which had been theirs in the past. Isolationist as the United States might try to be by its own choice, its position of power was established and recognized beyond possible cavil. Even if the Soviet Union was not yet very strong or especially active in the affairs of the wide world, the régime seemed to have achieved stability, and, in time, Russia could confidently be expected to become a very great power which might easily dwarf the other European. The past record of China made even more problematic the prospects of her latest successful revolution of the Nationalist forces under the leadership of Chiang Kai-shek. Nevertheless the possibility could not be ignored that China might find her way into the modern world, and certainly her potential was vast. Taking a long range view of things there was reason to entertain second thoughts about the future of the distinct units of Europe from the standpoint of their positions of power. If any kind of union of Europe demanded as a pre-condition the solution, or at least the softening, of a multitude of quarrels and suspicions, it was also possible that a union itself could serve as solvent of these ancient differences. To repeat, the climate of 1929 was suitable to thinking of this nature.

This is the background that explains the initiative taken by Briand, who by this time had been established for some years in his office; he was dedicated to the attempt to solve the French security problem through a strong pro-League policy and the reintegration of Germany into the community of Europe. More than any of the representatives of the great powers, his name and his policy were associated with Geneva and the League. It was thus eminently suitable that he should take the initiative best summed up in a quotation from the speech that he delivered before the Assembly of the League of Nations on September 5, 1929. Said Briand:

> I think that among peoples constituting geographical groups, like the peoples of Europe, there should be some kind of federal bond; it should be possible for them to get into touch at any time, to confer about their interests, to agree on joint resolutions and to establish among themselves a bond of solidarity which will enable them, if need be, to meet any grave emergency that may arise. This is the link I want to forge. Obviously, this association will be primarily economic, for that is the most urgent aspect of the question, and I

think we may look for success in that direction. Still, I am
convinced that, politically and socially also, this federal link
might, without affecting the sovereignty of any of the nations
belonging to such an association, do useful work; and I pro-
pose, during this session, to ask those of my colleagues here
who represent European nations to be good enough to consider this suggestion unofficially and submit it to their Governments for examination, so that those possibilities which I see
in the suggestion may be translated into realities later.

The priority given to economics is interesting. Although in
this and in the financial domain Briand was largely an innocent, the importance of economics in our time is not a
subject for debate. The political field was to him more congenial and in this he was careful to pay the proper homage to
the fetish of sovereignty. The fact that the proposal came from
the representative of France, the country more than any
other major state wedded to the preservation of the status
quo, gave it added significance. The initial reception was favorable, Stresemann among others endorsing it, though he also
used the occasion to remind others of the German view of
things.

Following consultations among representatives in Geneva
of the twenty-seven European states members of the League,[4]
Briand was entrusted with the task of pursuing the idea. In
May of the following year he produced a memorandum on
the organization of a system of European federal union. It
was a lengthy and closely reasoned document. It will suffice
to say that, starting with the assertion of the need to affirm
the "moral union of Europe and to place formally on record
the existence of the solidarity established between the States
of Europe," it went on to outline a possible machinery for the

[4] This, therefore, did not include the Soviet Union, who was not a
member of the League at this time. Turkey and Iceland, because of their
eccentric geographical locations, were also not included.

implementation of this purpose. This would take the form of a representative body, a "European conference," and an executive body, a "permanent political committee." Briand's memorandum went on to stress the "need for laying down in advance the essential principles which shall determine the general conceptions of the European committee." Under this rubric, "the general subordination of the economic problem to the political problem" was asserted, and it was suggested that the federation should be "based on the idea of union and not of unity," meaning by this the safeguarding of the principle of sovereignty. The long history of Europe clearly pointed to the desirability of a gradualist approach. Finally, the memorandum proposed that a subsequent meeting of the participants concern itself with "the study of all questions of practical application." Some of these were enumerated (e.g., general economics, financial, labor, inter-parliamentary relations, etc.), and the definition of methods of procedure should be examined as well.

Beyond a doubt here was a novel initiative and the seed of a potentially far-reaching development. The replies to the memorandum were prompt in coming—they had been received by the beginning of August—and served as a basis of discussion at a meeting called by Briand in September. Following this he presented the matter formally that same month to the Assembly of the League, which instituted a committee to examine these replies, a committee which first formally met in January 1931, appropriately under the chairmanship of Briand.

But in the course of the two years since Briand had first hopefully launched his scheme much had happened which is best epitomized by one of the first actions of the European committee, which was the issuance of a unanimous declaration denying the validity of any fears of imminent war. The

fears were hardly justified at this time, but that it was thought
necessary to allay them is a measure of the alteration that had
taken place in the climate of Europe.

In May 1930, at the very same moment that Briand produced his memorandum on European Union, the Young Plan,
final settlement of the problem of German Reparation, had
formally come into existence. A month later the anticipated
evacuation of the occupied Rhineland had taken place. But
these hopeful developments, apparent tokens of the return of
normality in Europe, were a misleading carry-over of the
euphoria of the latter years of the preceding decade. Other
happenings were a better reflection of the true state of things.
In the election of September 1930 the Nazi Party, hitherto
little more than a lunatic fringe in the German political
spectrum, increased its representation in the German Reichstag from 12 to 107 members. Especially in France, this
seemed a strange answer to Briand's policy of reconciliation
and concrete friendly gestures; Stresemann had died the preceding October, and seemingly with him the German policy
he had pursued in such close accord with Briand. The Young
Plan was hardly a year old before its operation had to be
suspended. The result of a direct appeal to the American
President from the German President, von Hindenburg, was
the Hoover moratorium, a one-year suspension of payment
on all internation financial obligations. The somewhat awkward manner of implementation of the Hoover proposal
created irritation, especially in France again; and the rather
clumsy announcement of a scheme of Austro-German customs
union, which followed in July, was hardly suited to the
prosperity of Briand's proposal, which at best could hope to
succeed in a climate of relaxing tensions. The fundamental
fact, exemplified in the isolated episodes just cited, was that
in 1930 and 1931 much of the world was plunged in deep
economic depression. The common plight was all the more

reason for co-operation at the international level, stressing the economic aspects of Briand's proposal, but the nations proved incapable of adopting such an approach, and their response was an intensification of unco-ordinated national initiatives. The autumn of 1931 saw the abandonment of the gold parity of sterling, and as the result the world was split between gold and sterling blocs. The catastrophic fall of commodity prices, unmatched by a corresponding adjustment of the prices of manufactured goods, a vast diminution of world trade, and fantastic levels of unemployment, were in large measure factors behind the Nazi success in the German election. All this indicated that the economic consequences of the war, dislocation in brief, had not been successfully absorbed. America was not primarily to be blamed for all this, as many, especially in Europe, are often wont to assert. It is true nevertheless that the economic and financial policies of the United States had contributed much to the concealment of the realities of international financial relationships. Once the golden flow of American capital began to dry up at the source it was not long before the Hoover moratorium was suggested.

The replies that were sent to the Briand memorandum of May 1930 conveyed a very different picture from the reaction which his initial speech had elicited in the preceding September. To the general idea of European union they continued to pay lip service, but the substance of their observations was unfavorable. As might have been expected, and as Briand fully realized, there was much sensitivity on the score of sovereignty; the Dutch alone were realistic enough to point to the inevitable infringement of that prerogative if unity or union was not to be devoid of substance. The British favored the idea, but disapproved of the method; others feared, or pretended to fear, that the scheme was but a devious device calculated for the further enhancement of the already too-dominant position of France. They proposed—as Italy did, for example—that the Soviet Union and Turkey be brought into the picture.

What discussion there was of Briand's plan in 1931 had no more substantive reality or prospects of concrete achievement than the futile perennial discussion of disarmament. The climate of Geneva was fast changing, the spirit of Locarno, as Mussolini put it, had evaporated; the heyday of the League was past history. More accurate expression of the reality of the day was the Manchurian episode, mainly significant because one member of the League, Japan, successfully reaped the fruit of its aggression against another member, China. Japan merely quit the League which had had the temerity of going the length of verbal—and only verbal—condemnation. Japan was far from Europe to be sure, and the conditions of the case were special; the precedent was nonetheless as important as it was discouraging. Briand was weary and aging, and one of his last acts was to preside over a meeting of the Manchurian committee which was held in Paris, in deference to his failing health. It was an appropriately sad epilogue, registration of the demise of high hopes. Briand fully realized that the times were not suited to the pursuit of his ideals of peace and European unity; pending the possible return of better days he felt sad and disillusioned. His resignation from office at the beginning of 1932, and his death which followed shortly, were apt symbols of the closing of an era.

The Collapse of the European System

The central and dominant influence at the beginning of the second postwar decade was undoubtedly the Great Depression. As pointed out, the effect of economic crisis was highly inimical to all forms of co-operation, whether for the world as a whole or in the more limited domain of European states alone. No more was heard of European union, and even what prospects there had been of some agreement on the control and limitation of arms were set back. The Preparatory Commission, set up in 1926, had accomplished little, and the calling of a Disarmament Conference in 1932 was rather in the nature of a gesture of desperation than the expression of serious hope of achievement. A more urgent reality had to be faced, in simplest terms that of the status of Germany in this domain.

Germany was disarmed, as she had been since her defeat. During the course of the disarmament discussions in Geneva, her representatives had taken the simple position that disarmament was indeed a welcome condition, but that since Germany herself was disarmed while others were not, her chief concern was with parity of position, *Gleichberechtigung*, on whatever basis might be agreed upon for all. It was a telling position, increasingly hard to refute, especially in the face of other gestures which asserted formally that Germany had worked her passage back. Her admission to the League in 1926 and the final evacuation of the Rhineland in 1930 could hardly be interpreted otherwise. At the end of 1932, wearying of futile discussion and delaying tactics, Germany quit the disarmament conference. A compromise resolution, which was a skillful exercise in diplomatic verbiage, but also fundamentally an evasion, because the French and the German positions were not really susceptible of accommodation at this point, brought her back for a time but not for very long.

This is the point at which a crucial change took place. The German economic crisis was particularly severe, and its political consequences had two distinct but related aspects. It may be attributed to the lack of experience of the German people in the operation of a democratic system that the Weimar régime, in contrast to the British, American, or French, was incapable of dealing with the strains to which circumstances subjected it. As in the case of Italy ten years earlier the parliamentary system in Germany broke down. This was one aspect of the German crisis, the other being the rise of the Nazi Party; from its first great success in the 1930 election it went on to ever greater heights; in 1932 its Reichstag membership rose to the figure of 230. Despite a setback in another election in November of that year, a murky political passage ended with the appointment of the Nazi leader, Adolf Hitler, to the Chancellorship of the German Reich on January 30, 1933. It is worth noting that in both the German and Italian cases, the proceedings were entirely constitutional; Hitler, like Mussolini, became head of the government with the freely given endorsement of the representatives of the people. In other words, in both cases a democracy committed suicide in accordance with the laws of its existence. In the German case, there was the additional fact of a very large, if not at first wholly overwhelming, authentic popular support.

It must be pointed out, however, that just as in 1922 many who endorsed Mussolini in Italy thought of him as a temporary expedient, after which democratic normality would return, so in 1933 many took a similar view of Hitler in Germany. Hitler himself encouraged this idea, taking the position that he would cure the troubles of the German people if they entrusted him with unfettered power for four years; the Enabling Act received an overwhelming majority. Nevertheless a question was raised, especially in view of the by now ten-year-old record of the Fascist state. What precisely did the Nazis want and stand for? Was their aim the limited one of ridding Germany of all disabilities, regaining true equality for her, and possibly redressing some concrete and not illegitimate grievances? Or were they truly set on a path of unlimited conquest to which their racial superiority gave the German people a right? Hitler himself had set it all down in *Mein Kampf*, but just because of the extravagance of his outpourings the tendency had often been to discount them. The demagogic rantings of electoral campaigns are familiar enough fare, and many a demagogue in irresponsible opposition has been turned into a reasonable man by the responsibilities of power. Who precisely, for that matter, were the real holders of power? Was not Hitler a front, a tool, that saner men would use and manipulate to their more moderate ends and then discard? We have found out the costly answer, but there was in 1933 room for divergence of interpretation. Still, a question there was.

Hitler soon clarified the weary discussion of disarmament. Germany withdrew from the disarmament conference and from the League as well, and from this point the discussion may in effect be regarded as closed. This specific breakdown, more generally the deterioration of the European situation, of which the Nazi advent to power was the most concrete manifestation, was the occasion for an interesting initiative. Appropriately enough it came from Italy.

Mussolini had always prided himself on being a realist and he hardly concealed his contempt for the League and general Genevan vaporings. The reality of the day was the national state and the competition of power. Italy, Fascist or otherwise, did not like the imbalance of power that the war had produced and the restoration of German power would be a useful counterweight to French. In addition, this would have the advantage of removing German grievances as well as getting rid of the pretense that Germany could and should indefinitely be maintained in an inferior status. This did not mean substituting German for French hegemony, but merely recognizing that equilibrium was a sounder foundation of the European order than the existing state of things. Such views appealed to many—they were widely shared in Britain for example—and had nothing to do with Fascism as such. The

way to translate them into effective reality was to bypass
the egalitarian pretense of the standing of states and frankly
acknowledge that, broadly speaking, there were in Europe
four equal great powers. These four—Britain, France, Germany, and Italy—should acknowledge their equal status and
openly assume the responsibility for maintaining the order of
Europe "by inducing others, if necessary, to accept their decisions." Within the circle of the four any excessive desire of
one would automatically tend to create a coalition of the other
three; thus, among other things, French fears of German aggressiveness could be allayed.

The concept was hardly original, it was essentially no more
than a revival of the nineteenth-century Holy Alliance, or the
Concert of Europe. The difference was that Mussolini proposed the formalization of the concept, committing it to a
treaty. This was his Four Power Pact proposal that he first
submitted to the British, from whom he received a sympathetic response. Somewhat more hesitantly, the French and
the Germans also agreed to entertain the proposal. This was
hardly a scheme for European union, yet, like the traditional
Concert of Europe, it did reflect an awareness of the community of Europe and a concern for its orderly functioning.
To be sure, the device could be used as a means to effect
revisions, on the map of Europe for example. Needless to
say, the smaller powers, especially the beneficiaries from the
war, read into it a threat and the Little Entente immediately
went on record voicing strong opposition. Clearly, the scheme
was wholly antithetic to the spirit of the League, as indeed it
was meant to be.

In the end nothing came of the Mussolinian proposal,
which was not rejected, but mainly through the operation of
French diplomacy, was instead effectively emasculated.
Faced with a choice between gambling her future security
on the Four Power Pact and relying upon the network of

alliances she had contrived, France opted for the latter. But the fact that she yielded to her allies' representations rather than taking the first initiative of opposition herself is highly significant and could do no other than induce doubts among her allies.[5] Mussolini's proposal had the effect of a warning and was an obvious challenge to the French organization of Europe. There were at this point three roads that were open to Europe: a League that would be made effective, the French system willing to use its power if needed, or the Concert of Europe as embodied in the Four Power Pact.

Clearly the French attitude was crucial and at the heart of this lay the German problem. Conditioned by an obsessive wish for security, consequence of an insufficiency of power, even Briand's conciliating policy had not completely removed German disabilities, and had not succeeded in making Germany a satisfied and orderly member of the community of Europe. Granted time, the continuance of favorable economic conditions, and some contribution from others, America and Britain most of all, the Briand-Stresemann policy might conceivably have succeeded and eventually given Briand's plan for European union a fair chance. But time was not granted, the world was in deep crisis, and the Nazis had come to power in Germany. In face of the challenge of the dissatisfied forces of change, the entire question of the future of Europe was reopened.

Something must be said at this point of the situation in France. Like others, the French people as a whole were overwhelmingly concerned with their domestic affairs. When the time came for elections in 1932 they gave the majority of their votes to the left, or left center, as normally happens in France

[5] Thus, the German-Polish understanding of January 1934 may be viewed in this context as a hedging operation, an attempt at reinsurance, on the part of Poland.

when conditions are reasonably normal; Herriot once more was Prime Minister. This at once created a dilemma for the French left, generally favorable to the Briand type of conciliating policy toward Germany, yet strongly repelled ideologically by the Nazi phenomenon. It was awkward for the French left to be cast in the role of guardian of French security at this juncture.

Moreover, albeit with some lag, economic conditions deteriorated in France as well, not in a catastrophic fashion, yet sufficiently to give added point to the economic and social questions. The net result was intensification of internal divisions, while on the opposite side of the political spectrum there were some who found increasing attraction in the social and economic aspects of the experiments being carried out across the Rhine and beyond the Alps.[6] There appeared in France the recurrence of a familiar phenomenon, *ligues* of diverse coloration, of which the Croix-de-Feu is the best known. In addition, the financial difficulties of the government resulted in more than usual government instability.

The tensions of the French milieu reached a climax in the rioting that occurred in Paris in February 1934. It was a small enough affair in itself, but nonetheless one of considerable significance. The gravity of the situation was judged sufficient to result in the formation of a Union government in which nearly the whole range of the political spectrum, save the extremes, was represented. But this was mere papering over of differences rather than a true resolution of them. One of

[6] The attraction of Fascism and Nazism for certain elements of the French right was largely for reasons of social outlook, independent of national considerations. It is nevertheless, understandably, from among these elements that certain individuals emerged who were willing to give "national" considerations second priority and hence were led to accept even German dominance for the sake of resisting the threat to the social order, especially that which Communism represented. But this did not happen until later, after German victory was an accomplished fact.

the aftermaths of the February rioting was the organization
of the Popular Front, a coalition of three groups, Communist,
Socialist, and Radical Socialist, dedicated to social reform and
to the defense of the régime against the Fascist threat in
France herself. The threat was more imagined than real, but
the Popular Front effectively alarmed the conservative elements, who glibly identified it in turn with a Communist
threat, another gross misrepresentation. The net result of it all
was that, to a point, France became the battleground of
contending ideologies, both of them alien. The former leader
of the progressive forces of political change in the eyes of all
Europe now seemed old and tired, fearful of change, incapable or unwilling either to lead or to prevent others from
doing so. Undoubtedly, the active forces of change, the leadership of the forces of movement, were to be found in other
places, in Fascism of the German or Italian variety, or in the
red star of the Kremlin. France's uncertain reaction to the
Mussolinian proposal of the Four Power Pact has already been
examined.

Yet France was still ostensibly the great power, whose combination of resources and connections had organized and still
might control the international order of Europe. She may be
said to have made one last effort to maintain the existing
situation. That effort found its best expression in the personality of Barthou, the man who came to her foreign office in the
new Union government that emerged from the February
riots. Barthou was an able and intelligent man, no longer
young, though full of vigor; he belonged to the more intransigent and determined school of French foreign policy of
which Poincaré had been the best-known advocate. Barthou
had been his right-hand man during the early twenties.
Barthou's plan was the simple one of confirming the existing

alliances while extending their scope. The prospect was not wholly Utopian.

On one side, the Soviet Union, although welcoming the demise of the Weimar Republic, was having second thoughts about Nazism being the last stage of a decaying capitalism. The death throes of the monster might not be devoid of dangers against which some reinsurance might be useful. The hitherto relatively pro-German and anti-French Soviet Union was effecting a reversal of position until the possibility appeared of a recurrence of the situation of forty years earlier. The facts of power lay at the root of the original Franco-Russian alliance, when the danger inherent in the rising German power had overcome strong ideological differences.

In another quarter, the concrete essence of the Franco-Italian difference was small, and Italy had no desire to substitute German hegemony for French. The initial Fascist welcome of Nazism seemed to dissipate very easily in the face of the attempted Nazi coup in Austria which, in July 1934, resulted in the assassination of Chancellor Dollfuss. Germany professed innocence of Austrian involvement, but Mussolini wasted no time in speaking the clear language of power: some Italian divisions appeared at the Brenner frontier, and Hitler understood very well. Italy's was in fact the only substantial gesture of protest. The continued independence of Austria was an authentic common Franco-Italian interest.

But two kinds of fundamental difficulties prevented the success of Barthou's policy. One was internal, stemming from the continuing uncertainties of France, economic and financial, and the more serious, increasingly sharp cleavage of opinion. The other difficulty was foreign. On the round of visits that Barthou undertook to the capitals of France's allies, he met on the whole more enthusiastic receptions from the people than from the governments, especially in Poland. There were doubts in Warsaw about the direction and reliability of French policy, on the latter score where Germany was concerned, on the former where Russia was involved. Polish feeling vis-à-vis Russia, whether wise or not, is wholly understandable; to attempt to drive a Russo-Polish team in harmony was more than France could accomplish. Poland followed the German lead in refusing to entertain the proposal of an Eastern Locarno, a scheme intended to stabilize the Eastern European situation by internationalizing the responsibility for its maintenance on the model of the original Locarno. Some of the same considerations that applied to the Russo-Polish situation had equal validity in the case of Yugoslavia and Italy. There is such a thing as trying to have too many friends who in turn are not friendly with each other. Thus, while discussions continued with the Soviet Union that eventually led to the conclusion of a Franco-Soviet Pact, the existing system of alliances was not revivified, and the Italian case took an unexpected twist that will be mentioned presently.

On the whole, Barthou's policy was hardly a success. His failure was dramatically registered in his assassination, together with that of King Alexander of Yugoslavia, in Marseilles in October 1934, when King Alexander was visiting France as part of Barthou's scheme of resoldering France's alliances. This deed, the attempted Austrian coup of July, the rioting of February in Vienna and in Paris, and the Nazi purge in Germany in June, taken together convey an adequate picture of the disarray of Europe in 1934.

But there was more to come. Mussolini, even if he may have indulged at the time in no more than in a flight of rhetorical fancy, had shown prescience, as early as 1927, when he had forecast that, about 1935, the European situation would be ripe for the assertion of Italy's rights. The possibilities of the changing and fluid condition of Europe—German resurgence and French passivity—he assessed quite correctly, at least from the narrow immediate standpoint of Italian interest and power. His decision may be dated to 1933 when he began to make military and diplomatic preparations to conquer Abyssinia. Matters came to a head with a border incident in December 1934. The fact that Abyssinia was a member of the League, just as Italy was, and put her case before that organization, had in the end no other effect than to introduce complications, and the main result was to accentuate the disintegration of Europe. France, who was courting Italy, was highly embarrassed and rent by greater dissension than ever by the Abyssinian issue in the League. Britain, partly for domestic electoral reasons, adopted at this time a strong pro-League policy, and was also highly embarrassed. British opinion, with a measure of justification, was highly critical of French machinations; and French opinion, also with some justification, was equally incensed at British ambiguity, preferably called British duplicity. The Soviet Union, newly arrived in the League, was at once cautious and puzzled.

In Britain, France, and the Soviet Union lay the effective power of the League. The Italian success in the face of ineffectual sanctions that the League eventually decreed had the effect of finally voiding the League of significance; Mussolini had contributed much to making true his contention that the competition of national power was the reality of the day. As much as any one he succeeded in destroying the Genevan institution, which, after 1935, was no longer a significant factor in the affairs of the world or of Europe.

Europe and the German Problem Again

There were indeed those, most of all Nazi Germany, who would gladly see the destruction of the organization of Europe which had been shaped after the war largely under French guidance. Hitler, like Mussolini, showed shrewd judgment in exploiting the situation. In March 1935, Germany reintroduced conscription, thereby clearly violating one of the major clauses of the peace. What mattered was that no one, not even France, reacted to so important a move. The meeting that took place in Stresa, of Britain, France, and Italy, condemned —with words alone—the German action, But especially in view of the simultaneous development of the Abyssinian imbroglio, it is little cause for surprise if the so-called Stresa front is best characterized by the later phrase "paper tiger." This was amply demonstrated a year later when Hitler took what may be called the last step along the road of removing what disabilities still remained from Versailles. Pretexting that the ratification of the Franco-Soviet Pact was a violation of the Locarno agreements, he proceeded to send German forces into the hitherto demilitarized Rhineland. Against the warnings of some of his advisors his intuition was proved right, and his prestige, both at home and abroad, was correspondingly enhanced. Again the French made brave speeches, but nothing more, while the British strongly urged them to inaction. It was the eve of an election in a France more than ever rent by political and social divisions, an election that would bring to power the Popular Front, which in some quarters was cause for the cry "rather Hitler than Blum."[7]

The period of the legislature that had been elected in France in 1932 was a crucial one for Europe; it is clear, especially in retrospect, that it marks the transition from what has been called the French system to what may properly be described as the German. One is tempted to recall the observation made after the Franco-Prussian War that Europe had lost a mistress and gained a master. What happened in

[7] This was a true expression of the intensity of dislike for the Popular Front, comparable to the views expressed in some American quarters in regard to the Rooseveltian New Deal. It had little to do with any literal desire of German control, the likihood of which at the time seemed wholly unreal.

March 1936 was the abdication of France from her position of responsibility and power, and French power was shown to be another paper tiger. Unchallenged for a time, it had been a pole of attraction, and had after a fashion worked out an organization of Europe, but now, in the face of change, it refused to assert itself.

The rest of the story is familiar, and the sequel in retrospect appears entirely logical, though it was possible in 1936 to take a more optimistic view of things. Many did so at the time, especially in Britain, where *The* (London) *Times* went on record with precisely such an interpretation of the remilitarization of the Rhineland.

The French had failed either to assert power or to effect an orderly transformation of Europe in which the legitimate grievances of the discontented, Germany most of all, could be redressed. It was no doubt regrettable that treaties and obligations should be broken, but reasonable and tolerant men, focusing on substance rather than legalistic form, could understand and condone the German mode of operation. They viewed it as the result of understandable desperation largely due to the unreasonableness of others—once again, mainly France—in refusing timely concessions. If anything, the French should be congratulated and encouraged in their new-found reasonableness. At least many well-intentioned people thought so.

The vital question at this point was that of the precise nature of the German aims. Were they the fantastic ones expounded in *Mein Kampf*, the unlimited rights of the German people based in the last resort upon the assertion of their racial superiority? Or was Hitler mainly a tactician who had succeeded in creating unity among the German people in order to use this asset of unity to assert no more than the claim to a legitimate place among others? Hitler was skillful and knew how to capitalize on the desire for peace which even in

Germany was widespread. For a long time it was one of the chief assets of his position at home that he contrived to gain concessions without carrying the threat of violence beyond the point of threat. Vis-à-vis the outside he was equally skillful and shrewd, and after each coup reasserted his peaceful intent, claiming the concession secured was his last demand. One may well be surprised at the blindness of the credulity which persisted in accepting the validity of this repeated assertion; it is only understandable in the context of the climate of the thirties, when, in the Western democracies especially, the reluctance to face the prospect of renewed conflict was such that "peace at any price" and appeasement adequately expressed the dominant tendency of opinion. What for that matter could a conflict mean for Britain and for France? If Germany could conceivably gain worthwhile advantages, Britain and France could at best hope to keep their own and maintain their positions. Even victory could only mean for them enormous effort, expense, and ultimate diminution. It might even be worth, and perhaps cheaper in the end, yielding some of their own. Only if threatened in some truly vital fashion could they be brought to rouse themselves to positive resistance.

There is no need to tarry on the story of the remaining three years of peace. The turning point was the remilitarization of the Rhineland and the abdication of France, and it had some sharp and almost immediate effects. The scheduled election in France brought to power, in June 1936, the coalition of the Popular Front under the leadership of the socialist prime minister Léon Blum. Blum was a cultured and a civilized man, better suited to the urbane discussion of literary and philosophical issues than to the rough necessities of politics, especially at a time of unwonted stress, both domestic and foreign. In addition, the focus of the Popular Front was social and economic reforms; these were indeed enacted, and there was never any real threat of civil war or revolution in France even if political tensions ran high. This was not a suitable background for the pursuit of a vigorous foreign policy; France could indeed mend her domestic military fences, and a substantial program of rearmament was undertaken which, except for air power, was on the whole effectively carried out. But this was essentially negative action.

The general state of Europe, the French surrender of leadership, and the peculiar domestic condition of France, led the government to the conclusion that it was indispensable for France to act in unison with Britain. This judgment was entirely sound and a proper reflection of the common fundamentally defensive position of the two countries. But from this correct premise an erroneous tactical conclusion was drawn. To put it in the simplest form, the fact was that, in the last analysis, the French Army was the single most concrete bulwark of peace in the existing European order; and there was abroad much respect for French force. British power was very great, but, as usual, was more in the nature of reserve and potential. France therefore could have, and should have, elaborated with Britain a common policy based on a partnership of equality. But instead of this France opted for the easier course—in a sense a consistent consequence of her abdication —of indeed procuring Anglo-French agreement, but on the basis of complete surrender to British leadership, a surrender one is tempted to describe as abject.

Unexpected circumstances almost immediately provided an acid test of this condition. In July 1936 an attempted military coup took place in Spain. The outcome was the worst possible of all, for the coup was neither a full success nor a total failure, and the country was plunged into civil war. Ordinarily, because of the eccentric position of Spain and the small degree of her power, Spanish coups or revolutions have a minimum of external impact. But in the Europe of 1936, badly torn by the intertwined rivalries of ideologies and power, the Spanish situation had widespread repercussions; Spain to a large extent became the preliminary battleground where these competing ideologies and powers first essayed a contest of force. Judging, or rather misjudging, that at small cost he could gain the asset of a sympathetic and beholden régime in Spain, Mussolini became committed to a victory of the rebel forces of General Franco, to whom from the beginning he sent some assistance.

It might be expected that the Popular Front government of France would want to assist a roughly similar government in Spain. But with one eye on the division of France, and another on Britain, it is highly significant that the proposal that all abstain from intervention in Spain should have been of French origin. A non-intervention committee was organized, which appropriately sat in London, Britain being the nearest thing to an authentic neutral in the affairs of Spain, although the government of the day was somewhat more sympathetic to the rebel faction than to the existing government of that country.

The non-intervention committee may properly be described as a farce, a shield behind which intervention and the victory of the Fascist forces was made possible. It was at best a safety valve and a political operation that, for a price, served the purpose of preventing the extension of the conflict beyond the borders of Spain. But the Spanish affair had another effect, of formalizing the hitherto *de facto* but unplanned co-operation between the two Fascist states of Europe, to whom the Abyssinian case had already shown the advantage of such tactics. The Rome-Berlin Axis was born in October 1936.

The cleavage of Europe into three centers of power was becoming sharper: the Anglo-French combination in the West, the Axis in the middle, while in the East the Soviet Union had just made a connection with France. The Soviet Union at this point may properly be described as a power of conservation, which was fearful of change though it remained suspicious of all. This was a source of reciprocal suspicion and of puzzlement to others, and it is relevant to mention that strange things were happening in the Soviet domain in this period.[8]

Germany in 1936 was not yet in a condition to assume the active reorganization of Europe; in simplest terms she was not yet rearmed. This was the fundamental reason for the relative pause while the Spanish war was dragging on to its appointed end. The British policy of seeking to break the Axis connection by courting alternately either end of it, especially the Italian, was a rational approach to the situation; in actuality, however, it had little effect other than offering opportunities for blackmail.

By 1938 Hitler felt that the combination of the effective power he had built up in Germany and the pusillanimity of the Western states warranted initiating his active program of change. Austria was the first to fall with little objection from the outside and no resistance within. In contrast with his 1934 behavior Mussolini approved; his position was changing from partner to prisoner of the Axis, but he saw no way of escape. There was still wishful thinking in England: were not the Austrians German, and therefore was not the *Anschluss* the removal of another legitimate grievance? Chamberlain's optimistic stance could still seem ostensibly reasonable,

[8] The world could only observe in astonishment the spectacle of the trials and purges that took place in the Soviet Union, when much of the original Bolshevik leadership and some of the high military leaders were cast in the role of traitors to the régime and many of them were liquidated.

though it had in effect become blind, wishful thinking. It reached its highest point in September, when he contrived the peaceful removal of yet another German grievance, and the Sudeten Germans of Czechoslovakia rejoined the fatherland.

Much has been written about the Munich episode and its settlement—the climax of the policy of appeasement. Yet British intentions were honest, and there is no denying that Chamberlain was at this point the authentic representative of the overwhelming bulk of his people. Britain is a democracy, and the "peace in our time" scrap of paper was largely taken at face value in that country. Chamberlain's French colleague, Daladier, was somewhat more skeptical, but it is also true that on the whole the French people were glad to have been able to avoid facing the reality of things. This is what gives some foundation to A. J. P. Taylor's thesis that Hitler, rather than being an unlimited aggressor, was at times embarrassed by things that were dropped by others in his lap.[9] In the face of such performances as Munich one may well understand that the idea should occur that there might indeed be no limit to the concessions that could be extracted from the Western democracies. Was not perhaps the bombast (and in large part it was just talk) about decadent democracy a true description of the state of things? Their behavior fostered this idea, and there is no doubt that the Western democracies did their best to mislead the would-be aggressors; this is not a light responsibility. However, craven as their behavior may have been, their intention was hardly to lay a trap for aggression.

Where France was concerned Munich was the effective and formal registration, and in a sense the logical consequence, of her failure to act in 1936. After 1938 the Franco-Czech

[9] Taylor, A. J. P., *The Origins of the Second World War* (London, 1961).

alliance no longer existed, even on paper, and the Franco-Soviet connection was effectively voided of content; the Soviet Union was not present at Munich. To take the position, in an orderly, peaceful, Europe, that Central Europe properly "belongs" to or with Germany is not unreasonable; for example, the stream of its exchanges is naturally far more directed toward Germany than toward France. But far closer to the true significance of Munich in 1938 was Bismarck's observation that he who controls Bohemia controls Central Europe; one must think at this time in the military and political sense rather than in the economic.

Europe had reverted to the competition of power in its crudest form, and was divided into the three great rival centers that have been mentioned. The rest of Europe, the smaller powers, could only observe in dismay the looming contest of the giants; Munich had duly impressed them and for them all it was primarily a case of *sauve qui peut;* some hoped for change, others feared it, but the main consideration for all was the desirability of judging correctly which of the powerful ones would gain the upper hand.

Contending ideologies helped to confuse the situation and to a point beclouded the realities of the struggle for power. On this score the most handicapped was the West, for the nineteenth-century democratic wave seemed to have spent itself. Britain and France gave the impression of fatigue; peace, peace at any price, seemed to be their overriding concern, and they certainly lacked either the desire or the vigor to conquer or to impose their ways on others. In contrast the Communist ideology continued to have widespread appeal, but its principal exponent, if it would seize an opportunity, seemed at the moment content to cultivate socialism in one country and appeared to have relegated the world revolution to some indefinite, dim future. What influence it had on Com-

munists abroad it used mainly with an eye to the limited
objective of the promotion of the interest of the Soviet Union
as a state among states. The Fascist powers loudly proclaimed
their energy and their vigor, forever stressing youth. They
posed as the self-appointed defenders of the old civilization
of Europe against Bolshevik barbarism, anxious to substitute
their own leadership for that of the tired, ineffectual, and
decadent democratic West. This outlook, too, had considerable
appeal. But, to repeat, the influence of the ideological factor
was secondary to the more immediate and limited role of
competing national interests.

To speak of any unity in Europe in this situation may seem
like an attempt to escape into fantasy. Yet if the competition
for power should break out into open conflict vast novel possibilities might be envisaged. The Soviet Union might resume
its crusading activity and stress once more the universal aspect
of the Communist ideology. Even if that aspect of the matter
was at the moment played down, the Communist belief in
the inevitability of war among capitalist states and in the
revolutionary possibilities that war offers had never been forgotten. Out of a conflict, a unity, even larger than the existing European states, might conceivably be born.

The Axis powers, because of their stress on the nationalistic
factor, were less suitably placed to issue a universal appeal.
Their success might indeed place them in the position of
being able to reorganize Europe in accordance with their
wishes, but this would be sheer conquest, and therefore might
be expected to arouse the opposition of other nationalisms.
Yet the attempt to unite Europe by conquest, if it had failed
so far, was also not an unfamiliar experience. Given the relative position of power of the two members of the Axis, such
an attempt must be essentially a German undertaking. Some
of the features of Nazism, the racial component in particular,
as well as the stress on some of the less attractive aspects of

the Germanic tradition, such as the glorification of ruthless-
ness and brutality, might seem especially repellant to others,
and therefore handicap the scope of the Nazi appeal. This
was indeed the case. But there were also compensating
factors. Not everyone objected to the racial views of Nazism,
which for that matter had long been familiar. The appeal
against Communist barbarism elicited a broad response in
many quarters, and it was recognized that the Fascist states
had made some marked contributions in the social and economic domains. Finally, mention ought to be made of what
might be called the response of the weary, the overcivilized,
and the weak, and the historically minded: even a Nazi
domination of Europe achieved without the exacerbation of
passions of open conflict might be the best way to put an end
to the suicidal quarrels of Europe. No doubt a measure of
unpleasantness—especially for some—would accompany the
process, but the extent of it would be minimized, and in due
time Nazism could be tamed and absorbed into the greater
bulk and the mainstream of civilized Europe, while on the
other hand open resistance and conflict would be sheer suicide.

Conclusion: The German Bid for European Unity

This was the condition and the climate of Europe during
the last year of uneasy peace following the settlement of
Munich. The active forces of change could not assert themselves without first breaking the mold of the existing structure
of states, and during that last year of peace there were
attempts at realignment among the three main centers of
power. From a set of three objects pairs can be made in
three different ways; there were therefore three possibilities:
a combination of the Soviet Union and the Western democ-

racies, forces of conservation and peace, might either deter, or in the last resort defeat, Axis aggression; or the Western states could contrive a compromise with the Axis on the basis of giving it a free hand in the East—a possibility the Soviet Union ever suspected and feared; or, and it seemed least probable at first, a Nazi-Soviet combination could emerge.

A short pause followed the Munich settlement while Germany digested her latest acquisitions and some other Central European rearrangements were made. But very soon it became evident that Germany could not abide even the remnants of an independent Czechoslovakia, when, in March 1939, German forces were "invited" to preserve order in Prague. The substance of the change was small; it could indeed be regarded as a logical corollary, a footnote, to what had happened six months earlier. At least such a conclusion fitted the interpretation of Munich as the surrendering of Central Europe to Germany; reasonable men in London ought to understand this without much difficulty. The occupation of Prague by the Germans, however, did not fit the fiction that all that had been done at Munich had been no more than the redressing of a minor German ethnic grievance.

Yet Chamberlain and the British people had sought to cling to that fiction. Their reaction was strong and swift; the British Prime Minister, who but a short time ago had professed little knowledge of a faraway Czechoslovakia, now suddenly discovered a more distant Poland. Britain issued a unilateral guarantee to Poland for which Poland had not even asked. This was an unusual piece of diplomacy, and its intention was not so much directed at Poland as at Germany— Britain would resist further Nazi encroachment. Chamberlain, in taking this position, was again, or still, the authentic representative of a finally aroused British opinion. To understand the psychology that lay behind this sudden British reversal was perhaps more than could reasonably be expected of the

Nazi mentality, especially in view of the past record of Britain.

The British action introduced into the situation a measure of confusion. It marked the initiation of a negotiation focusing on the Soviet Union. The Soviet view of things was closer to the German *Realpolitik* outlook, and this, in combination with the hesitant British approach, made it difficult to convince the Soviet Union of the authenticity of the British conversion. The French here, too, followed the British initiative. Thus the negotiations between the West and the Soviet Union were slow and did not prosper, and the West found it difficult in turn to accede to Soviet demands, which, if granted, would have convinced the Soviet Union of the dependability of the intent of the West.

Nazi Germany was not hampered by any qualms in disposing of the fate of other peoples. For all the intensity of their ideological differences the Soviets and the Nazis talked much the same realistic language of power, and although no love was lost between them or any real trust established, it proved possible, at least for the time, to reach an understanding. Russia was willing to divide Poland with Germany, and an astonished world was confronted with the announcement of the conclusion of a Nazi-Soviet non-aggression pact. This was on August 23. Peace lasted one more week, for in the meantime Hitler had discovered that he had yet another grievance—a German-Polish crisis had been developing along the now familiar lines, similar to the German-Czech episode of a year earlier.

The Soviet Union may have felt that in its crude handling of power it had displayed high sophistication and skill in defending its interest. Rather than be itself involved in war with the assistance of little trusted allies, the war could now take place between the Western countries and the Axis—all capitalist states. In 1939 it did not seem unreasonable to expect that such a war would be hard and protracted, exhausting all the participants alike, and meantime the Soviet Union could enjoy the desirable position of *tertius gaudens*. It was even conceivable that the war would create suitable conditions for a vast extension of the revolution, possibly to all Europe. This line of thought, if rational, was not divorced from an element of gambling; for the fate of war is always uncertain, as events were to prove before long.

On the German side there was similar rationality and gambling. Behind the shield of at least momentary Soviet acquiescence and neutrality, Germany was prepared to launch upon the bid for the conquest of Europe. Certainly it could be maintained—it has been by A. J. P. Taylor—that Germany wanted no more than the unfettered control of Central Europe. Once Poland was conquered, did not Germany offer peace to the West and even offer to guarantee the British Empire, apart from some secondary colonial demands? And might not this same West, until now so accommodating, take a reasonable view of things instead of pursuing the quixotic undertaking of assisting a Poland that no longer existed and that the West had not the means to assist, short of an all-out war with Germany herself? Such thoughts were entertained in many quarters, during and after October 1939, after Poland had been overrun and once again partitioned. But it is also difficult to conceive that the restoration of peace on the basis of the *fait accompli* would have created any sort of stability in Europe: it would have merely extended the pre-existing situation, with the one difference that Germany would have been in a better position to pursue the implementation of the Hitlerian program.

British policy in the preceding years may properly be judged in the harshest of terms and even charged with a heavy share of responsibility, albeit negative, for the pass to which Europe had been brought. Nevertheless, the past was past, and the British judgment was correct that if the German bid for hegemony was unacceptable, it must now be resisted to the bitter end. Britain was again cast in the familiar role of being the stanchest defender of the liberties of Europe, the continued existence of her separate entities, but also the greatest obstacle to the achievement of any European unity.

Britain, in the large sense, would in the end again be successful but this tale and especially the aftermath of it was to take a highly unexpected turn which will be examined in the last section of this book.

Part Four

AN IDEA THAT WILL NOT DIE

From what has been written so far it may appear that, while the concept of one Europe has reality, the accent in more recent centuries has been on the diversity of the component parts of that continent. The common strands in the culture—and the aspect of culture must be stressed—are both real and powerful, but within them the fact of difference seems to have asserted itself with increasing potency. The divisive creation of the sovereign state has triumphed over the common heritage of political unity that Rome had for a time realized, over the version of it embodied by Christianity, and over the surviving ideal that the Holy Roman Empire represented in its attempted fusion of the two.

Meantime the nation was also achieving increasing consciousness of itself and was becoming the kernel around which the state took geographical shape. By the sixteenth century several national monarchies had appeared, mainly on the Atlantic seaboard. Then came a change in the theory and practice of government which substituted the people for the individual monarch. The democratic seed was planted first in England, then in France, and through France, on the continent. The combination of the two concepts of nationality and of sovereignty fused in the nineteenth century to produce the concept of modern nationalism and self-determination. Though we may think it now an aberration, and certainly some of its more extreme manifestations have been such, nationalism at the beginning of the present century in Europe had become without a doubt one of the great moving forces of history.

It was strong enough to overcome the effects of other contrary forces of integration, which were primarily technological and economic in nature. In some of its aspects at least, the growth of large industry was inimical to the limitations imposed by the existence of national boundaries. So was the Marxist view of development, also born of economic considerations, which gave priority of importance to class instead of to nationality and was alien to the exaltation of the supreme value of the nation. But what happened in 1914 was clear evidence of the far greater strength of the national force, and the Second International collapsed quite easily in the face of it.

Appropriately, the First World War was a contest of peoples whose "national" consciousness was raised to an unprecedented pitch. As a consequence the settlement of that conflict purported to redraw, and to a large extent succeeded in redrawing, the political map of Europe along lines of ethnic separation.

Yet in a sense the madness had been overdone. Even though it was sanctioned in the moral condemnation of the defeated enemy and in the demand for unconditional surrender, there had been during the war itself a reaction against it. One aspect of the war registered the failure—in this case German—to establish a hegemony in Europe out of which unity might conceivably have emerged in time. It was too late for unity on such a basis; Napoleon's attempt was possibly the last that held any hope of success, and even that is doubtful. In any case Napoleon failed, though one may speculate on what he might have been able to accomplish had there not been an England. Britain in the First World War had filled her by now classical role of serving her own interest through the device of preserving the liberties—or the divisions—of

Europe. However, it is of the highest significance, especially in view of later developments, that this was not accomplished until a wholly extra-European power, the United States, had thrown its weight into the scales of the conflict.

The United States thought that it was a stranger to the quarrels of Europe, and at the time there was very little consciousness in America of the desirability, for its own safety and interest, of actually preventing the rise of a continental hegemony. There was even less indication of any American interest in fostering the unity of Europe. The peculiarly American contribution, the League of Nations, although it came to be largely a European institution, was originally of world-encompassing scope; and certainly America, as much as and rather more than most, was a highly jealous guardian of its own sovereignty. In any case, where America was concerned, the League was shipwrecked on the rock of senatorial opposition.

But the war also produced a revival of the socialist prospect in unexpected fashion and in an unexpected quarter. However, the outlook of the Bolshevik revolution, like that of the earlier French, was universal in scope rather than merely European, let alone narrowly national. Yet what prospects of revolution there were after 1917 were at first largely limited to Europe; this was consistent with the more advanced economic development of Europe, to which corresponded a more widespread familiarity with the socialist doctrine.

The Russian Revolution did not spread, and the League eventually failed. But it is perhaps all the more significant that within a short ten years, in the face of the virulence of exacerbated nationalisms that shaped much of the peace, the more modest prospect of European union, in large measure designed to save Europe from a recurrence of war, was sponsored by the French Foreign Minister. The fate of Briand's proposal and hopes have been examined.

One might see in that attempt the even more limited motivation of the satisfaction of the French desire for security, or,
alternatively—though in fumbling and instinctive fashion—an
expression of the consciousness of the demotion of the European states. Certainly all the great powers of Europe were
dwarfed, in terms of either status or potential, by the United
States; and if the Soviet Union was involved in the long and
painful process of recovering from chaos, de Tocqueville had
long ago foreseen the gigantic possibilities of the latent power
of Russia. But it would be a premature anticipation of our
story to speak at this time of any clear awareness that only in
union could Europe hope to continue to play the world role
that had been hers in the past.

It may be put this way. For the component parts of Europe,
especially the great powers, the war put an end to the age of
their world dominance. Yet the damage done by the war was
insufficient, save in the Russian case, to radically alter the
structure of society, while the momentum of European power
was so great that the abrupt reversal of a long-established
condition was not clearly perceived—it would take another
world war to do that. The consequence was deep malaise and
a fumbling attempt to return to the presumed normality of
prewar days. To take but one example, the British schemes in
the Middle East, which were an expression of the attempt to
maintain continuity of imperial development, are a good
illustration of the prevalent illusions. Their prompt collapse is
also a good measure of the degree of change that had
occurred. Although the war was insufficiently effective in
destroying the old, it did enough injury to prevent its unaltered survival, and herein lies the key to much of the
ambiguity characteristic of the uninspiring interval between
the two world wars.

This is what we have discussed so far. These fumblings
were reflected in the appearance of new political systems, first

the Italian, then the German, in varying degrees imitated by others, which in a way should be seen as attempts to adapt to altered circumstances. Like the economic collapse of the thirties, they were in a sense expressions of the inability properly to liquidate the consequences of the war by simply restoring the past. Thus the old ways persisted, in the sense at least that both Fascist Italy and Nazi Germany represented the highest exaltation of the value of the nation, and in the German case above all, embellished with the peculiar aberration of racism.

In 1939 Europe was therefore confronted with the prospect of two rival possibilities, which, in their antithetic ways, might have led to her unity. The Soviet Union for some years had been a conservative power, in the sense that it feared facing the risks involved in open clash; for the moment, wrapped in its own domestic stresses, it preferred to see the peace and the status quo preserved. It also always feared a revival of the capitalist coalition, which, in its simplest expression, might take the form of the Western democracies giving Nazi Germany *carte blanche* for an attack directed toward the East. Just as in the initial days of its existence, when Lenin had insisted on the acceptance of peace, even on Germany's dictated terms, the chief concern of the Bolshevik government in 1939 was to preserve the fruits of the revolution at home. It is of secondary importance whether this attitude is regarded as being primarily dictated by the desire to save the revolution or by the more limited interest of the Soviet state as such; for that matter, the two could coincide.

To prevent the formation of the dreaded capitalist coalition either of its main components might be dealt with. For a time, the Soviet Union supported collective security, and even after Munich, though she was naturally made suspicious by her exclusion from that settlement, would consider co-operation with the West. But the prospect of world revolution, the universal aspect of the Communist gospel, even if temporarily soft-pedaled or put in cold storage for reasons of momentary expediency, had never been wholly renounced. Certainly many thought so in the West. This inevitable element of mutual distrust lies at the root of the failure to achieve an understanding between the Soviet Union and the Western states. The Nazi stress on the crusade to save Western civilization from the threat of Bolshevik barbarism fitted nicely into this situation.

But there was another aspect to the classical Marxist interpretation, namely the belief that the adherents to the capitalist practice were fated by their rivalries to fall out among themselves. In this view the failure of world revolution immediately after the First World War would call for no more than a modification, rather than an abandonment, of the initial expectation; the passage of some time would provide another opportunity when the capitalist imperialist states would come to blows among themselves. For all the Nazi stress on anti-Bolshevism there was enough difference between Germany and the Western states to justify the possibility of such a clash. Out of this situation came the Nazi-Soviet Pact. From the Soviet standpoint this agreement was a rational act even if it involved a calculated risk. This risk did not seem very great at first in 1939, because it was reasonable to expect that a clash between Germany and the Western democracies would lead to a substantial and fatal mutual bloodletting, which would considerably enhance the prospects of Soviet gain and of world revolution.

The Nazi-Soviet Pact of 1939 therefore may be seen as having some of the same characteristics as the agreement contrived between Napoleon and Tsar Alexander I in 1807 at Tilsit. In exchange for the assurance of being left undisturbed, plus some immediate concrete gains in Poland and around the Baltic, Stalin would let Hitler proceed with the attempt to organize the rest of Europe. Even more, just as Tsar Alexander had initially joined Napoleon's Continental System, so would Stalin furnish some economic aid. Relevant to the central theme of this discussion is the fact that an eventual Communist revolution, if it would encompass all Europe, would be of far wider scope than the confines of the Continent and therefore would not be especially significant from the standpoint of its unity. A German success, on the other hand, would be a much more clearly European affair; where the rest of the world was concerned, it would reassert or confirm the supremacy of Europe. In any case, Germany in 1939 could proceed to implement her bid for European dominance out of which European unity might in some form emerge. Lastly, it must be pointed out, the 1939 German bid for hegemony was far more conscious and more sharply defined than that of 1914.

I. The Defeat of the German Bid: The Second World War

The stakes were clearly high, and there seemed to be universal reluctance to become irrevocably committed. Poland was destroyed in three weeks with expeditious ease, but it took another six months before the war truly got under way. How could the Western allies restore Poland save by destroying Germany first? Not a few thought that some accommodation could be found on the basis of an altered status quo in Central Europe, a logical extension of what the Western powers had been willing to accept a year before at Munich. Even in Germany, as pleasing as success had been, the taste for all-out conflict was not strong in the mass of the nation. Had not Hitler's most telling argument vis-à-vis his own people been that the rightness of his intuition had enabled him to achieve his succession of gains while preserving the peace? Even the Polish operation was hardly modern war in the authentic sense, despite the German insistence on displaying a measure of its capacity for frightfulness, used in the safety of largely impotent opposition. There were some thoughts of compromise and even some ineffective attempts at mediation, by the Dutch, for instance.

But to others the issue was clear. A new compromise *à la* Munich could be no lasting solution. The British had become by now adequately convinced of this. The "phoney war" was consequently no more than a pause before the dogs of war were totally unleashed. Some things that happened in the interim—Central European readjustments, the Russo-Finnish War—are but footnotes to the larger context.

The prelude was in April with the efficiently managed Nazi occupation of two Scandinavian countries, followed in May by the beginning of an all-out German offensive in the West. That, too, was efficiently managed, and the new version of the Schlieffen Plan, the invasion of France from the north, bypassing or turning the powerful Maginot Line, was crowned with total success; it happened so rapidly that the world was left in a state of breathless awe. The great bulwark of the West, the huge French military machine, quite comparable to the German in dimensions, and the object of world-wide respect, assisted by a small but high-quality British force, was dispersed like chaff before the wind. In six weeks France was destroyed and the British contingent wiped out.

This event forced the world, or a large part of it at least, to realize that it could not tranquilly attend to its normal pursuits behind the shield of French force. If the world had a stake in defending what French force had defended—not France as such, but larger matters; concrete interests as well as ideological positions—it would have to do this itself, and

this time without the asset of France. That asset, even in
defeat was not wholly negligible and was now in large
measure transferred to German hands.

The French collapse, far more than the Polish, raised in
sharp form the issue of whether there was point in continuing
the struggle. Since Britain was alone this meant a British
decision. The British offer of union with France, when France
was in the last throes of defeat, was an imaginative gesture
which might have had untold consequences had it been
accepted—certainly from the standpoint of the future unity
of Europe. Under the circumstances it may be regretted, but it
is hardly surprising, that it elicited little response.

Since Britain would not accept compromise, let alone yield,
the situation once more arose when a dominant sea power
faced one supreme on land; it had happened in 1805 after
Trafalgar and Austerlitz. The British margin of sea power was
adequate but none too comfortable, especially once the
French fleet had been neutralized. But there was now the
novel element of air power. After a brief pause the Battle of
Britain began, the outcome of which was similar to that of the
Marne in 1914. Both were negative successes which at the time
robbed Germany of full victory and insured the continuance
of the struggle, although the final outcome of German defeat
seemed in 1940 even more problematic than in 1914. At best
the future was uncertain.

Nazi-dominated Europe

As in Napoleon's time, a continental power was free to
organize the Continent outside the Russian domain. It mattered relatively little whether Germany was dealing with
friend or foe. Italy was formally an ally who hoped to share in
the spoils, and with little grace had joined in the kill of France
at the eleventh hour. But Italy had been for some time a

prisoner instead of an equal partner in the Axis, and the passage of time, especially in view of the quality of her own military performance, merely emphasized her dependent position. Others—Hungary for example or Rumania—mattered even less. In German eyes, even a defeated France might be a more valuable asset in war than an allied Italy.

Should France willingly accept the German primacy and dominance, this would constitute for Germany, from the standpoint of organizing the new order of Europe, an asset comparable in value to the physical resources of France, now at Germany's disposal for purposes of war. The rapidity and thoroughness of the defeat, induced a state of shock among the French people that needs no explaining. It behooved their leaders to make decisions on the basis of a cooler appraisal of circumstances and prospects. They called upon Pétain, a military man and revered figure, now nearing eighty-five. One is reminded of von Hindenburg in the twilight of the Weimar Republic. The decision that the war was lost implied a judgment of the prospects of British resistance. These were thought unpromising and it was felt that Britain, while she was still undefeated at home, could at best find an accommodation, which might even possibly be in part at France's expense. The facts of power are harsh.

One may be thankful that it turned out in the long term to be a mistaken decision.[1] It was nevertheless a rational judgment in which many on the outside concurred at the time. The next step was to make what adjustments could be made to the situation, and here, not surprisingly, much confusion arose. Patriotic Frenchmen, who refused to accept the decision, either went abroad, like General de Gaulle who proceeded

---

[1] Whether or not it was a wise decision from the more limited standpoint of French interest is debatable. France has had to pay heavily since 1940, but mainly as a consequence of defeat and of the demotion that that defeat represented.

to organize the Free French movement in Britain, or took up clandestine resistance in France. Altogether these were initially very few; the bulk of the French people were stunned, and willingly accepted the leadership of Pétain. Thus Vichy France came into existence; it represented a disparate merging of widely divergent tendencies and hopes, and was also in the reckoning a mean and uninspiring passage. There was little love for Germany in France, yet there were those—practical, sensible, realistic men, even men of some vision—who looked beyond the facts of war and defeat to the day when Europe would be one. No doubt many aspects of German leadership were repugnant, to say the least, yet in time Germany could be fused and absorbed into the more civilized traditions of Europe, and the making of Europe might be worth the price of passing unpleasantness and humiliation.[2] Such an approach is not to be either dismissed or uncritically condemned; it reminds one of some of the things being said currently about the evolution of the Soviet Union and the prospects of its integration in the Western tradition.

But, stupidly, the Germans themselves were the worst enemies of what prospects they may have had. To be sure, their behavior in France was vastly different from what it was in Poland; it was to a degree "correct," precisely for the reason that the German leadership was aware of the value of the moral asset of French acquiescence, either as a precedent for the same acceptance by others, or alternatively as a discour-

[2] Such views were but an extension of those held by certain elements in France even before the war had begun. They were held by a variety of people and for a variety of reasons, not least the fear of social upheaval, and their exponents, ironically enough, were to be found among the conservative elements, traditionally associated with the more intransigent aspects of French nationalism.

agement of their opposition. Yet, with a blind and obtuse
consistency, the Nazis insisted on the application of their
fantastic racial beliefs. Accordingly, their behavior was "soft-
est," or least harsh, in the Scandinavian countries, and in
Denmark especially they strove to establish a model. But
when it came to Slavs the Nazis could find in their book little
room for consideration, even for the barest dictates of humanity.[3] This attitude they soon found occasion to implement
and display, especially after their attack on Russia.

In the stalemate that resulted from continued British resistance, Hitler was led to a repetition of the Napoleonic
attempt. There were some preliminaries, of which the most
dramatic was the unexpected Yugoslav opposition to Nazi demands. Needless to say, Yugoslavia was forcibly brought into
line, while the episode served as an occasion to bail out the
Italians from their inglorious failure against Greece. Even in
North Africa, it was not long before the Afrika Korps had to
come to their rescue, marking a further occasion for the
demotion of Italy to the status of dependent satellite. Since
Hitler could not dispose of England he would eliminate in the
meantime the lurking danger constituted by the very existence
of the Soviet Union in his rear. For that matter, Nazi-Soviet
relations had been deteriorating, while from the Soviet point
of view the new face of the war might be cause for recon-
sideration. By the summer of 1941 German preparations were
complete, and on June 22, interestingly the same day that
Napoleon had crossed the Russian border, Nazi forces moved
against the Soviet Union.

The detailed story of the Russian war does not belong in

[3] The attempt physically to wipe out the Jews of Europe is one to
tax belief. Yet, because of the relatively small number of Jews in
Europe, the Nazi treatment of others, Slavs in particular, assumed even
greater significance from the standpoint of any claim to organize
Europe under German leadership.

this discussion. The war itself may be summed up by saying that, just as the Channel moat has served the traditional function of preventing the invasion of England, the traditional Russian assets, Generals "space" and "winter," saved Russia from defeat. This, too, had been Napoleon's experience, but in the latest case it took several winters instead of only one to accomplish the result. Certain things that happened in connection with the Russian war have considerable significance. Two in particular must be mentioned.

The Germans achieved considerable successes at first, and before long much of the Ukraine was in their hands. Their vaunted boast of fighting the fight of civilization against Communist barbarism did not seem wholly empty considering the degree of co-operation they initially received from those they had "liberated." But here again they proved their own worst enemies; the insanely consistent application of their racial beliefs where supposedly inferior Slavs—whether liberated or prisoners—were concerned, was the most effective argument in favor of resisting them. This in turn had the effect of emphasizing the national character of the war in place of the ideological; the war for the Soviet people became above all a great struggle for national survival in which the stress was on the alien national character of the enemy. There has been occasion to dwell on the divisive influence of the national factor in Europe.

The rest of the Continent felt an important consequence of the involvement of Russia in the war. The Nazi-Soviet Pact had been at first a surprise and a source of great embarrassment to Communists outside the Soviet Union. Yet, with very few exceptions, the factor of ideological allegiance prevailed, and when it came to war Communists overwhelmingly adopted the Soviet policy of benevolent neutrality toward Nazi Germany. In France, for example, during the period of the "phoney war," the outlawed Communists sabotaged the war effort and contributed to the confusion that undermined French morale.

The collapse of France did not alter their position, and for a time relations between them and the Nazis may be described as untrusting mutual neutrality. It is not surprising that the German attack against the Soviet Union changed all this. In the Communist rationalization that equates the best interest of the Communist ideology with that of the Soviet state, Communist parties outside the Soviet Union become expendable tools. This is again a situation where the premise may be fallacious but the conclusion is logical.

In any case the Nazi attack upon the Soviet Union made it imperative for good Communists in the occupied or subservient countries of Europe to resist the Nazi war effort. And this they generally did with both loyalty and effectiveness. But herein also lay the seeds of great future confusion. For, as the war dragged on doubts grew about Germany's chance for victory. As the Germans were led, whether for purposes of war alone or because of their own ideology, to increase their exactions and the brutality of their treatment, resistance to them became increasingly strong. In France, in Italy, everywhere, the *maquis* prospered; it was a vicious circle, for increasing resistance was met by growing harshness, on which further resistance flourished. Much of this resistance, quite naturally, had national roots, and for a time to be a good Communist and a good Frenchman, or a good anything else, led to the same concrete actions. Neither were the Communists themselves immune to the nationalistic emotion, which no longer posed for them the dilemma of divided allegiance. As it turned out, the Communists everywhere in Nazi-controlled Europe played a very large part in the Resistance, and their familiarity with clandestinity was a valuable asset. But this also had the consequence that the Communists, posing as good patriots, and because of the magnitude of their unstinting contribution—they did generously pay the blood tax—endeavored to annex to themselves the leadership of the resistance movements. Also their popularity increased among the many who were primarily moved by the national emotion. This is where confusion crept in, and we shall have occasion to return to the consequences of this state of affairs when a Russian bid followed the German bid for dominance of Europe after the war. Meanwhile some other things had happened.

The Impact of External Forces

From its experience in the First World War America had learned, or thought it had learned, a lesson, which in simplest form was expressed by the dictum "The quarrels of Europe are not our quarrels." America, the story went, had been taken in by such things as Allied propaganda and the sordid interests of its own bankers for example; these elements in combination had taken advantage of America's better instincts and inexperience in the domain of world politics. America in future must stick to its own last and guard against the influence of either its emotions or its special interests. There was little sympathy for the Nazis in America, but it is well to recall the degree to which many Americans leaned backward in an effort to disbelieve the accumulating evidence of what Nazism was and stood for; a false and undiscriminating wisdom had inured them against propaganda. Remember, for example, the First World War false tales of the hands cut off Belgian children.

When the international situation in Europe began visibly to deteriorate, with the Abyssinian War, German rearmament, the Spanish Civil War, the destruction of Czechoslovakia following upon each other in rapid succession, these events emphasized the necessity of more stringent precautions against any possibility of involvement. The answer was the series of measures called the Neutrality Acts, a curious passage that amounted to an attempt to deny that America was part of this planet, and which had, among other things, the effect of considerably hampering the implementation of American foreign policy.

The outbreak of the war altered all this very little. If sympathy was predominantly on the side of the Western democracies, this was all the more reason for caution and impartial behavior. America eliminated the possibility of becoming involved either through insistence on its rights as a neutral at sea or through financial commitment. In addition, there was the comforting—wishful as it turned out—expectation that the British and the French alone would ultimately be successful.

The collapse of France was a shock to America, but Reynaud's pathetic appeal for "clouds of airplanes" showed the distance that separated America from the conflict; the airplanes were not available, and even had they been, there was, in June 1940, not the faintest possibility of their being sent. The government, especially the President, took a less simple view of things, but against the tide of opinion—America *is* a democracy—it must proceed with caution. The domestic reaction to that tentative feeler, Roosevelt's 1937 Quarantine speech, had been highly critical, and now that war had come, the best that could be done, stretching neutrality to the utmost, was such arrangements as the transfer of some overage destroyers to the hard-pressed British, a useful but small thing. Even that arrangement, matched by the lease of certain British bases to America, could be presented as primarily intended for the defense of the Americas, their more effective insulation from whatever effects the conflict might have elsewhere. The concept of fortress America had appeal to isolationist feeling, and the 1940 election is reminiscent in some respects of that of 1916, when one of the slogans had been "He kept us out of war."

Gradually, there was some shift in public feeling—if outright interventionists were few, there was a substantial number of those who would not have stinted help to Britain regardless of its consequences. But the unrealistic debate went on in an inconclusive fashion, centering around the issue of America's precise place, if any, in the affairs of the wide world, until it was resolved by the Japanese bombing of Pearl Harbor. As Germany and Italy, perhaps unnecessarily, took the initiative of declarations of war, matters were made clear in sudden and brutal fashion; America was at war with all three members of the Rome-Berlin-Tokyo triangle.

Of the role of America in the war it is enough to say that it confirmed the unique tradition that America does not lose wars. In December 1941, American military power was still largely potential. But the barriers of two oceans, which air power could not overcome, played the same role for America that the Channel has traditionally played for Britain—it made possible the undisturbed mobilization of resources. After a year, sufficient military power had been created to make itself effectively felt; in the Pacific and in North Africa the tide began to turn. It took three more years to finish the task, and, to be sure, America did not win the war alone, though it is essential to bear in mind the extent of the American contribution to both the British and the Russian wars.

Especially after the turn toward the end of 1942—the invasion of French North Africa coincident with the battles of El Alamein and Stalingrad—hopes rose in Nazi-controlled Europe. And, quite naturally, any assistance that could be added to their efforts from within Europe was welcomed by the Allies. Because the status of different countries varied this led to many complications. Some governments, the Norwegian and the Dutch for example, had fled to continue the struggle, mainly from the shelter of Britain. Others, like the Danish, had not. Among governments-in-exile there were at times factions, and they were even challenged by sufficiently powerful resistance movements that developed at home; this happened in Yugoslavia and Poland. And what to do with France? The Vichy government was undoubtedly legal, but the Free French were actually fighting. "Our [America's] Vichy gamble" gave rise to many qualms, much difficulty, and not a little confusion. And what of Italy where, in 1943, Fascism collapsed and the new régime sought to enlist itself among the Allies? It was granted co-belligerent status, while Mussolini, rescued by the Germans, set up a Social Republic in the North.

Nevertheless, in the present context, all these developments are secondary to the general fact that everywhere opposition to German rule put great stress on national difference. The one exception appeared in the East where the Russians insisted upon dealing only with régimes sympathetic to their own; the seeds of future complications and dissensions were being planted.

The Looming Shape of the Future: One World?

Needless to say preparations began to be made for the peace long before the fighting was over. Such a declaration as the Atlantic Charter, an Anglo-American statement, issued in August 1941, antedated the American intervention. It is reminiscent of the Wilsonian Fourteen Points, though far less precise, contenting itself with the general endorsement of the independence of all peoples, meaning their national allegiance as well as the nature of their governments. In addition, the Atlantic Charter acknowledged the importance of economic matters and the related social question. It also spoke of the desirability of reducing the burden of armaments, but made no concrete reference to the possibility of international organization.

Once the United States had joined the war contacts with others inevitably became closer, and since power is always of paramount importance, the views of three states—the United States, Britain, and the Soviet Union—were of especial significance. More narrowly this meant three men, Roosevelt, Churchill, and Stalin. This reminds one of the Big Three of 1919. At this point a major problem arose, and its consequences and manifestations are with us to this day. The coalition that won the First World War, if it had to contend with the problem of conflicting national interests, was not rent by ideological differences; it had no difficulty in authentically underwriting the democratic slogan, and in large measure it could also subscribe to the idea of self-determination.

This was not the case in the Second World War, for the ideological rift between the Western states and the Soviet Union was profound. While the war was in its active phase, the common purpose and the common danger provided an adequate bond that to a degree concealed this difference; some were even led to think that differences were small. Churchill and Roosevelt indeed spoke the same language, and relations between them were always close and generally easy, although the thinking of the former was clearer on the score of the realities of power. Where power was concerned Stalin was very clear indeed, but the dire straits in which the Soviet Union found itself and its vital need of American material assistance, caused him to be amenable to a degree. Thus a measure of agreement was outwardly preserved that nevertheless concealed the depth and the reality of difference. The meetings that were held, for purposes of co-ordinating the war effort and then for arranging the future, in Teheran and especially at Yalta, laid the bases for the note of ambiguity on which the war came to a close.

It was an undeniable fact that Fascism, especially in its German form, was the great enemy. There was authentic agreement on the desirability of its complete extirpation—a somewhat naïve hope, perhaps. It also seemed wholly reasonable that Russia should wish to have friendly, or at least not avowedly inimical, régimes on her borders. But words can be used to confuse as well as to express agreement. Whether it is honest difference of opinion, or the result of deceitful intent, the fact is that terms like "democracy" and "friendly" were used in the loosest of undefined fashions.

The past ever casts its long shadow on the present and nothing is easier than to make the simplist assumption that the opposite of an error must be the correct answer. Two such errors—if errors they were—were widely thought to have been committed in connection with the First World War and its settlement. The pre-armistice commitment to the Wilsonian program that the Allies had made vis-à-vis Germany was in large measure responsible for the subsequent German claim of having been deceived and taken advantage of. Things would be clear this time, and to the enemy nothing more would be offered than unconditional surrender.[4] Secondly, the incorporation of the Covenant of the League into the Treaty of Versailles had been the very cause of the American rejection of that settlement. Again the reverse course would be adopted, and the peacemaking process would be carefully divorced from the endeavor to create a world organization.

The United States set great store by the last provision and certainly the desire for lasting peace was world-wide. As

[4] There has been considerable criticism of that decision, but this is largely the wisdom of retrospect. By the time the war was drawing to a close, the possibilities of a negotiated peace, given the circumstances, were small; hence the effects of the policy of unconditional surrender were of secondary significance.

early as September 1944, when the outcome of the war was
clearly visible, a meeting took place at Dumbarton Oaks,
where the main features of the future United Nations were
agreed upon. This meeting was followed by another gathering
in San Francisco, in April of the following year, where the
United Nations was formally born. There were some difficulties at San Francisco, omens of future greater ones, especially between the United States and the Soviet Union, but
this is not the place to dwell on them, any more than there
is cause to go into details about the nature and the structure
of the world organization. It was a fairly close replica of the
all but defunct League of Nations, of which it formally became
the heir. Both consisted initially of the victorious coalitions,
but their scope was universal, and, in time, unrestricted membership would make the whole world one.

On this note the war ended. In contrast with 1918, the
supreme German leadership of 1945 did not consist of sane
and reasonable men. Hitler must realize his boast, or threat,
that if he could not succeed in laying the foundations of the
thousand-year Reich he would bring down the house of
Europe. He had his *Götterdämmerung;* with a tenacity worthy
of a better cause his armies fought to the last, and he put
a fitting climax to the weird and gruesome episode with his
own macabre performance in his Berlin bunker. On May 8,
1945 VE-Day dawned on Europe. The United States elected
to precipitate the end in the Pacific. On August 9 the world
could but stand in awe before the spectacle of the first
atomic bomb that was dropped on Hiroshima.

That decision and that gesture have been the source of
much controversy and of divergent judgments. Yet that perhaps is of but secondary importance. For once man had un-
locked the secret of atomic power, that he should fail to use
it, for purposes of either war or peace, was as likely a prob-

ability as the suggestion sometimes heard that scientific development should in some manner be controlled or held back.
Man is launched on a course from which, whatever its end
point may be, there seems no possibility of turning.

What is of the highest significance is the fact that, in 1945,
the United States stood on a pinnacle of unique power, the
height of which had no precedent. From the war itself the
United States had, unlike others and alone among others,
derived immediate and concrete advantage in the sense that
the war had given a great boost to the acceleration of its
material development. Now, in addition, it possessed the monopoly of nuclear power. The uniqueness of the American
position was far more clearly marked in 1945 than in 1918.
Therefore, what the United States would do and how it would
exercise its power, was of the utmost significance to all.

That is the reason why this background has been sketched,
which in other respects may seem extraneous to and far removed from a discussion of the unity of Europe. But the
shape of Europe, collectively or in her separate parts, could
not but be deeply affected by American action. America
did not intend to abuse her power, and for a brief time it
might even appear that America would re-enact the withdrawal that followed the First World War. Certainly the dis-
mantling of the huge American military machine was alarm-
ingly precipitate, but the peculiar accident of the monopoly
of nuclear power was an adequate substitute and served to
maintain the effective presence of American power.

Even during this interval America was firmly committed to
the world organization. Appropriately, the American outlook
was global, rather than limited in scope to Europe or any
other section of the world, for all that military priority had
been given to the European war. The conflict was after all
European in its origins and at the heart of it stood the German
bid for power, with, among other things, the possible con-

sequence of European unity in some form and enhanced world subordination to Europe. The German bid, like others, Napoleon's for example, had been defeated, and this outcome had been accomplished in the fundamentally classical fashion. After France had collapsed Britain was left alone for a time. Circumstances eventually made Russia her partner, but it is doubtful whether the combined power of Britain, Russia, and whatever internal resistance existed in Europe would have sufficed to bring Germany down. Britain in the mid-twentieth century no longer possessed the margin of power that she had 150 years ago; Russia was badly mauled; and internal resistance was useful but weak, especially so long as ultimate prospects and goals were clouded.

The power of America was needed successfully to tip the scales, and from this may be drawn the conclusion that America had fallen heir to the historic British position. As the twentieth century opened Europe was still in large measure mistress of the planet, and two world wars had been born out of Europe's inability to compose her differences and unite. It is highly significant that, on the second occasion, the traditional liberties of Europe, her division into separate sovereign segments, had been preserved by the intrusion of an unquestionably non-European power. The other two chief contributors, Britain and Russia, while European, are only so with the qualifications that were pointed out in the earlier pages of this book.

Having defeated the German bid for dominance, hence incidentally for possible European unity, America and Britain looked to the restoration of the traditional divisions of Europe, although there were some in Britain who perceived that the separate parts of that continent could no longer expect to play their former roles in the world and perhaps should join together in some manner. The position of the Soviet Union was

different, and it is one of the ironies of the Second World
War that the defeat of the German bid for control should
have immediately been followed by the rise of another.

II. The Defeat of the Russian Bid

The point has been made earlier that the First World War
effectively put an end to the supremacy of the powers of
Europe, yet that it did not cause sufficient damage to effect
the collapse of the previously existing structure and make
possible a totally novel start. From this standpoint the Second World War is merely an extension of the previous episode
and the completion of unfinished business.

In 1945 the task seemed complete. All Europe, save a few
minor neutrals, lay thoroughly prostrate and dependent on
outside—largely American—assistance for the most elementary
necessities of existence. The effects of the war were in some
ways contradictory and confusing. The loathesomeness of
some aspects of the German performance had naturally exacerbated national sentiments, though largely in a negative,
anti-German sense. There was also infinite weariness, profound revulsion against war and the sterility of national quarrels, and, even allowing for what pride could be felt among
Germans from the quality of their country's military performance, there was nowhere room for the pride or elation of
victory. For all in Europe, allowing for some qualification in
the British case, were defeated, and even in Germany the
extent of defeat and the madness that had finally brought it
about left the country permeated with a sense of stunned
passivity.

The Soviet Union had been badly hurt, yet had survived
and could indeed take pride in its contribution to victory.
Moreover, the relative primitiveness of Russian conditions, in

combination with the nature of the controls that prevailed in the Soviet state—the structure of both party and state emerged intact from the war—made it possible for the Soviet Union to contemplate a very large future role in the world.

In the years immediately following the 1917 revolution the Soviet leadership had clung to the hope of world revolution. The renewal of war after a pause of two decades furnished the possibility of a readjustment in the Marxist belief in the inevitability of conflict among capitalist-imperialist states that might open once more the door to opportunity. The Soviet Union did two things. The agreements that it had made with its American and British allies put the Red Army in occupation of a very large section of Eastern Europe, Poland, Czechoslovakia, Hungary, Rumania, and Bulgaria, plus sections of Germany and of Austria.[1] It was not long before it became evident that Soviet ideas were both simple and clear, while their implementation was ruthless. The passage was somewhat tortuous, and at first the gesture was made of allowing some participation of others than Communists in governments, but very soon it was apparent beyond a doubt that the Soviet Union interpreted "friendly" to mean "wholly subservient." Given the Marxist outlook and the nature of the Soviet state itself this should perhaps not have been cause for surprise, and it is even understandable that the Russians may in turn have been surprised at American objections to Soviet interference with the operation of the democratic process as understood in the United States. Although the words are used, what is the meaning of "democracy" and "freedom" in the Soviet context? Perhaps it was Americans who had been simply guilty of naïveté.

The other thing the Soviet Union did was to attempt to

[1] The Baltic states were essentially absorbed into the Soviet Union proper, with the exception of Finland. From Yugoslavia the Soviet forces withdrew, leaving control in native, though Communist, hands.

operate in the rest of Europe, in the section outside the physical control of the Red Army, through the agency of the Communist Party. The highly important and very honorable role of Communists in the resistance movements has been mentioned. At the very least they could not be denied participation in the governments. The new government of France, for example, was based on a three-cornered coalition of which the Communists were part[2]; they commanded larger popular support than any other party, receiving the allegiance of between a fourth and a third of the electorate, a fact which was measure of the extent of the revulsion against previously existing régimes. A similar condition existed in Italy.

France and Italy, the former even more than the latter, were the crucial countries. If in either or both the Communists, by ostensibly constitutional means, should secure control of the government, the likelihood would have been very strong that Communism would dominate virtually the whole of the Continent. It might be noted, in passing, that a new version of the argument that had been used by some in favor of the acceptance of Nazi dominance reappeared at this point. Among Western Communists (not all of whom were insensitive to national sentiment, and aware also of the backwardness of Russia), there were those who contended that in a Communist Europe the Russian influence would become dissolved and absorbed into the more advanced and civilized traditions of the rest of the Continent. Nor would it have been an easy thing to undo the outcome, except by direct intervention, which would be fraught with innumerable difficulties. America was understandably concerned, and the last years of the decade of the forties were a difficult passage. A

[2] The coalition consisted of the Communists, the Socialists, and the newly formed *Mouvement Républicain Populaire,* a Catholic party that covered a wide range of political and social opinion.

number of things happened, however, which once again saved the liberties—and the divisions—of Europe, or of what remained of Europe in freedom, from this latest possibility of union under the banner of Communist, or Russian, leadership or control.

If the appeal of Communism was considerable, so was the rejection of it, even though the opposition was not, unlike the Communist parties, organized in a disciplined bloc. It was in May 1947 that the Communists were ejected from the governments in both France and Italy. The operation was a skillful political maneuver, but in the larger sense must be seen as a rallying of the anti-Communist forces in those countries, which, despite their divisions, commanded a majority of popular support. The Communists had to abandon their infiltrating tactics and, for the moment at least, turn to outright opposition, a dangerous enough matter if one bears in mind their very large hold on the labor unions.

America promptly gave a powerful boost to this resistance to Communism. The imaginative idea launched by Secretary Marshall in a speech he made at Harvard University in June 1947 grew into the Marshall Plan. It proposed to deal with Europe as a whole through a co-ordinated and long-range scheme of massive instead of piecemeal assistance as had been the case until then. It is probable that Secretary Marshall's ideas were not initially too precise, and the proposal was originally open to all. But it seems fair to say that the Soviet Union, unduly constrained by its ideological interpretation of the behavior of others, missed at this point an opportunity, which conversely was seized by others, particularly by the anti-Communist forces of Europe. In any case the Marshall Plan unquestionably did become an effective and powerful tool for the economic recovery of the states of West-

ern Europe, while it induced at the same time a measure of
co-operation among them. Even though this was not its
initial intent, the Marshall Plan became an important element
in the sharpening struggle between Communism and the free
Western world, more narrowly between the Soviet Union and
the United States. Europe was placed between the two, an
understandably coveted prize, for, despite the wreckage and
the demotion, in Western Europe lay the greatest reservoir
of developed resources and skills in the world, second only to
the American.

The struggle that we call the Cold War, sharpening into the
Soviet-American rivalry, was growing in intensity. It is worth
noting that the Truman Doctrine preceded the Marshall Plan
by four months. In March 1947 President Truman asked of
Congress an appropriation for assistance to Greece and to
Turkey. The significance of this concrete act far exceeded the
limited bounds of its application. America was giving notice
to the world that she was taking over a policy and a responsibility that Britain could no longer carry, that of resisting the
establishment of any hegemony in Europe. Also, between the
Truman Doctrine and the Marshall Plan, whatever doubts
may have existed about America playing a conscious and full
share in the world could henceforth be definitely laid to rest.

In the sharply delineated contest moves and countermoves
followed one after another. In 1946 the Communist Party had
received 38 per cent of the popular vote in an election in
Czechoslovakia; this was the highest record ever achieved
anywhere in a free consultation. But, despite so promising a
prospect, the Soviet Union would not wait; in February
1948, President Beneš found himself cast in a role reminiscent
of that of his predecessor, Hacha, in 1939. Czechoslovakia was
brought into line, *gleichgeschaltet* once more, and Beneš's
hopes of authentic co-operation between the Soviet Union and

the West were buried with her briefly recovered independence.

Germany had been divided into zones of occupation and Berlin was under joint quadripartite control. The integration of the three western zones and the introduction of a new currency in them precipitated Soviet retaliation in the form of an attempt to isolate Berlin. Because of the success of the airlift the Berlin blockade was a failure, but tension had run high, and Germany was clearly being broken into two parts, which in fact soon became two distinct states, the Federal Republic, whose capital was situated in Bonn, and the German Democratic Republic, whose government was located in the Russian sector of Berlin.[3]

Any prospects of German reunification on the basis of a free consultation of the German people clearly must be put off to the Greek kalends. And if the weakening of Germany by her division could, because of the war, have equal appeal to peoples on both sides of the Iron Curtain, that division was also expression of the increasingly sharp cleavage of Europe into two ever more sharply differentiated segments.

The crowning climax of division may be seen in the signature in Washington, in April 1949, of the treaty that created the North Atlantic Treaty Organization. NATO in many respects is an old-fashioned military alliance designed to withstand a Soviet military threat. However, what is significant in NATO is the fact that it was an expression of American leadership, American power being so much greater than that of any of its other members, or even the combination of all of

---

[3] In addition to the division of Germany into two distinct states, the section east of the Oder-Neisse line has been virtually incorporated into Poland, and East Prussia has been divided between the Soviet Union and Poland. These *de facto* arrangements have not, however, received the formal sanction of incorporation into treaties.

them.[4] Based on the authentic common interest of these members, because of the discrepancy of power, NATO raised the question of whether a part of Europe was not merely becoming a collection of American satellites. But just because of this demotion of Europe the possibility could also be considered of a closer integration of these parts. Paul Reynaud in 1951 published a small book with the significant title *Unite or Perish* (Simon and Schuster). We must now return to some aspects of internal European development.

III. The Reconstruction and Integration of Europe

The cry contained in Reynaud's appeal was not original with him. Even allowing that the physical wreckage of Europe at the end of the war represented a passing stage and that peace would bring with it reconstruction and tolerable conditions of life, it seemed as safe to predict that the day of the former great powers of Europe was gone as it was to observe that their inability to adjust their differences had brought about their common plight. Clearly, America and the Soviet Union were and would continue to be entities of a different class. In unity, however, even free Europe alone, once the wreckage had been made good, still represented a great deal. But the divergent effects of the war, as mentioned before, brought common consciousness of defeat while they exacerbated national feeling, especially the anti-German aspect of it. Yet it is clear that Europe without Germany can-

[4] Greece and Turkey after a time also became members of NATO, thus completing the European, or Western, arc of Russian containment. The encirclement of the Soviet Union has been extended into Asia through CENTO (Central Treaty Organization), which covers the Middle East, and SEATO (Southeast Asia Treaty Organization), which extends to the Philippines.

not have any meaning. Some things will therefore have to be said about the special case of Germany. But before doing this it may be well to consider another special case—Great Britain.

Britain and Europe

Britain had gone through the war in most honorable fashion, in moral terms more so than anybody else, if one thinks of her role in 1940. Appropriately at the end of the war she was one of the Big Three, alongside the United States and the Soviet Union. Her wartime leader, Churchill, had done a magnificent job of both leading and representing her, and he certainly intended that Britain should maintain her place in the world; he had asserted, among other things, that he had not assumed his current position in order to preside over the liquidation of the British Empire. Britain at home is but another European state, roughly comparable to some others, but empire had put her in a category apart. But Churchill was also a realist, who understood power, and had during the war deferred to both Roosevelt and Stalin. It is of great significance that the election of 1945 in Britain, with the war just finished in Europe but not yet in the Pacific, resulted in the rejection of his leadership and the advent for the first time of Labour in unfettered control of the country. This, in the simplest form, expressed the fact that the prime focus of concern of the mass of the British people was looking inward toward domestic issues. Quite properly, since it was its mandate, the Labour government inaugurated a great program of social reform and nationalization.

Foreign policy had lost none of its importance, but it tended nevertheless to receive second priority, certainly when it came to the taking of large initiatives. As proved to be the case, one could expect from the Labour government genuine support of the United Nations and a liberal policy toward empire. The control of India was relinquished in 1947, to the accompaniment of some perhaps wishful thinking that this might be no more than another step along the well-established path of liberalization that would serve to maintain the reality of the Commonwealth.

But there was another factor at work, and it was essentially national rather than associated with party. Distrust and often profound dislike of Germany ran deep in Britain instead of the soft sentimentality that prevailed soon after the First World War. In terms of power and position, Britain did not feel that she was in the same category as other European powers. In this connection the French wartime performance was highly significant; Britain did not after all belong in the club of the defeated. While it might be nearer the mark to say that the very cost of victory had caused Britain an injury comparable to France's in the First World War, it is hardly surprising that a clear perception of this should have been lacking in Britain.

There were, scattered in a variety of quarters, those who hoped that just because of her standing, yet combined with diminution, Britain immediately after the war might assert a bold leadership in bringing Europe together. We do not know what might have happened had she tried, but it is not unreasonable to think that such leadership would have been welcome to Europe in her prostrate condition, and that not a few Europeans might even have been willing to become in a sense "annexed" to Britain. Such a prospect would at least seem far less objectionable than union under either Nazi or Soviet control. In any case it was not done. The weariness of war and the deep traditional consciousness of separateness combined to prevent Britain from seizing what may have been a unique opportunity. Subsequent ones would be missed as well, as we shall presently see. The Anglo-French Treaty of Dunkirk of May 1947 was little more than a revival of the prewar alliance and had the same anti-German focus, although a year later its scope was somewhat enlarged with the inclusion of the three Benelux countries in the Treaty of Brussels.

The consciousness was deep among Europeans that the fate of the old Continent had been settled by essentially external forces, and this tended to create a common desire to avoid being at the mercy of such forces, especially as it became increasingly clear that the two superpowers were drifting into a relationship of sharp rivalry. Picking up older threads, a movement was taking shape promoted by the efforts of a variety of groups and associations. The European Movement may be said to have been launched with the meeting at The Hague, in May 1948, of the International Committee of Movements for European Unity, which was attended by some eight hundred delegates from sixteen countries. As early as September 1946, Churchill had accepted the chairmanship of the movement; he had expressed enthusiastic support for it, though even he was not free of the usual British reluctance to make things too precise. It is significant, nevertheless, that the Hague meeting was simultaneous with the signature of the Treaty of Brussels, and that a month before in Paris the creation of the OEEC (Organization for European Economic Cooperation) had brought the Marshall Plan into formal existence.

The connection and the difference between the limited economic and defensive aspects, and the broader possibilities contained in these arrangements was not clearly defined, and in the discussions that followed the Hague congress the British dislike of assuming far-reaching commitments toward the Continent was again in evidence. But the Consultative Council established by the Treaty of Brussels was able to effect a compromise between British and French proposals that led to the signature of the Statute of the Council of Europe, in London, in May 1949. Italy, the Scandinavian countries, and the Irish Republic joined the initial Brussels combination, thus bringing together an appreciable segment of Europe.

The Council of Europe was organized in the normal representative pattern of two organs—a committee of foreign ministers and a Consultative Assembly. The more optimistically inclined saw in this the prefiguration of an authentic future European parliament. Its first session was held in Strasbourg, in the late summer of 1949, when the admission of Germany was the most important issue considered. As mentioned before, there is no meaning to "Europe," even in the most restricted sense, unless Germany is included in it. But it is not surprising that, in 1949, feeling toward Germany should still be such as to militate against her acceptance. The matter was put off for the time being.

France, Germany, and the Franco-German Relationship

But if Europe, any Europe, exclusive of Germany is an impossible conception, geography alone clearly dictates that Europe without France is even more impossible. France had now reason both to fear and to dislike Germany even more than three decades earlier. But because of the events of the war, France did not now command the place of importance that had been hers after the earlier conflict. By contrast, if in America there was little love lost for Germany, there was also no fear. Instead, America was now primarily concerned with the containment of the Communist threat. In American eyes the reconstruction of power in Europe, her economic recovery first of all (*vide* the Marshall Plan), were consequently desirable, even pressing, ends. Germany, from the American standpoint, was as much a part of Europe as were France and others, and the local details of Franco-German and other relations rated but a relative minimum of attention. Germany was still the defeated enemy, divided and under occupation, with whom formal peace had not been made[1]; yet Germany contained much potential that could not be simply dragooned. Neither could France, weak as she was, be coerced beyond a certain point. This is the proper place to say something of Germany and of France and of the Franco-German relationship. If Europe can have no meaning without either France or Germany, clearly some sort of solution of the Franco-German problem must be found.

The American initiative in bringing about the merger of the three western zones of Germany, the currency reform, and the organization of the Federal Republic have been indicated. As for Germany, even though she was on probation, it was inevitable, under any dispensation, that she should strive to recover her place. The emergence of Adenauer in control of Western Germany, who was dedicated to the building of a democratic Germany reintegrated into the mainstream of European civilization and culture from which she had departed, facilitated things. The comparison between Adenauer's role and that of Stresemann after the First World War is valid: both sought to restore the place of their country through a policy of conciliation and fulfillment. The American desire to reconstruct a German force that could be added to the rest of Europe's was obviously a highly valuable asset of German policy, though Adenauer did not seek to exploit it, and, where France was concerned, he did his best to create trust instead of fear. Although there were, especially among

[1] Reversing the procedure adopted after the First World War, peace was made first with the secondary, or satellite, enemies. With difficulty this was accomplished in 1947, except for the Austrian case, which was deferred until 1955. But peace with Germany, contingent upon the reunification of the country, has been held in abeyance.

the American military, thoughts of choosing *either* France *or* Germany as the pivot of American policy in Europe, with a possible preference for the latter, so divisive, not to say self-defeating, an endeavor was not pursued very far.

Adenauer was ever willing to make concessions to France which ran counter to German national feeling, in the Saar for example.[2] For this he gained French acquiescence in Germany's admission to the Council of Europe in 1951. However, the most promising line of development was not to come from that institution.

On the French side the war had, among other things, the effect of confirming the failure of the policy that France had adopted toward Germany after the First World War. Whether that policy had failed because of lack of power, or because of deficient will, or a combination of both, beyond a doubt it had failed. An attempted return to it seemed an unpromising prospect, especially once it appeared that America was bent on reviving German power. Yet the German problem remained. It is out of this dilemma that was born the ingenious initiative of the Schuman Plan.

The proposal may at first seem remote from our topic, yet it is very intimately connected with it. The point of it was the integration of the coal and steel production of France and Germany. Launched in 1950, the treaty was signed a year later, in April 1951 that brought into existence the European Coal and Steel Community. This treaty joined, in addition to France and Germany, Italy and the three Benelux countries. The subject was economic, but in many minds the economic aspect was not the most important, although its significance

[2] France endeavored again, as in 1919, to detach the Saar from Germany. This attempt led to long and intricate negotiations and a variety of proposals, but the issue was finally eliminated with the French acquiescence in the reintegration of the Saar into Germany in 1955.

should not be minimized. The advantages of a large free trade area need no explanation. The structure of the Coal and Steel Community is fairly involved. It consists of four elements: a High Authority, empowered to make decisions and recommendations; a Council of Ministers, made up of delegates of the governments; an Assembly, which controls the High Authority, and in which representation is on a proportional basis; and, finally, a Court of Justice. Of the greatest importance is the fact that the powers of the High Authority entail the surrender by the participating governments of some aspects of sovereignty, and this set a most unorthodox precedent. This was indeed the deliberate intent of the sponsors of the Schuman Plan.

It was in a sense an ingenious attempt to solve the Franco-German problem by creating a state of affairs where war between the two countries would be made very difficult, if not wholly impossible, through the "scrambling" of their production of two such vital commodities as coal and steel. This aspect of the matter was important enough, but the experiment, if successful, could be enlarged to include other sectors of the economies. It will be noted, moreover, that the scheme involved six countries, not just Germany and France; also, the political implications were large and were in fact uppermost in the minds of its makers. The name of the plan comes from that of the French Foreign Minister at the time, Robert Schuman, who indeed shared these views and hopes. But credit for the idea belongs as much to Jean Monnet as to anyone else. To repeat, here was an imaginatively novel approach to the old problem of French security; no doubt it did seek to capitalize to a degree on French advantage vis-à-vis Germany, yet for Germany it also meant much, and, to repeat again, beyond the limited Franco-German problem, and beyond the limitation to two commodities, coal and steel, the deeper motivation was that of the making of Europe. Finally, it should be noted that the initiative was largely French and that the British evinced little interest in the scheme, a significant aspect to which there will be occasion to return.

The Schuman Plan was a first step, imaginative and full of significance. As a first step, it might or might not be followed by others, and indeed it might even be undone. Such forward-looking men as Monnet and Schuman were in many respects ahead of their country's opinion, which they were seeking to coax along an untried path. To seek solution of the Franco-German problem first was a proper approach to a solution of the larger problem of Europe, because the two countries involved are the most important states of the Continent and their differences have been the source of so much trouble for all. But mechanical schemes would probably founder unless a change took place at the deeper level of feelings.

There was soon occasion to test the lack of sufficient confidence in France. It was in response to the American desire to add the asset of German force that long discussions took place and a variety of proposals were produced. There is no point in rehearsing them in detail; it will suffice to say that a treaty was signed in May 1952 that created the European Defense Community. But the French signature to it was given with reluctance, and the French Parliament gave its prior consent only after hedging it with conditions and reservations. France was not ready to be reconciled to German rearmament of any sort, and fearful governments put off the day of ratification lest parliament give a negative answer. France was out of line with others and the patience of all was being tried until finally the energetic and decisive Mendès-France undertook to put an end to the uncertainty. He himself was unenthusiatic about the arrangement and he sought some modification of it, which he failed to obtain from the other participants. He met with little but impatient annoyance, understandable in the light of the drawn-out French tergiversation, and submitted the treaty to parliament where it went down in defeat.

There was abroad, not least in the United States, combined dismay and irritation; after so much patient forbearance, designed to accommodate French wishes, to have the result of so much effort destroyed seemed adequate cause for discouragement. Yet it was temporary, and the day was momentarily saved by the mediating intervention of the British Prime Minister, Anthony Eden. Discussions in London were shortly followed by the Paris Accords, which provided for the termination of the occupation régime in the Federal Republic. The Federal Republic, together with Italy, would be included in a Western European Union, an enlargement of the Brussels Treaty combination. The outcome may not appear devoid of irony, for it constituted a major step in the rehabilitation of Germany, especially if one considers that it provided for her rearmament as well as her membership in NATO, whose ultimate control of her forces was the sole guarantee against their independent use.

The success of the new arrangement obviously depended upon its acceptance in both Germany[3] and France. With difficulty, ratification was obtained from both, and the path was opened thereafter for whatever course the future might disclose. It may seem strange that France, after having wrecked EDC, should accept a potentially less favorable compromise. The answer to this acquiescence is to be found in the current condition of France, which was outwardly dif-

[3] There was in Germany at this time very qualified enthusiasm for the reconstruction of armed force, which in fact proceeded at a very slow pace. This, however, proved to be but a momentary lag, and by the beginning of the next decade Germany's was the largest European force in existence.

ficult and therefore minimized her ability to make her weight felt. These difficulties were of two kinds, quite distinct though by no means unrelated.

After the liquidation of the wartime Vichy régime France had experienced difficulty in putting her political house in order. A new constitution, laboriously adopted by a minority vote, had installed the Fourth Republic, which was soon said to be but a more awkward version of the Third. The easygoing ways of that régime may have been well enough suited to days of relative normality; it had even survived a great war, though not the defeat of a second. New political formations appeared—the Catholic *Mouvement Républicain Populaire* and the Gaullist *Rassemblement du Peuple Français* for example—but it proved more difficult than ever to produce stable governments, and ministerial crises seemed to become even more frequent and more recalcitrant to resolution than they had been in the past. In 1946 General de Gaulle had withdrawn in disgust and, in contrast with the British management, French finances offered the dreary spectacle of repetition of their immediate prewar course.

Moreover, the termination of hostilities in Europe had not meant peace for France, who soon found herself involved in imperial difficulties. But in any case it appeared that France in the mid-fifties might not be in a good position to play even an adequate role in Europe, let alone one of leadership. Germany by contrast seemed to be in better health, for it was becoming evident that the stunned prostration which had followed defeat was but a passing phase rather than a lasting condition. Peace was not made with Germany, as initially intended, and instead Germany became the battleground of the Cold War. This, however, did not mean continued disorder. As the lines of the contest between the Soviet Union and the United States became drawn with sharper clarity, especially after the attempted Soviet blockade of Berlin in 1948 and the outbreak of war in Korea, it became clear that Germany was the locale of two separate states. As we have seen, America strove to restore the western part, with economic assistance and through the fusion of the three western zones of occupation. Once this was done the Federal Republic, West Germany, emerged for all practical purposes as another full-fledged European state. It was a much reduced Germany—the ironic outcome of senseless Hitlerian ambition—and it was even burdened by the influx of more than ten million refugees, from East Germany and from other parts of Europe, Poland and the Sudetenland for example, from which Germans had now been expelled. But in the end even this influx proved an asset rather than a liability, and one began to hear about the German "miracle." The more attractive qualities of the German character—order, discipline, the capacity for work—had not been destroyed by the war; they now began to reassert themselves until one was reminded of the quip that whereas most people work in order to live, work is the chief objective of the Germans' existence.

In any case the combination of German application with outside, mainly American, assistance had the effect of marked revival; out of the rubble and destruction a new Germany arose which resumed the momentarily interrupted practice of sending the output of her factories to the far corners of the world in successful competition with others. Gold accumulated in Germany and the Deutsche Mark was before long to become a harder currency than even the American dollar, increasingly drained of its gold backing.[4] One is also reminded

4 Within roughly a decade of the end of the war, recovery had been such that the United States was confronted with an increasingly competitive position. The dimensions of its favorable balance of trade were severely reduced and no longer sufficed to make up for other American foreign commitments and expenditures.

of the phenomenon that had occurred thirty years earlier, when the Dawes Plan had inaugurated an era of German prosperity such that the contrast between conditions on either side of the Rhine was cause for the wry query as to who had, in fact, won the war.

But things were also different. If there was point to the parallel between Stresemann and Adenauer, in so far as both strove to restore their country through a policy of fulfillment and a Western orientation—and granting that the shape of the unborn future is unknown—there seemed to be little question of the authenticity of the new Chancellor's desire.

The economic rebirth of Germany may be seen as a recurrence, or a continuation, of the trend that has been characteristic of Germany for a long time, particularly since her unification almost a century ago. The change across the Rhine was fundamentally of deeper significance; for if the politics and the finances of the Fourth Republic tended to convey a picture of ineffectual continuity, they concealed a deeper reality that has by now become quite apparent. How and why change should have been initiated in France is a highly interesting question, the analysis of which may be left to various brands of social science. We may remain content with noting that change did occur, beginning roughly at the time of the Second World War. Humiliating as defeat may have been, and burdensome as were German wartime exactions, not to mention the physical damage which was in its total greater than in the earlier war, the last war had at least a clarifying effect; for one thing, it certainly did not place France in a false position of power.

But already during the war a band of men, many of them young economists, had been quietly at work on plans for reconstruction. Here again the name of Jean Monnet stands at the fore though there are many others. This work was fruitful, and behind the seemingly shaky façade of its politics the Fourth Republic caused—or allowed—to be initiated a far-reaching renovation of the French economy, in combination with a measured dosage of nationalization and an extension of the social reforms that the prewar Popular Front had inaugurated. Incomplete though it still is, the modernization of French industry and agriculture achieved marked results, breaking through the traditional conservatism and relative backward timidity characteristic of much of French enterprise. The ability of French steel to compete with German in Germany has properly been noted as a concrete symbol of the change that was taking place.

This would seem to have been, in part at least, the consequence of psychological modification, even more clearly registered in the demographic situation. The French had preceded other peoples in achieving stability of population, a condition reflected in the fact that they were probably the oldest nation on earth in terms of the age median of the population. It used to be the general prediction of demographers before the war that economically developed countries were all tending toward a similar pattern, a prediction everywhere invalidated after the war. But the significance of this is especially relevant in the French case because it meant the reversal of a trend long established and thought to have been permanent.

For want of better words, and in default of adequate causal analysis, one must speak of a new spirit in France. This new spirit made possible the imaginative approach to the solution of the German problem adumbrated in the above-mentioned Schuman Plan. But the integration of sectors of diverse national industries could only achieve desirable results if a rough parity of position existed between them, and there were indeed those who foresaw in the arrangement the wedge of an eventual German dominance; hence it was highly desirable to raise the French level.

The sequence is significant of the coming into effect of the Schuman Plan in 1952, followed by the French rejection of EDC a year later. This rejection bespoke French uncertainty and fear; yet it is also worth noting the altered tone of the Franco-German relationship in a larger context. If there is no love lost on the French side, there is also little trace of the intense feeling toward Germany that was characteristic of the post-First World War period; and if German visitors to France are no novelty, large numbers of French travelers, especially the young, in Germany are indeed an innovation.

The Common Market—and the European Free Trade Association

This is the climate that made possible the meeting that took place in Messina, in June 1955, where it may be said that the seeds of the European Economic Community were planted. Already the preceding December the Common Assembly of the European Coal and Steel Community had called for the study of possible extensions of the community's function, and this was emphasized by its proposal the following May that further steps be taken toward European integration. When the foreign ministers met in Messina they had before them three governmental memoranda, from the Benelux countries, from Germany, and from Italy, respectively—one will note the French abstention. Out of this came the appointment of a committee made up of national representatives, appropriately placed under the presidency of Paul-Henri Spaak, sometimes dubbed "Mr. Europe." For Spaak was a sincere believer in European integration, in pursuing which he did not allow, like some others, his socialist convictions to create suspicion from the fact that much of the leadership of the movement was in Catholic hands; it was in fact the weight of his influence which contributed to the conversion of the reluctant German Social Democrats.

The degree of consensus that prevailed at the highest level, that of the foreign ministers, who used their influence to prod instead of hinder the work of the committee, was highly significant. Thus they adopted the so-called Spaak Report, and the committee was entrusted with the further task of elaborating draft treaties. This, considering the complexity of the matter, was done with expeditiousness, and on March 25, 1957 these treaties were signed in Rome; they came into force on January 1, 1958, following their intervening ratification.

This is in brief the story of the birth of the European Economic Community, usually known as the Common Market. In view of their importance a few words must be said about the possibly epoch-making Rome agreements.[5] In addition to the EEC proper, the Common Market in the narrow sense, a European Atomic Energy Community (Euratom) was established; also it was provided that a single assembly and court would serve for the three organizations, the Common Market, the Coal and Steel Community, and Euratom, absorbing those organs which had so far existed for the Schuman Plan alone.

The Rome agreements therefore must be seen as the culmination of a long and steady process, of the aims and direction of which the promoters were highly conscious. None had been more persistently assiduous in this endeavor than Jean Monnet himself, whose efforts deservedly have earned him the title "father of Europe." It was in order to devote

[5] In view of the nature of the present treatment no attempt will be made to go into a detailed discussion of the technical aspects of the Common Market and its operation. Such discussions can be found in many places, some of which are indicated in the bibliography.

his energies to this work of European integration that Monnet, in October 1955, had organized the Action Committee for the United States of Europe and had resigned from his post with the Coal and Steel Community. Devoid of official position, from his residence in Paris, he quietly but with un-relenting steadiness of purpose furnished the guiding hand and energy that were needed.

The crowning of his efforts by the success registered in the Rome agreements was greatly aided by the fact that he was moving with a larger tide.[6] Not the least significant aspect of European integration lies in what may be seen as a common consciousness, even if dimly perceived in many quarters, of the necessity for Europe to unite if she were to maintain her place in the world. "Unite or Perish," as Reynaud had put it, if dramatic in form, was fundamentally sound in judgment. The Common Market was not the work of starry-eyed idealists of the Mazzini type, but of men whose feet were firmly planted in the solid realities of economics. If it is true that Monnet and his followers were looking far ahead to an ultimate goal of political union, they were for the moment content to deal with more concrete and limited matters. The lesson of the German *Zollverein* may be appropriately recalled at this point.

The heart of the Rome agreements was the creation of a free-trade community among the six initial participants. Clearly such a result could not be accomplished by a mere stroke of the pen, for it would have induced too drastic disturbances in the respective national economies. The final aim therefore of the total elimination of tariffs among the Six was set for

[6] The idea of integration may be said to have been in the air. In addition to the already established grouping of Benelux, which had brought together Holland, Belgium, and Luxembourg as early as 1947, a variety of combinations was being talked about—Finabel, Fritalux, and others, the Common Market combination of the Six being the one that was eventually realized.

the end of the following decade, that point to be reached through agreed steps of gradual reduction. Nor was there lack of doubting Thomases, most prominent perhaps among the representatives of French industry, a fact which lends added significance to the French contribution in the leadership of the experiment.

For clearly here was an experiment, and its ultimate fate was in the lap of the future. After the passing of the better part of a decade that fate is not yet sealed, but before looking at subsequent developments it is worth pausing for a while to indulge in some considerations about the state of affairs at the time of the launching of the experiment, the year 1958.

One may well see a connection between what was done in Rome in 1957 and both the Marshall Plan of ten years earlier and the North Atlantic Alliance of 1949. These last two, it will be noted at once, were to a large extent American initiatives; both looked to Europe outside the Russian domain, as a whole, and in both cases the American and the European motivation of defense was strong. What happened in Rome was a more purely internal European development, and in Rome there were only six European states. This calls for some comment.

The German *Zollverein* has been mentioned, yet the validity of it as a precedent or parallel may seem open to question. For if undoubtedly the free-trade area that was the *Zollverein* had been a valuable asset to the economic development of Germany, it is significant that the participants in it shared the political fact of common nationality. That the larger free-trade area of the Six should be, eventually at least, of common benefit to all seemed a reasonable expectation, but it was not so predictably beneficial where nationality was concerned. Especially when it came to France and Germany there is no need to stress the familiar record of strife between the two; whether shared material advantage could eventually suffice to overcome profound national difference and deep-rooted rivalry was at best an open question—hence the importance, indicated before, of the future evolution of the Franco-German relationship.

Secondly, the Six, which in combination embrace an area reminiscent of Charlemagne's empire, are but a part of Europe, which contains much else in addition, most important by far the United Kingdom. The original scope of the makers of Europe, men like Monnet himself, was by no means confined to so limited an horizon as encompassed by the Six alone. In the French case, for instance, the tendency had rather been, especially in political matters, to seek the British association, for added protection, if necessary, against a too strong a Germany. However, despite sweet utterings about the blessings of European unity, when it came to the test, the traditional insularity of the island kingdom proved more than could be overcome. It mattered little in the last resort whether Britain was ruled by a Conservative or a Labour government—the prospect of becoming "a province of Europe" was one that deeply ran against the British grain. This should not be very surprising, for it is nothing more than expression of the very special position that Britain has occupied in relation to the whole European continent, more particularly of the long arbitral record of British power that had prospered from, and fostered, continental divisions. If the association with France before both wars had been expression of the decline of British power, or at least of the margin possessed by that power for more than a century, the vicissitudes of the last war had again the effect of emphasizing British separateness. And if the wartime position of Britain as one of the Big Three did not in fact correspond to the realities of the postwar relationships of power—Britain, too, had needed American assistance—one can readily understand the lag in thinking and in the adaptation to the altered circumstances of the British milieu.

The fact is that Britain in effect looked askance at the continental tendency to combination, partly in fear, partly in skepticism of the possibility of success of the movement, although there were those, more farsighted, who took another view in Britain. Thus Britain had not joined in that first successful manifestation of the integrating movement in Europe that had been the organization of the Coal and Steel Community in 1952. Then came the Treaties of Rome in 1957, and although the British had closely followed the discussions, Britain was not among the original members of the Common Market.

Should the operation succeed despite British skepticism, a possibly troublesome question arose, for which again the German *Zollverein* could furnish a precedent. If the *Zollverein* had been a great asset to Germany, in political no less than in economic terms, its integrating benefits had not extended beyond the German borders; instead of this the German free-trade area had generally turned protectionist vis-à-vis the outside—just as had the American, for that matter. Might not a free-trade area embracing the Six do precisely the same thing, especially as it envisaged the adoption of a common tariff toward the outside world?

Britain alone remains a very important commercial nation, whose exchanges with some others are of crucial importance to them. One recalls the formation of the sterling bloc when the pound went off gold in 1931. Britain's response to the emergence of the Europe of the Six was the organization of the Europe of the Seven, comprising in addition to herself the three Scandinavian countries, Switzerland, Austria, and Portugal. It must be borne in mind that the division did not occur before extensive negotiations had taken place between the Common Market and Britain. These failed, however, mainly because the Six found it impossible to accede to what appeared to them excessive British demands for a privileged position. Again in this one should see a reflection of the peculiarities of the British situation—Commonwealth associations for instance—for, rather than look to limiting restrictions, the founders of the Six looked to free trade among themselves as a preliminary to further and closer integration. Theirs and the British outlook were authentically divergent. In any case the signature, in November 1959, of the Convention of Stockholm, which was promptly ratified, brought into existence the European Free Trade Association, EFTA for short, the Europe of the Seven. When this happened the Common Market was already well launched, having at the beginning of the year implemented the contemplated first step in tariff reduction among its six members. Would Europe, even a reduced Europe consisting of the part of it outside the area of direct Soviet control, find itself, to use the title of a recent book, at Sixes and Sevens?[7]

We do not know the answer, but it may be suitable to use the closing pages of this essay for a discussion and analysis of what has happened since 1957 and the significance of these happenings for the possible development of the integration of Europe.

IV. Prospects and Possibilities

Since its formal coming into existence, on January 1, 1958, the European Economic Community has belied the doubts and reservations of skeptics, and the economies of its members have continued to grow at faster rates than either the American or the British. Also, the exchanges among its members have increased in notable fashion, by more than 60 per

[7] Benoit, Emile, *Europe at Sixes and Sevens* (New York, 1961).

cent during the first four years of its existence. Thus it became
the fashion to sing the praises of the Common Market and
to credit it in large measure with the economic prosperity of
its members. Perhaps this is unwarranted, and we may have
a situation where it is difficult to distinguish with assurance
between cause and effect.

For it is easy to point out that the economies of the Six
had been growing at a substantial rate even before they decided to join and that the rising pace of their mutual exchanges
had been no slower during the years preceding 1958. Especially if one recalls the reaction to the advent of the Great
Depression, the *sauve qui peut* which had led all to seek
the deceptive shelter of economic nationalism, the raising of
impediments to international exchanges, one is tempted to
feel that the fact of expanding economies made easier the
adoption of a more liberal approach to trade.

But it may not matter too much whether we can with cer-
tainty disentangle the causal connection between the two
phenomena, and perhaps much credit for current prosperity
should go to a better understanding of the operation of economics. Certainly Keynesian ideas have converted much of
the economic fraternity, though there have been appreciable
differences in the manner of management in different countries. Rapid recovery, followed by expansion to levels substantially above those of the prewar period, was the similar
consequence of a variety of methods: British austerity and
Labour rule in Britain; a much less stringently controlled,
hence financially more chaotic, situation in France; the task
that Erhard did in Germany; and what was done in Belgium
and in Italy. All were, especially at first, powerfully assisted
by a massive and generous American assistance, a rare case
of enlightened self-interest, and all adopted a combination
of free enterprise with planning, in varying proportions but
in marked degree, directed by the state. Analysis of all this

may be left to the debates of economists and academicians.

What may well matter more are two things. One is the fact that if the process of integration and "scrambling" continues along the path it has so far successfully pursued, a point of no return might be reached. Powerful interests, not least those of private enterprise, some of which were initially reluctant, will have been enlisted, and the "nationality" of an enterprise may become an increasingly difficult matter to determine. This, to be sure, is not a simple process, and it is only natural that the greatest difficulty should have been encountered in the agricultural sector, where the conservative, individualistic peasant is hardest to convince.

The other fact, already indicated before, is that the instigators of economic integration—Monnet, Spaak, Hallstein, and their ilk—are looking far beyond what they envisage as a necessary preliminary step toward the much larger goal of the political making of Europe. That the internecine quarrels of Europe have led to the defeat of all and to the loss by Europe of her place in the world is hard to gainsay. And if one think of the British exception to the fact of actual defeat in the limited military sense, it may easily be retorted that the emphasis should rather be placed on the real damage, the very cost of victory, that the war had caused Britain. If the prewar British appeasers may properly be charged with the onus of failure, their basic motivation was sound in so far as it stemmed from the judgment that from war, even if ultimately successful, Britain could only reap hurt and diminution.

The British Position

The uniqueness and peculiarity of the British position cannot be overemphasized. The roots of it reach far into the past. Unlike all other European states, Britain has not had the experience of enemy forces on her soil for nine hundred years, a fact which in the last analysis is a consequence of simple geography, her island position. This has powerfully contributed to the creation of an insular mentality; the British consciousness of difference has a flavor that is wholly *sui generis* in comparison with that of other nationalisms. In more recent times the consciousness of difference has further been confirmed by the primacy of British power. This, to be sure, has been of shorter duration than the immunity from invasion, yet it has lasted long enough also to strike deep roots among the British people; moreover, for a time at least, it obtained recognition from others.

Thus, from the British point of view, the Second World War could be seen as in considerable measure the repetition of a familiar phenomenon—the successful defeat of a dangerous bid for hegemony on the Continent. Hitler, the Kaiser, Napoleon, Philip II were but successive embodiments of the same recurring threat. To be sure there were differences, not only among the impersonators, but in Britain herself, and to these the British people, reputedly hard-headed and practical, were not wholly blind.

But here a distinction is necessary. Where the bare facts of power are concerned, the awareness of relative diminution can already be perceived toward the end of the nineteenth century; it is what began to draw Britain out of her isolation before 1914 and placed her increasingly in the same defensive position as France before 1939. This condition, however, if it registered at the level of some at least of the directors of British foreign policy, does not invalidate the psychological factor of consciousness of difference and uniqueness of position, one that is deeply rooted in the mass and from which much of the leadership is also far from immune. Moreover, there have always been, even in the heyday of empire, little Englanders in England. The modern rise of the mass, the spread of the franchise, have given this last tendency added strength. Labour has been critical of imperialism and an advocate of internationalism. At least it has been so officially and where verbal expression is involved, for at the psychological level Labour has been, if anything, even more provincial and suspicious of the outside than its political rivals.

It is out of this situation that were born the ambiguities of British policy after the Second World War. Because of the importance of Britain, in the world at large and without question in Europe, something must be said about them. The first reaction of the British electorate after the war was to repudiate the wartime leadership of Churchill. The chief significance of that decision, in the present context, lies in the emphasis that it placed on a domestic, inward-looking approach.

Where empire was concerned the British people proceeded —through the Labour government first, but the returned Conservatives have continued the same policy—to belie Churchill's wartime boast mentioned before. The relinquishment of India in 1947 was the most striking single manifestation of the new orientation; it could be regarded as but a continuation of the liberal policy that goes from the 1867 Dominion of Canada Act to the Statute of Westminster of 1931. But here something went wrong. Though fully independent and sovereign, India and Pakistan, technically at least, retained the Commonwealth connection. This precedent was followed by the major part of the other areas that have subsequently emerged into independent statehood out of the vast British complex. The more favorable or optimistic view was that this world-encompassing complex that may be called British was merely continuing along its evolutionary course. But the question must be raised at this point of the reality of the content of Commonwealth, and it seems difficult to avoid any but a negative answer.

Even among the older dominions—those of primarily British

settlement, as Canada and Australia for example—if the sentiment of Britishness remains strong, the facts of power have not failed to register. Like it or no, Canada has been increasingly sucked into the American orbit, and certainly her defense, like that of Australia or New Zealand, must primarily depend on American power. This is a simple and inevitable manifestation and consequence of the shift in the relative places that British and American power have come to occupy in the world.

There is more. The rest of the states that constitute the Commonwealth are of predominantly non-European composition. They represent a wide range of economic and political development, and though they have retained many of the outward forms of British institutions, the meaning of these forms is often questionable, while the use of them has been seriously strained. Also, the foci of their interests are widely divergent, their clearest common ground sometimes consisting in their common devotion to the demise of imperial control—a situation clearly registered in the manner of their voting in the United Nations.

The case of South Africa deserves special mention, for it illustrates with sharpness the strength of the disintegrating force in the Commonwealth. The Union of South Africa has adopted, under the name of *apartheid,* a strongly racialist policy of discrimination, which has naturally been highly unpalatable to others, particularly to the non-white members of the Commonwealth. These now constitute a majority, and South Africa was, in 1961, expelled from the Commonwealth. The point is not the rights and wrongs of South African domestic policy, but rather that the broader principle of association in difference, however great, was rejected in favor of a far more limited one, morally meritorious though it may have been, of racial equality. Here was perhaps the most concrete example of the disintegrating wedge that had entered the Commonwealth.

Britain retains many important economic positions and much trade with the Commonwealth, and her acceptance of devolution unlimited may be commended for its wisdom. This does not alter the fact that an experiment seems to have failed. The failure may even be regretted, for the possibility seemed to exist for a time that a world-encompassing association of most varied peoples, freely contrived, and which some thought to have sounder roots than such more ambitious devices as Leagues of Nations or United Nations, might have come into existence. One might even go further and say that far worse things could have happened to the world as a whole than to have fallen under a common rule the guiding hand and heart of which would have been British. At all events that is apparently not to be and the Pax Britannica has gone the way of the Pax Romana.

A vicious circle is involved where the decline of British power gives a boost to the disintegrating force, the effects of which in turn further diminish the British position. This condition might in itself have been expected to throw Britain back upon her nearer European background and connections. But the effects of so vast and radical a change, not surprisingly, are slow in registering. Thinking in terms of Commonwealth, world-wide association, more particularly that limited aspect of it that includes the English-speaking peoples, most of all the relatively new American giant, have contributed to color much of the British outlook at all levels. This, and the outcome of the war, the emergence of Britain as one of the Big Three, in contrast with the defeated collectivity of Europe, have served to emphasize, in British eyes, the separateness of Britain. Here was the supreme irony whereby victory was from one point of view highly injurious.

However that may be, the fact remains that the background just sketched had much to do with the previously mentioned failure of Britain to exploit or seize some opportunities: those offered to her by the continental chaos immediately after the war, by the birth of the Coal and Steel Community in 1952 and by that of the Common Market in 1957. Thus, in 1959, Europe, even reduced free Europe, was split between the Six and the Seven.

The initial success of the Common Market has also been indicated. In contrast Britain seemed to be doing less well economically. Britain, like others, had recovered from the war, and the standard of living of her people rose above prewar heights. Nevertheless, her rate of growth appeared to be markedly slower, and the position of the pound seemed recurrently threatened. The impact of her altered position in the world, the continuing uncertainties of her economic condition, and the example of the Six across the Channel finally combined to induce a major step on her part: in August 1961 Britain applied for membership in the Common Market. It was also understood that her acceptance would entail the fusion of the Six and the Seven.

Whether or not, as has been suggested, the application was mainly motivated by the search for an issue and a possible success in the foreign domain on the part of a Conservative administration aware of the decline of its popularity, the application intensified the debate in Britain. There had been all the while those who had favored the continental connection and who had now for their view the official action of the government; yet the debate went on in somewhat unresolved fashion and among shifting moods of popular opinion. Meanwhile negotiations were taking place in Brussels between Britain and the Six; these were technical in large measure, their focus being an attempt to reconcile the stress on uniformity among the Six with the special position and interests of the British.

The discussion was lengthy, close, and laborious, the very duration of it tending to dampen the initial enthusiasm. Nevertheless, it was widely believed that grounds of difference were approaching the vanishing point, when a *coup de théâtre* put an abrupt end to the negotiations. In one of his occasional press interviews, always surrounded by suitable stage setting, General de Gaulle declared that Britain was not adequately prepared to join the rest of Europe and that he therefore was opposed to granting her petition.

Since the decisions of the Common Market demand unanimity, the French veto effectively put an end, at least for the time being, to the discussions in Brussels. The action of the French president created a sensation of the first magnitude in many quarters—in Britain most of all, where the sudden and harsh manner of it was taken as deliberate slight; among the rest of the Six, where it was said that matters had come close to agreement and sentiment was favorable to the acceptance of Britain, even if some compromise were needed; even in France there were voices of dissent. The American reaction of combined surprise and irritation was not the least intense. For America had taken a sympathetic view of the union of Europe, encouraged the development of the Common Market, and made clear her desire that Britain join it, even using the weight of her influence in the form of some pressure on Britain. The fact of the changed British position —her decline, if one will—was easier to perceive and accept in the United States than in Britain herself. To some degree, it may even be said that the American treatment of Britain was cavalier and unfeeling. For America, in her impatience to see Europe unite, was understandably prone to underrate and minimize the differences among Europeans in favor of realistic, if perhaps rather crude, considerations of power. To be sure, some form of European integration might eliminate that troublesome factor of internecine European quarrels which, in American eyes, still "are not our quarrels." This could be useful to all, not least to Europeans themselves, but America focused too narrowly on the desirability of organizing power in Europe mainly with a view to the containment of the Russian danger. One is reminded in some ways of the previous case of the EDC, which also foundered, interestingly enough, on the rock of French opposition.

The French Position

Since the rejection of the British application and the resulting failure to fuse the Six and the Seven was clearly the result of a French action, it is necessary to say something of the French case and position. Without trying to delve into the distant past, the more immediate roots of the French situation go back to 1940 and the wartime experience. There is no cause or room in this discussion to rehearse the intricate and often confusing details of French developments since that time, yet a few things must be culled from the record.

However much one may resort to explanations and search for alleviating circumstances, the fact remains that for France the war was a deeply humiliating experience, which in addition did little to dissolve the differences between French and French. Things looked bright for a moment, when the passage through limbo that was Vichy France came to an end and the Free French led by de Gaulle took in their hands the reins of power. France was even accorded in the United Nations the position of privilege of which the veto power in the Security Council is expression. But in the case of France—as in that of China for that matter—the veto power was not the recognition of any existing power commensurate with that of the other three; it was in some respects a courtesy gesture, even possibly a wise one, the validity of which the future alone could justify or disprove.

For the rest France became the previously mentioned Fourth Republic. But the fact that the constitution of this new régime was finally adopted by a minority of the electorate, more in weariness than from positive conviction, may be regarded as manifestation of the uncertainty that prevailed in the French body politic as a whole. The quip one heard after a while, "The Fourth Republic is dead, long live the Third Republic!" and the title of the perceptive analysis by Swiss writer Herbert Luethy, *France Against Herself*,[1] were apt comments; the French may have insisted on asserting the high value of individualistic difference, as an entity France seemed to be out of line with others and unable to function in adequate fashion. The record of the politics of the Fourth Republic is hardly an inspiring one, and the management of public finances was such that France was repeatedly placed in the position of making calls on the patience, not to say the charity, of others.

In addition to this the Fourth Republic was beset by the difficulties of empire. Over the very long term the French colonial record, especially when it comes to relations with non-European peoples, compares not unfavorably with others —for example, the British. But this has no longer been the case in our century. The very insistence of the French on the aspect of non-discriminating assimilation has indeed successfully transferred to others certain aspects of French culture; it has in fact been so successful as to produce a class of people who have quite thoroughly absorbed such French values as the Rights of Man and the trinitarian slogan of the revolution

[1] The title of the original German version, *In Frankreich Uhren gehen anders*, which became in French, *A l'heure de son clocher*, is even more expressive of the apartness of France, seemingly immune from, or willfully rejecting, much of the modern world.

embody. Thus we come to the understandable paradox that French education has very effectively trained what in the twentieth century constitutes a reservoir and backbone of leadership of nationalist rebellion against French control.

On this condition the war itself had divergent effects. On the one hand it gave a fillip to both the desire and the prospects of colonial rebellion, while on the other it made France all the more reluctant to yield to the demands of such rebellion. The long-term background and the immediate circumstances explain to a considerable degree why Britain found it easier to yield India in 1947 than France to do the same in Indochina seven years later. But the result for France was, in the imperial domain, confusion that was the counterpart of ineffectual domestic operation. Some attempts at reorganizing the whole imperial structure into a French Union need not be considered, owing to their lack of success.

In fact, confusion is too mild a word. It is worth bearing in mind that since 1940, with a brief interval at most of two years, from 1945 to 1947, the year 1963 was the first in which France was wholly at peace. Trouble began in 1947 when the failure to reach an accommodation with the still moderate demands of Southeast Asian nationalism led to the outbreak of hostilities. In terms of the measurable components of power —material resources—France could subdue Indochina; but other, more elusive factors were involved, and the distant conflict was so unpopular in France herself that use could not even be made of the conscript army. Modern guerrilla warfare is for that matter not an easy task—the current woes of the United States, more powerful than France by far, in the very same locale are enlightening. In any case a long, confused, and in many ways sordid, struggle came to an end when, in the face of increasing difficulties and costs, the energetic Mendès-France succeeded in cutting the Gordian knot. After the manner of Korea, Vietnam was divided in two: the northern section became a Communist preserve, while the South, together with Laos and Cambodia, was launched upon an uncertain path of unstable neutral independence. Mendès-France also paved the way for the relinquishment of French control in both Tunisia and Morocco.

But the promising path of imperial devolution upon which France seemed at last to have embarked was soon brought to an end by domestic complications while the standard of revolt was raised in Algeria. This was an unusually difficult situation, for in Algeria there was no native governmental structure as in the neighboring Arab states; Algeria was instead, in terms of constitutional arrangements, an integral part of France. Moreover, Algeria had to a point become a land of European settlement, some 10 per cent of its population being of European extraction. Again in terms of measurable material resources France might be expected to subdue the rebellion. France indeed made an enormous effort, certainly a very costly one financially, and the bulk of the active part of the French Army became involved in Algeria.

THE FIFTH REPUBLIC

What is of relevance to this story about the Algerian rebellion—and the reason why it is mentioned—is that the peculiar conditions of the Algerian case caused it to have important repercussions in the metropolitan French milieu and in French politics. Perhaps most significant of all was the fact that the leaders of an army that had become embittered and disgruntled by a long succession of humiliations for which it tended to blame, not wholly without justice, the political leadership of the country, showed signs of taking things into its own hands. Thus the Algerian situation gave rise to a wholly different problem, that old perennial bugaboo of France, the place of the military in the state. The question of the point at which the individual conscience may justify disobedience to the commands of duly constituted authority is one that has troubled our time with special acuteness. In any case, Algeria and the army in politics finally brought France to a pass where the prospect of a military coup and the specter of civil war became concrete and immediate possibilities. This was in June 1958.

It was a tense moment and a difficult passage, an open clash being avoided by calling General de Gaulle out of his political exile to assume the Prime Ministership of the country; his past record and prestige made him the only person acceptable to all. Never a man to flinch in the face of danger or difficulty, de Gaulle was willing to undertake the task of salvation, but only on his own terms. That his assumption of power was constitutional it would be impossible to deny. But it is significant that parliament, having entrusted him with full powers for six months, entrusted him as well with the task of constitutional change. The Fourth Republic like the Third had died, voluntarily surrendering in the acknowledgment of its incapacity to deal with a situation. Shades of Vichy and Pétain, France, the continental home of democratic governance, seemed herself incapable of operating the system with success.

Thus the Fifth Republic was born, and it will suffice to say that its constitutional arrangements put very extensive powers in the hands of the executive. Inevitably, the memory of the Napoleonic performances could not but cross many minds, in France as well as outside. The details of French domestic affairs will not detain us, save as they may impinge upon our main theme—the unity of Europe—and on this more will have to be said.

Brief mention must also be made of the particular case of Algeria, out of which the change in France had occurred. Were it not full of much tragedy the tale might be summed up as a comedy of errors. Many—not least the near mutinous elements of the Army—thought that de Gaulle would save Algeria for France. Instead of this de Gaulle abandoned it. But it took four years to achieve that result, during which time the cruel war went on. The lag was due to the fact that it was necessary to educate French opinion to the inevitability of accepting abandonment, while the loyalty of the Army had to be maintained in the process, a most delicate operation. This called for the utmost skill in maneuvering and for all of de Gaulle's personal prestige. Little wonder that much bitterness was engendered and that several plots and attempts were aimed at his life, for some regarded him as guilty of no less than treason—for the second time in twenty years. In addition to relinquishing Algeria, de Gaulle went on to solve the rest of the French imperial problem through the simple but radical device of thorough liquidation. Though important economic and cultural connections remain,[2] especially with francophone Africa, the process of devolution has been more extensive than even the British.

At this point we may properly rejoin the story of the course and prospects of European integration. Since Europe without France is an empty concept, the French position inevitably is of paramount importance; understandably, it has been and is being, heatedly discussed. And since the observation is also fundamentally correct that de Gaulle is the master of France; since in addition, barring unforeseeable accident, he will retain his office until 1965 and is expected by many to succeed himself for another seven years, it is necessary to give him and his views some further consideration.

General de Gaulle remains, as he has always been, a highly

[2] It is worth mentioning that, in proportionate terms of national income, France is the country that contributes the largest share to foreign aid, substantially greater than the American proportion, for example.

controversial figure. The butt of frequent jibes, it is perhaps significant that even his sharpest critics often preface or conclude their attacks by granting him the attribute of greatness. De Gaulle is highly impervious to either jibes or the shifting sands of opinion, whether parliamentary or popular, nor is he given to confidences, preferring to exploit instead the effect of the impact of occasional oracular pronouncements. Of the asset of showmanship and his own inimitable style he is fully aware and a past master in their use.

He is often accused of delusions of grandeur, for himself and even more for his country, and the wartime American President's quip about the combination of Joan of Arc and Napoleon is familiar. That the quality of greatness appeals to General de Gaulle may be granted without question. It may be observed that the assertion of the possession of that attribute by America has nothing startling in it, any more than Churchill's wartime claim of it for England. It may also be mentioned in passing that the two English words "greatness" and "grandeur" have only one equivalent in the less rich French language, a fact that is sometimes the source of some confusion. With greatness goes a quality of nobility that need have no relation to delusions of grandeur. Since de Gaulle's pronouncements are often open to widely varying interpretations, one is reduced to speculation, but some possibly useful clues may be gathered from a brief glance at his past record and performance.

That General de Gaulle is of conservative background, an authentic adherent of the Catholic faith, and that for a career he chose the Army, are simple, well-known facts, as are the facts that he reads books and that he has a deep interest in as well as a highly developed sense of history; over his own literary style he also takes considerable pains, with impressive results. The First World War, when he was a young officer, gave him, through captivity, firsthand acquaintance

with the German milieu. Significant likewise is the fact that
in the interval between the wars, rather than resting content
with the contemplation of the French accomplishment and
preparing to fight the last war over again next time, he became one of the early advocates of the war of the future. As
it turned out his was a case of a prophet without honor in
his own land, where his voice was lost in the wilderness of
republican politics. In a Germany unhampered by the prestige
of victory and spurred instead by the necessity of reorganization, he found a more receptive audience. The merits of his
views were adequately tested in 1940, not least in France.
These observations seem to indicate valuable attributes of intelligence and open-mindedness in the French President.

De Gaulle's wartime record is also well known and the
quixotic gesture—as it appeared to many at the time—that he
made in June 1940 when he launched the Free French movement from London. Precisely because his power was largely
nonexistent, de Gaulle during the war was deliberately a most
difficult ally. Everyone knows Churchill's quip about the
Cross of Lorraine being the heaviest he had to bear, though
Churchill, unlike Roosevelt, understood and respected his
cantankerous associate. De Gaulle fought hard for recognition,
against heavy odds and the necessities of wartime allied politics. Another thing worth mentioning during this period is
the manner in which he contrived, amid the shoals and the
intrigues of French politics, in exile and especially later on in
Algiers, to emerge in a position of acknowledged control. That
operation, highly complex and not always necessarily pleas-
ant, points to political skill of a high order. One is in fact led
to suspect that General de Gaulle is primarily a political,
rather than a military, figure. His talents in the latter field
have been revealed and given full scope by the accidents of
the war and its aftermath. If one adds to this the consideration of the manner in which he dealt with the French empire

after 1958, the possibility presents itself that, rather than the monolithic, rigid, and intransigent character that he is often thought to be, de Gaulle is a highly flexible man, endowed with a keen sense of the possible. He is also a shrewd and skillful politician, aware that the unorthodoxy of his methods can be a useful asset.

De Gaulle returned to power in the same year that the Common Market came into existence, and it will be recalled that in some ways France had been the most hesitant participant entering the association. But it must also be stressed that the economic rejuvenation of France had taken place under the Fourth Republic, in spite of the confusing and uninspiring, and for that reason also misleading, record of its politics. The Fifth Republic thus was the beneficiary, rather than the creator, of a highly favorable situation, credit for which is often erroneously given to it. But the Fifth Republic also did two highly useful and important things. The devaluation of the franc that was one of its early actions greatly helped the French competitive position and the successful participation of France in the European Economic Community; this led in turn to widespread acceptance of the Common Market by French enterprise. In addition, putting French finances in order—not too difficult a task in view of French resources—has also been a highly valuable accomplishment. It may also be pointed out, in passing, that the French decision to embark upon the development of nuclear weapons is one with which de Gaulle had nothing to do since it dates from the Fourth Republic. De Gaulle, to be sure, found it highly congenial.

What matters, therefore, and can hardly be overstressed, is the basic fact of French economic recovery. When this is seen in the context of the changed demographic situation and the past record of French economic practice and thinking, the degree of change will appear to be very great and more significant perhaps than in the cases of Germany or Britain.

Britain, France, and Germany

But the making of Europe is in the last resort above all a political matter, and General de Gaulle is more sensitive to political than to economic considerations. We must therefore return to the political aspect of things among the Six, and between the Six and the Seven, more particularly Britain.

Despite a certain recent slackening in its rate of expansion, the Europe of the Six has continued to prosper and there is reason to believe that the mutual benefits of the association will prove a strong enough incentive to hold it on its path of further integration. Operation is at times difficult, which is hardly surprising in view of the multiplicity of interests that have to be adjusted in compromise, but it seems fair to put emphasis on the fact that at the eleventh hour—sometimes a little later—agreement somehow is reached. The case of the discussion of agricultural problems, the most difficult of all to adjust, at the end of 1963, and the relative ease and rapidity with which agreement was reached on that occasion belied the prophets of gloom who had foreseen disaster for the Common Market.

One hears nevertheless a good deal—perhaps overmuch in America—about a measure of difference between France and the rest of the Six. In simplest form the issue centers around the fear that France indeed wants a united Europe, but only one in which she will have a dominant place. From this it is an easy step to conjuring up visions of Louis XIV and the first Napoleon, visions which are easily fed by the belief in the intensity of Gaullist nationalism.

The strength and authenticity of de Gaulle's patriotism are

questioned by none. But here again it is revealing to observe that he has merely continued to pursue the policy toward Germany that the preceding régime had initiated—a solution of the German problem through reconciliation, absorption, integration as one will, instead of through external forcible control. It is in fact precisely because de Gaulle is de Gaulle that it has been easier for him than for others to extend to the German people the hand of friendship and to tell them, in their own land and their own language, that they are a great people. Some of his speeches have indeed proved startling to French ears, yet it is highly significant that they have not induced marked opposition.

The fate of the integration of Europe in the last resort depends on that of the relations among three peoples—the French, the Germans, and the British. That Franco-German unity in some form should be the central core of Europe seems a wholly natural precondition. This, to be sure, raises some questions and even fears. The recent Franco-German treaty of amity was for that reason looked on askance by some who feared too close co-operation between the two countries, though from that point of view its results have been frustrating. Others have expressed concern over the possibility that such union would be the first step toward a renewal of the bid for German domination, or alternatively that France should permanently "annex" control of the partnership, from there to seek to rise to further heights of dominance. Perhaps one might leave it to the French to run the risk of German domination, but in more limited fashion the possibility might also exist of authentic parity. Indeed, if the previously suggested interpretation of de Gaulle's chief characteristics—flexibility and a strong sense of the possible—be accepted as sound, one may be warranted in surmising that the aims of his policy are merely this: feeling that France has been unduly demoted, to restore her to a proper place, one of rough parity with Germany on the one hand and Britain on the other; then on that basis to build Europe. Even to achieve so much would be a sufficiently ambitious program.

No doubt, even if such parity were established—if it be correct interpretation—one may expect competition and a degree of playing for position. Of course France will seek to obtain for her agriculture as dominant a position as possible in as much of Europe as possible; the interests and the desires of French agriculture are in this respect precisely of the same nature as others, American for one, and we are dealing here with entirely normal and equally legitimate interests, which will contend and compete, but which are, given good will and willingness to acknowledge each other, adjustable. They are best handled not in the context of ethical considerations.

The interpretation of French aims just suggested is a surmise that may of course be wrong. One knows the tendency of power to feed upon itself, the ease with which a leader can become convinced of his own indispensability. But if the aims of France, with or without de Gaulle, go to unreasonable hopes of real dominance of others, the result will be certain defeat. What matters in the end is the relationship of power, and French power, however much renovated, cannot in any reasonable view be stretched to such lengths. The fear sometimes expressed of the virulence of French nationalism seems excessive in the light of its record over an appreciable time; it should not be confused with the not unreasonable desire to undo the legacy of humiliation and exaggerated demotion, in its own no less than in foreign eyes. For the rest, any French hegemonic attempts will be successfully resisted; the most that they could do would be to prevent the success of the integration of Europe.

We have just suggested that one of the aims of present French policy is the achievement of parity with Britain, a possibility that will shock many in England. This is not in the least surprising in the light of what has been previously said of the British outlook and position that stresses contrast between itself and others. But the almost twenty years that have passed since the end of the war call for drastic revision of this image. Though taken with good grace and a stiff upper lip, the extent of the British loss of position, as well as its failure fully to penetrate the British consciousness, must here be borne in mind.

General de Gaulle has made no secret of his suspicion of what he calls the Anglo-Saxons. This is with him a point of undue sensitivity. Certain aspects of it are not devoid of humor; for in its different way French insularity is no less strong than British. The British have taken just pride in the legacy of their institutions to so much of the world, not least to what they sometimes see as wayward America, and the American connection in particular has been highly valued by them. There is no denying that a special wire has run between London and Washington, for all that there is now direct connection between the White House and the Kremlin. This last point is, however, full of significance, for in spite of the very real Anglo-American affinity, the fact is also that America has been operating in realistic terms of power; its attitude toward Common Market Europe and Britain may again be recalled.

The reality, therefore, and the significance of the special Anglo-American connection can be exaggerated, though the British have tended to set great store by it. It is no doubt exaggerated by General de Gaulle, who translates it into the image of Britain as an agent or wedge of American control over Europe. This, and the British insistence on the Commonwealth link, is the sort of thing he had in mind when, in January 1963, he declared that Britain was not ready to join Europe. What de Gaulle means by British readiness is, to put

it in perhaps somewhat brutal fashion, the abandonment by
her of a position in any way different from that of other
European powers—in short truly becoming a province of
Europe. This may seem harsh. Yet is it, when one considers
the true reality of those supposedly special links, with the
Commonwealth on the one hand and the United States on
the other?

Of course if Britain is to join the rest of Europe without
any conditions of privilege, she will have to make certain
adjustments. Yet how drastic? There is significance in the
rapid expansion of the exchanges between Britain and Common Market Europe and perhaps some irony in the fact that
the fastest-growing of all has been Anglo-French trade since
de Gaulle's high-handed rejection of England. Perhaps there
is here room for some rethinking.

The point has also been made that Gaullist nationalism is an
obstacle to integration because of its too-rigid insistence on
the attribute of sovereignty and the preservation of national
distinctness. And here also there is irony in the fact that in
this respect the British and the French positions are closest;
the British reaction to the prospect of becoming a province
of Europe has been indicated. We are dealing here with
two somewhat divergent approaches to a similar goal, the
respective merits of which it is difficult to judge in advance.
On the one hand there are those who contend that fortune
should be seized by the forelock, that such possibly adventitious and uncertain conditions as common prosperity and
rapid growth should be used to push integration very far
and very fast at all levels. Others maintain that integration
will be a sounder and more solid outcome if the result of more
gradual and organic development, as is the case with institutions that have struck deep root; that it is futile and unrealistic
to pretend that the historic record of European differences

and struggles can be so easily erased. While this is true, it is equally true that the new pace of change has been vastly accelerated and that it is possible to miss opportunities.

The Anglo-French relationship has been stressed, properly so since the rejection of the British application to the Common Market was the result of a concrete French action. Yet we have in America perhaps tended to exaggerate the cleavage between France and the rest of the Six. These differences no doubt exist, but one should not forget that the development of the Common Market has continued. One must presume therefore that the feeling of common advantage is shared by all its members. Germany fills a very large place in Europe; she may make concessions to French interest and desire, but to think of her as a mere French appendage verges on the absurd.

Ex-Chancellor Adenauer was sometimes charged with undue submissiveness to French leadership, especially that of de Gaulle. No doubt Germany still remains to a point on probation, and suspicion of her has not vanished. Yet mere atonement cannot constitute for her the center of policy, which is instead rehabilitation and recovery of position. There are still those who fear a resurgence of aggressive designs on her part, or even, in more limited fashion, Germany's assumption of a strong enough position in Europe to involve the rest in a struggle for the recovery of her eastern losses. Her record having been what it has been such fears are wholly understandable and not to be lightly dismissed.

Even allowing that modern conditions of war put a new light on the prospect of its occurrence, there is no denying that the German position is crucial and that much will depend on what Germany does. The state of feeling of the German people, about which contradictory reports are heard, remains therefore of capital importance. Here one must speculate while realizing that conditions—economic, for one—can have considerable influence on the state of popular feeling; the Nazi phenomenon itself is a good case in point.

For the rest, certain risks may be worth taking. The French policy toward Germany after the First World War was not at all devoid of logic. But it was predicated on the assumption that German aggressiveness was incurable, an assumption largely rejected by others at the time. In any case that policy, improperly implemented, proved to be a failure. However much others may have come around to the former French view, there is no possibility of putting Germany back into a state of impotent subservience, and the other nations must deal with her and her power.

This need not mean mere blind, prayerful trust. There was after the First World War the view, contrary to the French, which believed that the avoidance of a punitive policy and the absence of economic distress might give the Weimar Republic a chance. This we shall never know, though the possibility cannot be a priori excluded. And the long-term evolution of France is also an enlightening thing to consider in this connection, for all that one may not simply assume the repetition of it in the German milieu. But there would seem at least to be promise in the attempt to integrate or "scramble" Germany into the rest of free Europe in such a way and to such an extent that an exclusive German leadership and control would be no more possible than any one other. As to those who have such regard for German capacity that they feel that a Europe that includes Germany is bound to be a German Europe, the only thing that can be said is that if they are right, if the rest of Europe together cannot absorb and contain Germany, then perhaps it is time that the rest abdicate. There is no warrant for such deficiency of faith.

On a basis of rough parity, Britain, Germany, and France, each in her way, at some point acts as mediator between the

other two in the achievement of European unity. Each
—especially Germany and France—also can prevent such an
outcome. A Europe without Britain can be conceived, if not
wished, as a viable entity; one without either France or Germany has no meaning. This, incidentally, points to the most
desirable course of American policy at this juncture: most important of all, do not separate Germany and France, but instead persist in the endeavor to reconcile Anglo-continental
differences. In any case it is not possible to coerce any one
against his will in such an undertaking where free consent
is indispensable. The catastrophic view taken by some of the
rejection of Britain has proved exaggerated fear, and there
is a growing number who believe that it may have been no
more than a postponement.

Europe in the Larger World

Whatever the intensity of his own French nationalism,
General de Gaulle is authentically European. Europe to him
does not extend across the Atlantic; he fears that too strong
an American influence might dilute or dissolve the special
qualities, as elusive as they are real, that characterize the
culture of Europe. This feeling of the uniqueness of Europe,
be it in terms of culture or of power position, is one that
many Europeans share, and the French position thus in a
measure represents Europe rather than France alone. But this
in turn has led to some misunderstanding in America, where
there has been an insufficient capacity to distinguish between the authenticity of the French spokesmanship for
Europe on the one hand and equally authentic European opposition to any possibility of French dominance.

Where France in particular is concerned the American record has been a combination of immense generosity, considerable patience, and an equal measure of faulty understanding.

It is no classified secret that irritation and annoyance with France have been intense, not least at the governing level; some would use stronger words. As a state among states it is the wholly proper function of American policy to concern itself above all with the defense of the American interest and to appraise others, including the French, in this light. But this criterion applies equally in reverse. The game of politics, whether domestic or foreign, is harsh; but sentiment, ideals, and ethics also play a large part in deciding the actions of men. That is why the troubled domain of the interrelation between power and ethics will always command interest and uneasy thought, in which confusion is likely. Of American policy no more can be demanded than that it should with effective intelligence defend the national interest—a large enough assignment which implies first of all a clear definition of and agreement upon what that interest is.

Survival and defense are obvious first prerequisites, in which respect the Soviet danger has since the war largely filled the horizon. The common interest of that portion of Europe that has escaped Soviet control is here the simplest initial reality. NATO, largely an old-type defensive military alliance, was the simple and natural response. But with the United States so much more powerful than the rest put together, the alliance is one among unequals. So long as the danger remains the cement of the alliance can be counted on to retain its solidity, and there is no reason to doubt the authenticity of Gaullist or other declarations on this score. But this in no manner excludes either the possibility of divergence of views in regard to tactics or the implementation of an agreed large common policy, or some desire to have a larger voice in decisions. There is some resentment, too, all the more understandable in the light of Europe's large and recent record of power. This tendency, in somewhat varying degrees, is shared by all European states.

Self-defeating would certainly be the wrong word to characterize American policy toward Europe since the end of the war. But the very success of the American contribution to the recovery of Europe was bound to have the consequence of inducing greater assertiveness by Europe. This is a simple fact of life and of politics, that should be cause for neither recriminations nor tears. Nor is there cause for either surprise or alarm in a measure of criticism issuing from Europe, even if at times couched in harsh and unfair terms. Two things may be said at this point.

One is that, understandable as it may be, American policy has been somewhat unduly colored by the military aspect of defense. It is basically the same motivation that made America so anxious to obtain the ratification of EDC at the beginning of the fifties and caused her to encourage European integration, more narrowly the admission of Britain to the Common Market in the latter part of that decade and the beginning of the next. We have in fact heard a good deal about the Grand Design of an Atlantic Community, a proposal that America is especially well placed to promote, and where it may seem wholly simple and natural.

This is without doubt an attractive vision, but it is premature, partly because the easy fusion of European components in the United States is a fallacious parallel, partly because of the overwhelming degree of American power. However much all of Europe may be becoming Americanized—a process that is going on at a rapid pace and by free imitative choice —differences are still considerable between Europe and America as well as among the various parts of Europe.

A more modest accomplishment might hold better hope of success while providing a more solid basis on which to build the future. This is sometimes described by the homely phrase, the "dumbbell" solution, by which is meant the creation of two roughly equal centers of power—the American and the

European—whose partnership would span the Atlantic. Even the Six alone—the modern version of Charlemagne's empire—in population, resources, wealth, and skills, represent an impressive collection which, save in square mileage and for its current (but perhaps temporary) deficiency in nuclear armament, can constitute a match for Soviet power.

An objection may be raised at this point in the form of the query: what assurance is there that the partnership spanning the Atlantic will survive the revival of power in Europe? The answer is that there is none, which leads to the second fact that we wish to mention: the bipolarity that has dominated the postwar period is and has been for some time in the process of breaking down. Some brief observations alone will suffice on this score.

On the Soviet or Communist side the process was initiated by the Yugoslav break of 1948. Yugoslavia is a small country, but her role and her significance in this matter have far exceeded the absolute and material extent of her power. For, given the nature of the Communist ideology and milieu, its monolithic character and its emphasis on discipline, it was no less than the issue of heresy that was raised by the Yugoslav defection. The consequences of heresy not suppressed or not reintegrated into the orthodox fold are fatal to orthodoxy in future. The peculiar circumstances that made success possible in this case—the personality of Tito, Soviet fears of larger conflict, skillful American exploitation of an opportunity—are mere details. What counts is the success. The fact that Tito's Yugoslavia has remained an adherent of the Communist faith made this episode far more telling than would have been the abandonment of the true faith by Yugoslavia, for thereafter the monopolistic claim of the Muscovite Church was voided of content. The process of fragmentation has since, not surprisingly, prospered, though one may wonder at the extent and rapidity of its progress. China, because of her vast potential, is a far more serious matter from the standpoint of Communist power. Even the harsh Soviet action in Hungary in 1956 does not matter too much in this context when one bears in mind the development that has since been taking place among the European satellites, including Hungary, of the Soviet Union. By this time we can contemplate a proliferating variety of increasingly diverse and competitive Communist centers.

Looked at from a different angle what this development means is that Communism has failed to break through the existing mold of the world of states. One may well understand —even to a degree sympathize with—the frustration of those who started it all with a vision not devoid of nobility, one aspect of the recurring dream of mankind that sees it united and rid of the bane of human exploitation. At any rate Utopia is not yet to be, and, like the aftermath of the French Revolution—it, too, was in some of its aspects a universalistic dream —Communism is in process of being integrated into the world that is.

The process of loosening fragmentation which has been taking place in the Communist world has been paralleled by a corresponding one in its chief rival, the Free World, and this is a development pregnant with possibilities. The devolution of empire has, for all practical purposes, reduced this last to its North Atlantic core—America (including Canada) on the one side and Europe on the other—while much of the rest of the world seeks above all to escape involvement in either camp and endeavors to exploit both. There is no parallel among the Free to the theological type of cleavage that rends the Communist camp, but the revival of Europe, as indicated before, has created certain stresses and made her less amenable to the unquestioning acceptance of the wishes and views of American leadership. There are differences among the Free, but they are of degree, and if de Gaulle's France has been the most vocally cantankerous ally, there has been a tendency in America to be perhaps unduly concerned with the search for an elusive, stable dependability. An American policy too exclusively oriented toward Britain, or Germany, or France might well be self-defeating, and the preference for and encouragement of Free Europe as a unit is the sounder approach, whatever local and momentary difficulties may at times intervene. The component parts of Europe share the desire to play a world role as they share the understanding that they cannot singly do so. This is a strong cement that offers reasonable grounds for believing that they will not again insist upon magnifying their ancient rivalries to their common detriment, though, to be sure, national folly can be without limits.

What has been happening is a loosening of the bipolar structure when for a time it seemed as if only two real powers were in existence in the world. This was a dangerous stalemate. The proliferation of centers of power is not without its dangers too, and the story of European power rivalries is familiar and recent; but it also contains the possibility of greater flexibility and of relaxation of tensions. Until the world is one, a preferable but not immediately realizable prospect, there may be virtue in the resurgence of Europe in union.

A one Europe has not happened yet, although prospects have reached the point of reasonable expectation, and we may bring our whole discussion to a close by raising once again the question of what precisely is Europe.

Europe, it has been rightly said, is an idea, and the early part of this essay has deliberately stressed the importance of the cultural elements that give that idea reality. But just as a revolution is an idea that has found bayonets, so likewise the idea of Europe must have a definable territorial domain.

One may begin with the Little Europe of the Six, where the Franco-German combination is an indispensable core, though one that need not and must not, seek to impose its will on the rest. The rest of Free Europe essentially consists of the Seven, which for all practical purposes means Britain, and here we come again to those states which were mentioned earlier as the two marginal and peripheral entities that are Britain and Russia.

Britain alone may indeed prosper economically. Size and power are not for this indispensable, as the Swiss case well shows. But Switzerland has never played a world role, and in the new dimensions of power those of Britain alone are no longer sufficient. As the leader of an evanescent Commonwealth, or as a spearhead of America, the prospects of British influence seem unpromising. Britain as an island off Europe is also hard to contemplate, for all that some in Britain have envisaged that role. Britain has meant too much and she still has too much to offer merely to abdicate, even in Swiss-like contentment. Only in and with Europe can Britain make an adequate contribution, one that involves an important function of leadership. To accept this for her may be demotion—all the individual parts of Europe have in singleness been demoted—and may indeed entail some painful readjustment. Britain must clarify her relations with others, in which respect there was indeed some foundation in the Gaullist charge of unreadiness. But this can be done, and if done would be to the greatest advantage of all, Britain's no less than the Continent's.

The Russian case is different for reasons both of dimensions and potential. It is again the same de Gaulle who has expressed the view that fundamentally Russia is European and will eventually return to the fold. This may seem like Olympian detachment, dealing with such long-term prospects as to have little concrete significance. Certainly this is not a

practical consideration of the moment, and it may be noted
that it is also de Gaulle whose attitude toward the Soviet
Union has been the most intransigent of all. Yet there may
be point in again drawing attention to two aspects of the
Russian development that have been mentioned before: first,
the very fact of the success of Marxism in Russia can be interpreted as the final conquest of Russia by Europe, in terms
of ideas especially; secondly, the course of revolution is
being integrated into that of existing culture and preceding
history, a development assisted by the impingement of Asiatic
pressures. But, to repeat, any discussion of European integration cannot at the present time give serious consideration to
the inclusion of Russia.

Perhaps one more development may be mentioned, one
which may seem far-fetched and extraneous, yet conceivably
might turn out not to be so at all. Certain recent initiatives
in the body of the Roman Church, centering in particular
around the second Vatican Council, called into being by the
late Pope John XXIII and continued by his successor, have
been cause for not a little surprise. One can no more than
speculate on the unfolding of a process which is in course
of development. But certainly it is a fascinating possibility
to envisage the closing of a chapter initiated by Luther. One
of the major components of the idea and the culture that
are Europe is undoubtedly the Christian, and the territorial
domain of Europe may roughly be equated with that of
Christendom. Even though much of the story of Europe in
the past two centuries has been one of de-Christianization,
and even though Christians have in the past fought with
each other savagely, in face of the loss of position as mistress
of the planet, in face of the revival and impingement of pressures from much of the rest of the world, Europe may be
in some unconscious manner drawing upon so basic an ele-

ment of distinction to reassert her separate unity vis-à-vis the rest of the world.

This, once again, is mere speculation that some may call unwarranted. Yet in whatever form and shape the separate identity of Europe, out of which stems the drive for unity, may manifest itself, the current strivings constitute a fascinating tale that is one of the potentially most pregnant happenings of our time. The idea of Europe persists in refusing to die.

BIBLIOGRAPHY

The following list is intended to offer some useful suggestions for additional reading. It makes no pretense at exhaustiveness and, as will appear, is oriented toward the more recent developments.

Barker, Sir E., Sir G. Clarke, and P. Vaucher, eds., *The European Inheritance*. 3 vols. (London, 1956).

Beloff, Max, *Europe and the Europeans: An International Discussion*. (London, 1957).

Benoit, Emile, *Europe at Sixes and Sevens*. (New York, 1961).

Brugmans, Henri, *Les origines de la civilisation européenne*. (Liége, 1958).

Coudenhove-Kalergi, Richard N., *Pan-Europe*. (New York, 1926).

Dawson, Christopher, *The Making of Europe*. (New York, 1945).

Dehio, Ludwig, *The Precarious Balance*. (New York, 1962).

Dewhurst, J. Frederic, et al., *Europe's Needs and Resources: Trends and Prospects in Eighteen Countries*. (New York, 1961).

Gerbet, Pierre, *La France et l'organisation de l'Europe*. (Paris, n.d.).

Halecki, Oscar, *The Limits and Divisions of European History*. (New York, 1950).

Hallstein, Walter, *United Europe—Challenge and Opportunity*. (Cambridge, Mass., 1962).

Hay, Denys, *Europe: The Emergence of an Idea*. (Edinburgh, 1957).

Heilbroner, Robert L., *Forging a United Europe: The Story of the European Community*. (New York, 1961).

Holborn, Hajo, *The Political Collapse of Europe*. (New York, 1951).

Jaspers, Karl, *Vom europäischen Geist*. (Munich, 1947). Also available in English and in French translations.

Kitzinger, U. W., *The Challenge of the Common Market*. (Oxford, 1961).

Kohn, Hans, *The Idea of Nationalism*. (New York, 1944).

Lange, Chr. L., *Histoire de l'internationalisme*, 2 vols. (Christiania and Oslo, 1919, 1954).

Lauret, René, *France and Germany: The Legacy of Charlemagne*. (Chicago, 1964).

Lichtheim, George, *The New Europe: Today—and Tomorrow*. (New York, 1963).

Lippmann, Walter, *Western Unity and the Common Market*. (Boston, 1962).

Madariaga, Salvador de, *L'Esprit de l'Europe*. (Brussels, 1952).

Mayne, Richard, *The Community of Europe, Past, Present and Future*. (New York, 1962).

Monnet, Jean, *Les États-Unis d'Europe ont commencé*. (Paris, 1955).

Mosse, George L., *The Culture of Western Europe*. (Chicago, 1961).

Pryce, Roy, *The Political Future of the European Community*. (London, 1962).

Renouvin, Pierre, *L'idée de fédération européenne dans la pensée politique du XIXe. siècle*. (Oxford, 1949).

Robertson, A. H., *The Council of Europe, Its Structure, Functions and Achievements* (London and New York, 1956).

———, *European Institutions*. (New York, 1959).

Rougemont, Denis de, *Vingt-huit siècles d'Europe*. (Paris, 1961).

Saitta, A., *Dalla Res Publica agli Stati Uniti d'Europa*. (Rome, 1948).

Voyenne, Bernard, *Petite histoire de l'idée européenne*. (Paris, 1954).

Zurcher, Arnold J., *The Struggle to Unite Europe, 1940–1958*. (New York, 1958).

For those interested in the unfolding of current developments in the realm of European integration, there is a steady stream of publications issued by such organizations as *The European Community Information Service*, with offices in Brussels, London, and Washington, *The European Parliament*, the *Service des Publications des Communautés européennes*.

Abyssinia, 238, 239, 243
Adenauer, Konrad, 287–88, 294; de Gaulle, 325
Aehrenthal, Count von, 165
Afghanistan, 128
Africa, 11, 121, 125–26, 127, 129, 264
Age of Reason, 32
Aggression, 228; defined, 218, 218 n; Germany, 163, 164, 174, 191, 198–99, 209; image importance, 163, 166; Munich, 245
Agriculture, 112–13, 115, 304, 320
Air power, 261
Aix-la-Chapelle, 144
Albania, 17
Albertini, Luigi, 171 n
Alexander, King of Yugoslavia, 237
Alexander I, Tsar of Russia, 94, 258, 259
Alexander II, Tsar of Russia, 79, 86, 89, 90–91
Alexander III, Tsar of Russia, 94, 147
Alexandria, 10
Algiers, 314–16
Allegiance, 61–62. See Sovereignty
Alliances, negative nature, 162
Alsace, 61–62, 76, 102–3, 131
America, ix, x, 1–4, 9, 56–57, 119; Bill of Rights, 59; Civil War, 3 n, 4, 122; Communism, 286; Constitution, 57, 60; containment, 213; Declaration of Independence, 56–57, 59, 111; democratic concept, 186; Depression, 227; England, 310, 323, 324, heir to, 275, 280; ethnic groups, 18–19; Europe, 256, 286–87, 299, 303, contrast, 1–6; foreign policy, 213, 280, 287–88, 327, 328–30, 332; France, 327–28; Germany, 286, 287, 288, 293; Hiroshima, 273; immigration, 3, 3 n; independence, 121; isolationism, 205, 222, 268–69; leadership, 281, 331; League of Nations, 205; Monroe Doctrine, 146; nationality, 3, 103; Neutrality Acts, 268; New Harmony, 134; oceans, 269; power, 2, 201, 274, 275, 281; Revolution, 111; Rooseveltian New Deal, 239 n; Soviet Union, 184–85, 280, 292–93, 328; unity, 4, 6; war-guilt clause, 199; World War I, 182–86, 208 n, 255, 267; World War II, 268, 269
Anarchy, 40, 139
Anglo-French Treaty of Dunkirk, 285
Anglo-Russian Agreement (1907), 128
Anschluss, 244
Anti-clericalism, 141
Appeasement, 173, 241; climax, 245
Aquinas, Thomas, 13
Arabs, 8, 18, 82; Iberian peninsula, 16, 17
Arbitration, 218 n
Argentina, 119
Aristotle, 8, 13, 18
Armaments: danger of, 167; merchants of death, 120; Russia, 119
Asia, 48, 128
Asia Minor, 16
Atlantic Charter, 270–71
Atlantic Community, ix, 329
Atlantic Monarchies, 33–34
Atomic power, 273–74
Ausgleich (of 1867), 104
Austerlitz, 70, 261
Australia, 307
Austria, 20, 100, 104, 151, 301; An-

schluss, 244; France, 154; Germany, 101, 157, 226; government, 143; independence, 236; Italy, 95, 96, 102, 102 n, 145; Napoleon, 70; Nazis, 236; Netherlands, 93; peace treaty, 287 n; Poland, 47 n, 94; Prussia, 154; Sardinia, 97; Serbia, 172
Austro-Hungarian Empire: birth, 104; collapse, 190, 194, 203; imperialism, 123
Avignon, 61, 62, 78
Axis, 247, 262. See Rome-Berlin Axis

Bakunin, Mikhail, 139
Balance of power, 41, 42, 44, 77, 83, 86, 142, 150, 155, 164–65, 206, 208; Balkans, 151; Bismarck, 155–59; Congress of Vienna, 86; principle of, 45; Wilhelmine Germany, 159–64
Balance of Terror, 167
Balkans, 123; Austro-Russian rivalry, 156; nationalism, 104–8; terrorism, 171; Turks, 16, 17; wars, 106, 150–51
Baltic, 48, 95, 195
Barbarians, 82
Barbusse, Henri, Le Feu, 180
Barthou, Louis, 235–37
Battle of Britain, 174, 261
Battle of the Marne, 174, 175, 177, 261
Beauharnais, 71
Belgium, 2, 20, 298; Congo, 126; ethnic groups, 93; France, 215; independence, 146, 147, 152; Industrial Revolution, 109, 110; nationalism, 92–94; Ruhr, 212; Russia, 94; World War I, 173
Benelux, 288, 298 n
Benes, Eduard, 280
Benoit, Emile, Europe at Sixes and Sevens, 302, 302 n
Berchtold, Leopold von, 172
Berlin-Baghdad railway, 152; blockade, 281, 293; Congress (1878), 149–50; Treaty of (1878), 165
Bernadotte, King of Sweden, 72
Bethmann-Hollweg, Theobald von, 173, 175 n
Big Three: World War I, 271; World War II, 283, 300, 308
Bipolarity, 330 ff, 332
Bismarck, Otto von, 101, 108, 122, 127, 143, 150, 154, 163–64; Cavour, 101; on Central Europe, 246; dismissal, 159; France, 101; Kulturkampf, 139; Realpolitik, 102 n; "reign," 155–59; Reinsurance Treaty with Russia, 157, 160
Bismarckian system, 156, 157, 158, 158 n, 160, 164, 216; French, 164
Black Sea, 48
Blanc, Louis, 135, 137
Blum, Léon, 239, 241
Boer War, 128
Bohemia, 39, 95, 98 n, 195
Bolshevism, 181–82, 184, 195, 213, 255; Fascists, 247; Germany, 214
Bosnia, 17; -Herzegovina, 150, 165
Boubons, 39, 71, 78
Boxer Rebellion, 128
Briand, Aristide, 219, 220, 221, 222, 223–28, 233, 255; reconciliation policy, 226; Stresemann policy, 233
Brunswick Manifesto, 62
Brussels, Treaty of, 285, 286, 291
Bulgaria, 106, 150, 151, 177

Bülow, Bernhard von, 130, 161, 162, 166
Burgundians, 15
Burke, Edmund, *Reflections*, 64
Byron, Lord, 105
Byzantium, 12, 21 n

Caesar, 11, 14, 22
Calvinism, 36; ethos of, 32
Cambon, Paul, 162, 163
Canada, 307
Capital, 113, 118
Castlereagh, Viscount, 79, 86, 87, 89, 90, 91
Catherine, of Russia, 48, 49–50, 55, 64
Cavour, Camillo, 100, 101, 102 n
Central Africa, 127, 129
Central Europe, 35, 51
Central Powers, 166, 175, 177, 178
Central Treaty Organization (CENTO), 282 n
Cervantes, Miguel de, 28
Chamberlain, Houston Stewart, 132
Chamberlain, Joseph, 117, 161
Chamberlain, Neville, 244, 245, 249
Charlemagne, 21, 22, 77, 300
Charles V, Emperor, 34–35, 41–42, 82
Chaumont, Treaty of, 85
Chiang Kai-shek, 214 n, 223
China, 121, 214 n, 228, 311, 331; Boxer Rebellion, 128; Nationalists, 223
Christ, 12, 13, 16
Christianity, 12, 13, 15, 37, 76, 253; Balkans, 104; democratic idea, 13–14; ethic of charity, 113–14; legacy of, 12–14, 81; structure, 14; unity and, 142, 334–35; universalism, 55, 138
Church-state conflict, 22–23, 30, 62 n
Churchill, Winston S., 271, 283, 285, 306, 317; De Gaulle, 318
Cispadane Republic, 68
Class struggle, 137, 138, 181, 184, 187
Clemenceau, Georges, 193, 206, 209
Coal and Steel Community (European), 288–89, 296, 297, 298, 301, 309
Cobden-Chevalier Treaty, 115
Coexistence, xi
Colbert, Jean, 111
Cold War, 280, 292
Colonialism, 121, 127. See Imperialism
Columbus, Christopher, 33
Common Market, vii, 297, 298–303, 320, 329; England, 309–10, 327; France, 319, 325; Soviet Union, 330. See European Economic Community *and* Europe of the Six
Communism, 182, 234 n, 246–47, 259, 330–31; democracy, xi; Europe, ix; integration, 331; reaction to, 279; universality, x, 247
Communist Manifesto, 137–38, 139 n
Communists, 139 n, 278; Nazis, 265–66; in resistance, 278
Comte, Auguste, 136, 137
Concert of Europe, ix, 143, 144–52, 199, 232; breakdown, 145, 154, 171 ff; operation, 147; Ottoman Empire, 149
Congo, 127
Congress of Vienna, 85–90, 106, 109, 115, 202; accomplishments, 92; leaders, 143; Paris Peace Conference (1918), 192; slogans, 143; *status quo ante*, 142
Constantinople, 16–17, 105
Containment, 282 n

Continental System, 72–73, 74, 111, 259
Convention of the Straits, 148
Copernicus, Nicolaus, 31–32
Coudenhove-Kalergi, Count, 222
Council of Europe, 285–86, 288
Crimean War, 106, 107, 148–49
Culture, 81, 83, 133, 141, 168, 253
Customs union, 226. See Zollverein
Czechoslovakia, 20, 195, 215, 280–81; Communist Party, 280; France, 215; Nazis, 249

Daladier, Edouard, 245
Dante, *Divine Comedy*, 28
Danube, 11, 15
Danubian Monarchy, 168. See Austro-Hungarian Empire
Danzig, 194 n, 196–97, 215
Das Kapital, 137, 138
Dawes Plan, 213, 221, 294
Decision-making, 193
Declaration of Gallican Liberties, 38
De Gaulle. See Gaulle, Charles de
Delcassé, Théophile, 130
Democracy, 84, 90, 186–87, 197, 253; Communism, xi; Greek heritage, 76; principle, 200
Democratic idea, 10, 13–14
Denmark, 194 n
Depression, the Great, 226–27, 228 ff, 257, 303
De Tocqueville, Alexis, 256
Diderot, Denis, 50
Diplomacy, 149, 161–62, 174; Central Powers, 178; England, 249; France, 232; Germany, 158; of power, 178; secret, 184, 187
Disarmament, 167, 199, 220, 221, 228; Conference (1932), 229; Germany, 229, 231
Disraeli, Benjamin, 123–24
Dollfuss, Engelbert, 236
Dreikaiserbund, 156, 157
Dual Monarchy, 104. See Austro-Hungarian Empire
Dumbarton Oaks, 273
"Dumbbell" solution, 329–30

Eastern Church, 142
Eastern Question, 146, 147–52
East-West conflict, xi
Economics, 113, 115, 117–20, 152, 303; contrary effects of, 109–29; divisive effects, 15–17; European union, 224–25; free trade and social question, 110–17; imperialism, 120–29; utopian, 136; World War I, 195 ff. See also Common Market; Depression; Imperialism; Marshall Plan; Schuman Plan
Eden, Anthony, 291
Edict of Nantes, 38
EFTA. See Europe of the Seven
Egalitarian principle, 59
Egypt, 148; England, 124, 124 n, 127, 129; Napoleon, 68, 74; nationalism, 124 n
Eighteenth century: beliefs, 59, 65; legacy, 133–34; tone, 83
Empire-building, 121. See Imperialism
England, x, 20, 24–26, 27, 42 ff, 59, 119, 140, 309; agriculture, 112–13; America, 2–3, 57, 191, 268–69, 323, 324; army, 73; Axis, 244; Channel, 265, 269;

Chartists, 136, 140; Common Market, 300; Commonwealth, 284, 302, 306–8, 323, 324, 333; Congress of Vienna, 86; Continent, 25, 26, 33, 44, 45, 283–86, 300; Corn Laws, 112; democratic idea, 10; Dominion of Canada Act, 306; Egypt, 129; empire, 44, 116, 161, 283, 284, 306; foreign policy, 50, 86, 89, 283, 306 ff; Four Power Pact, 232; France, x, 24–25, 43, 44, 45, 64, 67, 68–73, 144, 161–62, 206–11, 242, 325; geography, viii, 25, 44–45, 81; Germany, x, 117, 127, 161, 208, 208 n, 284; Glorious Revolution, 42; government, 67, 143, in exile, 269–70; imperialism, 25–26, 121–27, 131–32, 157; Industrial Revolution, 109, 110, 113–14; invasion, 25; isolation, 157, 161, 300, 305; Labour, 283, 306; leadership, 261, 284, 308; League of Nations, 238; liberties of Europe, 252, 254–55; Luddite riots, 114; monarchy, 33, 42–43, 64; Munich, 245; Napoleonic Wars, 77, 81; national superiority, 131–32; naval power, 43, 44, 68, 70, 73, 157, 161, 165, 261; Nazis, 249–50; necessity to Europe, 333; Netherlands, 43; "permanent interests," 208; Poland, 249; position, 304–11, 323; power, 44, 50, 242 (see naval; position); readiness, 323–24, 333; Reform Bill, 112, 153; Russia, 69, 86; Schuman Plan, 290; Spain, 36, 111, 243; Statute of Westminster, 306; trade, 111–13, 116–17, 121; Treaty of Chaumont, 85; uniqueness, 24–26, 45, 46, 284, 300, 308; utopian socialism, 135; World War I, 206–7, 208; World War II, 264, 283, post, vii, 276, 283 ff

Enlightenment, 50–56, 57, 76, 186
Entente Cordiale, 126, 128, 130, 153, 161, 163
Erasmus, 28
Erhard, Ludwig, 303
Estonia, 195
Ethnic groups, 18–19, 21, 196–97
Europe: America, vii, 1–6, 274; Christian, 12; community of, 65; culture, 52, 65, 79, 253; defined, 332–35; diversity, 4, 35, 36, 39, 65, 78, 79, 103–4, 200–1, 253, 281–82; equilibrium, 79; Europeanness, 51–52; evolution, vii–viii, 84–91, 152–55; fluidity, 237; Four Power Pact, 232; Franco-German relationship, 211; Free, 332, 333; geography, 17, 27; German problem, 238–48, 263, 263 n, 286; heritage, viii, x, 28, 105; an idea, viii; "inner-outer," 110; Islam, 17, 18; liberties, 69, 208, 252, 254–55; "little," 81; medieval contribution, 14–24; meaning, 1–79; after Munich, 246–49; Napoleon, 71; order, 91; organization, 204 ff, 211–21, 239 ff, 263–64, 264 n; overseas, 120–29; past, 6–27; peoples, 20, 105; position, 327–35; power, x, 4–5, 243–44; recovery, x, 331; revolution, impact, 56–76; traditions, 65; uniqueness, 327; unity (see Unity); Western, 280; World War I, 204 ff; World War II, 276

Europe of the Seven, 301–2
Europe of the Six, vii, x. See European

Economic Community and Common Market
European Atomic Energy Community, (Euratom), 297
European Defense Community (EDC), 290–91, 296, 329
European Economic Community, vii, 296, 297. See Common Market
European Movement, 285
European System, 228–38
European Union, 221–28. See Briand and Unity

Far East, 121
Fascism, 234 n, 248, 257, 270; Bolshevism, 247
Fashoda, 126, 161
Fellow travelers, 68
Ferdinand, Archduke Franz, 171, 172
Ferdinand, King of Spain, 33
Feudalism, 14
Fichte, Johann, Addresses, 75, 98
Fifth columists, 68
Finabel, 298 n
Finland, 74, 195
Fontainebleau, Treaty of, 75–76
Fontenoy, 45
Foreign aid, 316 n
Foreign policy, 211, 213, 214. See under name of country
Fourier, François, 134
Four Power Pact, 231–33
France, x, 3, 20, 35, 36–37, 59, 107, 108, 115, 119, 131, 139, 153, 224, 234, 238, 242; American Revolution, 57; ancien régime, 88; army, 185, 242, 260; Austria, 154; Belgium, 215; Boulanger episode, 108; characteristics, 24, 132, 323; Communist party, 278, 278 n, 279; Congo, 129; Congress of Vienna, 202; constitution, 60, 63; cordon sanitaire, 213; Czechoslovakia, 215, 219, 245–46; Declaration of Rights, 59, 60; democratic idea, 10; diplomacy, 161–62; Directory, 66; economy, 294–95, 319–20; Egypt, 124; empire, 312–16, 318–19; England, x, 24–25, 43, 44, 45, 64, 67, 68, 70, 72–73, 144, 206–11, 242, 325; Estates General, 56, 58; fall of, 260, 262, 262 n; Fascism, 234 n; Fifth Republic, 314–20; foreign policy, 209, 213, 214, 235 ff, 322–23; Four Power Pact, 232–33, 235; Fourth Republic, 292, 294, 295, 312, 315; Free French, 263, 270, 311, 318; Germany, x, 102–3, 130, 211, 212, 239, 239 n, 263, 286, 288, 288 n, 321, 326, problem, 218, 289, 290, 291, 295, 296, 299–300; government, 34, 63, 67, 71, 72–73, 143, 292; imperialism, 121–22, 125–27; industry, 109, 110, 119; Italy, 119; leadership, 241, 242, 292; militarism, 216, 260, 261; monarchy, 33, 38–42; nationality, 103; National Assembly, 60, 61; Nazis, 234 n, 260, 263–64; necessity in Europe, 286, 316; North Africa, 121; Peace of Westphalia, 40; philosophes, 52; "phoney war," 265; Poland, 215, 219; Popular Front, 235, 239, 239 n, 241–42, 243, 295; position, 311–14; power, 36–37, 38, 44, 51, 52, 55, 60, 85, 240, 314–15 (see French Revolution and Napoleon); Prussia, 154; resistance, 263, 266; Rumania,

215; Russia, 119, 125, 213–14, 216, 244, 246; satellites, 68; Second Empire, 107, 115, 123, 154; Second Republic, 153; security system, 209–10, 211, 216, 218, 223, 232–33, 237, 256, 289; Spain, 73; spirit, 295; Tennis Court Oath, 58; the Terror, 63; Third Republic, 108, 125; utopian socialism, 135; World War I, 206–7; World War II, 311; Yugoslavia, 215. See French Revolution, Napoleon and Vichy

Franchise, 59

Francis I, King of France, 28, 34

Francis II, Emperor of Austria, 74

Franco, Francisco, 243

Franco-Prussian War, 108, 125, 155, 239

Frankfurt, 154; Parliament, 98–99, 98 n; Treaty of, 157

Frederick the Great, 55

Free trade, 113, 114, 115–16, 153; principle, 112; and social question, 110–17

French Revolution, 58–64, 66, 66 n, 78, 115, 133, 142, 152, 182, 204, 255; ideals, 83–84, 85; influence, 187; purposes, 65; results, 83; slogan, 76; spirit, 59; the Terror, 66, 66 n; universal relevance, 59, 138

Fritalux, 298 n

Galileo, 32

Gaulle, Charles de, 262–63, 292, 311, 316–20, 332; Anglo-Saxons, 323; Common Market, 310; England, 323–24; Europeanness, 327; nationalism, 320–21; policy, 321–22; Prime Minister, 315; Soviet Union, 333–34

Geneva Protocol, 218

Genoa, 87

Geography, viii, 25, 26–27, 44–45, 81

George, Lloyd, 186, 193, 207

German Confederation, 87, 95, 98, 98 n, 154

Germanic world, 34, 51, 98

Germany, 20, 99, 100, 116, 118, 119, 123, 160, 230, 281, 293–94, 326; agriculture, 115; Austria, 157, 226; Bismarck, 155–59; "century," 155; character, 52, 101, 103, 132, 293; colonialism, 101, 102, 127–28, 179; conscription, 239; Democratic Republic, 281; depression, 229–30; diplomacy, 161, 174; disarmament, 221, 231; division, 281, 293; East, 293; Einkreisung, 163, 166; Enabling Act, 230; England, x, 117, 127, 161; equality desire, 218–19, 223, 229, 233; Federal Republic, 281, 291, 293; foreign policy, 157, 162, 203, 325; France, x, 102–3, 130, 212, 289, 290, 296, 299–300 (see Adenauer); imperialism, 129, 157; Industrial Revolution, 109–10; Italy, 119, 157–58; leadership, 263, 263 n; League of Nations, 217, 219, 220, 231; Napoleon, 74; nationalism, 75, 98, 101–2, 108; navy, 160–61, 165; Near East, 152; necessity in Europe, 282–83, 286; Paris Peace Conference, 192 n; Poland, 197, 233 n; position, 325–26; power, 164; problem, 193–94, 203, 233, 238–48; rearmament, 290, 291, 291 n; Reichstag, 103, 175 n, 226, 230; reparations, 226; Russia, 157, 159–60; suspicion of, 325; unification, 98, 101, 154, re-, 281; Wilhelmine, 159–64;

World War I, 173, 174–77, 189–90, 202–3, 212; World War II, 276; Zollverein, 115, 117, 298, 299, 301. See Hitler and Nazis

Gibbon, Edward, 51

Gioberti, Vincenzo, 132

Gladstone, William, 124

Gobineau, Joseph de, 132

Government, 67, 88–89, 143; theories, 85, 118, 253

Greece, 5, 7–8, 10, 18 n, 105, 132, 264; independence, 105 n, 146–47, 148; legacy of, 7–10, 81, 105; Truman Doctrine, 280

Grey, Edward, 163

Grotius, Hugo, 46

Habsburgs, 34, 35, 37, 39, 40, 50, 71, 92, 97, 101, 194; domain, 95, 99, 104

Hacha Emil, 280

Hague Court of Arbitration, 167

Hegemony, 305; France, 174, 216, 275; Germany, 174, 175, 184, 202, 251–52, 254, 259, 275, 276; Russia, 267, 277–82

Henry of Navarre, 36, 37

Herriot, Edouard, 218, 234

Hindenburg, Paul von, 226, 262

Hiroshima, 273

History: analysis, function of, 165; force, 201; repetition in, 6

Hitler, Adolf, 230–31, 238–41, 258–60, 293, 305; aggressor, 245; Mein Kampf, 230, 240; Mussolini, 236; Napoleon, 67; program, 251

Hofer, Andreas, 74 n

Hohenzollerns, 99, 101

Holy Alliance, 90–91, 143, 232

Holy Roman Empire, 21–23, 34–35, 36, 39, 82, 253; death, 71, 87; Napoleon, 71, 72

Hoover, Herbert, 226, 227

House, Colonel Edward, 183

Humanists, 28–29

Hundred Years War, 24, 44

Hungary, 20, 98 n, 99, 104, 262, 331

Iberian peninsula, 16, 17, 73

Iceland, 224 n

Ideas, impact of, 130–42

Ideologies, 271

Immigration, 3, 3 n

Imperialism, 120–29, 131, 138, 150. See under name of country

India, 121, 123, 284, 306, 313

Indochina, 122, 313

Industrial Revolution, 109–10; second, 117–20, 123

Industry, 114, 116, 117–18, 121, 254

Inquisition, 32

Integration: American-Europe, 329–30; economic, 296, 298, 298 n, 301, 302, 304, 311; forces, 254 (see Nationalism); key, 320–27; obstacles, 324; political, 304, 311; Soviet Union, 333–34

International Committee of Movements for Europe on Unity, 285

International law, 46, 149

International organization, 46

International politics, 26

International relations, 119

International Workingmen's Association: First, 138–39; Second, 139, 140, 179, 254

Interval between the wars, 256–57
Intervention, propriety of, 89
Invasions, 14, 15, 17, 24, 25
Ionian Islands, 86
Ireland, 107, 117, 222, 286
Iron Curtain, 281
Isabella, Queen of Spain, 33
Islam, 16, 17–18, 18 n, 35
Isolationism, 205. *See under* name of country
Istanbul, 17
Italy, 20, 71–72, 115, 135, 152, 154, 179, 185, 193, 206, 230, 286, 288, 291; Austria, 95, 96, 102, 102 n, 145; Communist party, 278, 279; disunity, 34; France, 67, 68, 69, 96, 119; Germany, 119, 157–58; imperialism, 129; Jacobins, 68; nationalism, 96–97, 101–2, 132; peninsula, 95; Pope, 23; Renaissance, 27–28; resistance, 266; Risorgimento, 102; Turkey, 150; unification, 96–97, 100, 100 n; World War I, 178; World War II, 261–62, 264. *See* Mazzini: Mussolini
Izvolsky, Aleksandr, 165–66

Jacobins, 68
Japan, 228; England resemblance, 25; World War I, 178, 193
Jaurès, Jean, 140, 179
Jefferson, Thomas, 56–57
Jews, 10, 12, 264 n; chosen people, 12
Joan of Arc, 24, 317
John XXIII, Pope, 334
Joseph, King of Spain, 71–72, 73

Kant, Immanuel, 75
Kellogg-Briand Pact, 220, 222
Keynes, John, 198, 198 n, 303
Kipling, Rudyard, 131
Kitchener, H. H. (Earl), 126
Klein-Deutschland, 99
Korea, 313
Korean War, 293
Kruger, Stephanus, 127

Laissez faire, 111, 112. *See* Free trade
Language, 19–20, 29, 52
Latvia, 195
Law, 12, 188, 188 n, 199–200
League of Augsburg, 41, 43
League of Nations, 91, 143, 188, 191, 194 n, 196, 201, 204, 217, 220, 228, 255, 308; Abyssinia, 238; Briand, 223–24; Convenant, 199–200, 205; failure, 255; Germany, 229; members, 224; power, 238; purpose, 217; spirit, 232; UN, 273; Wilson, 199
League of Virtue, 75
Legitimacy, 86, 88, 230, 240; of rule, 143, 147
Lenin, Nikolai, 138, 181, 182, 184, 257; New Economic Policy, 214
Leo XIII, Pope, 141
Leopold II, Emperor, 60–61, 64
Leopold III, Emperor, 67, 68
Liberalism, 153–54
Liberty, 40, 45, 65
Libya, 129, 150
Lithuania, 194 n, 195; Poland, 47, 47 n
Little Entente, 215, 232
Locarno Agreements, 218–19, 220, 222, 237, 239; spirit of, 220, 228
Locke, John, 57

Lombardo-Venetia, 95, 96
Lombardy, 87
London, Treaty of (1840), 148
Long Armistice, 202–52; Anglo-French divergence, 206–11; European system, 228–38; European union, 221–28; Germany, 238–48; bid for European unity, 248–52; organization of Europe, 211–21
Lorraine, 102–3
Louis XIV, King of France, 38–39, 41, 42, 66, 78, 320
Louis XV, King of France, 51, 54
Louis XVI, King of France, 57, 60, 64
Louis XVIII, King of France, 78, 88, 90
Louis-Philippe, 148, 153
Low Countries, 92
Ludendorff, Erich, 175 n
Luethy, Herbert, 312, 312 n
Luther, Martin, 28, 29, 30, 31, 35, 334
Luxembourg, 298 n

MacDonald, Ramsay, 218
Macedonia, 5
Madrid, international act (1880), 128
Magyars, 104
Malta, 86
Malthus, Thomas, 134; theory, 113
Manchuria, 228
Marie Theresa of Austria, 71
Marlborough, Duke of, 43, 73
Marseillaise, 139
Marshall, George C., 279
Marshall Plan, 279–80, 285, 286, 299
Marx, Karl, 136–38, 139; *Communist Manifesto*, 137, 139 n; *Das Kapital*, 137, 138
Marxism, xi, 114, 179, 181, 187, 254; universal aspect, 138
Maximilian, Emperor, 122
Mazzini, Giuseppe, 96, 135–36, 138, 298
Medieval Ages, 14–24
Mediterranean, 7, 11, 16, 33; Agreements (1887), 157
Mehemet Ali, 148
Memel, 194 n
Mendès-France, 290–91, 313–14
Mercantilism, 111
Merchants of death, 120
Metternich, Klemens von, 89, 91, 95, 98, 99, 143, 144, 145, 147, 153; design, 156; Italian unification, 97; Napoleon, 74
Mexico, 122–23
Militarism, 160–61, 165. *See under* name of country
Mill, John Stuart, 136
Mitteleuropa, 98–99
Monarchy(ies), 33, 38, 253; constitutional, 60, 64; divine-right, 38, 40, 60, 67
Mongols, 15
Monnet, Jean, 289, 290, 294, 297, 298, 300, 304
Montaigne, 28
Montesquieu, 60
Morocco, 128–29, 130, 162–63, 314; German-French difference, 129, 130, 131
Moscow, 74, 181
Munich Agreement, 245–49, 257, 259, 260
Murat, King of Naples, 71
Mussolini, Benito, 228, 230, 231–33, 235, 238, 243, 244, 270; Axis, 244; Hitler, 236

Napoleon, 67–76, 83, 84 ff, 111, 124, 142, 185, 202, 204, 208, 254, 258, 305, 315, 317, 320; achievements, 69–70; Continental System, 72–73, 74, 111, 259; Grand Army, 74; Hundred Days, 84; Russia, 264, 265; unity of Europe, 69–76

Napoleon III, 107–8, 122, 154–55, 155 n

Napoleonic Wars, 76–77, 81, 121, 202

National consciousness, 75. See Nationalism

Nationalism, ix, 75, 84, 90, 95–108, 124 n, 131–32, 141, 154, 168, 202, 253–54; culture, 133; defined, 102 n; divisive force, 92–108, 147; duality basis, 103; economics, 114, 115–17, 303; French Revolution, 65, 187; imperialism, 131; Mazzini, 135–36; Napoleon, 75; readiness for, 77; Realpolitik, 102 n; Southeast Asia, 313; unity of Europe, 91; utopian, 135; World War I, 202. See also under name of country

Nationality, principle of, 178, 179, 197, 200

Nation-state, ix, 18

Nazis, 67, 231, 233, 234 n, 236, 237, 247–48, 258, 260, 263, 265; aims, 251, 261–67; America, 267; Communists, 265–66; Czechoslovakia, 249; racial theory, 230, 240, 247, 248, 257, 264; resistance, 266; rise of, 226, 227, 230; Soviet Pact, 250, 258, 265

Near East, 11, 150, 152

Negroes, 3 n

Netherlands, 20, 35, 87, 93, 298 n; England, 43; Spain, 92–93; World War II, 260

Neutrality, 161, 215, 268

Newton, Isaac, 32, 52–53; Principia, 52

New Zealand, 122

Nicholas II, Tsar of Russia, 147, 180, 181, 194

Nineteenth century, 142, 144

Normans, 21, 24

North Africa, 11, 121, 264

North Atlantic Treaty Organization (NATO), ix, 281, 282 n, 291, 299, 328

Norway, 106

Odessa, 27

Old Testament, 12

Organization for European Economic Co-operation (OEEC), 285

Origins of the War of 1914, 171, 171 n

Orwell, George, 59

Otto, King of Greece, 147

Ottoman Empire, 104, 105 n, 177, 178; Concert of Europe, 149; decline, 50, 104–6

Owen, Robert, 134

Pacific, imperialism in, 121–22

Pakistan, 306

Palmerston, Henry, 122, 148, 153

Pan-European Union, 222

Paris: Accords, 291; capital of Europe, 52; Commune (1871), 139; Congress of 1856, 106, 149, 150, 154; Pact (see Kellogg-Briand Pact); Peace Conference (1918), 1, 190, 192; Treaty of (first), 76, 84, 85 (second), 84–85, 144

Passive resistance, 212

Pax Britannica, 308

Peace: "at any price," 241, 246; critique of, 192–202; desire for, 272–73; Germany, 240–41, 287, 287 n, 292; "in our time," 245; organization of, 199; World War I, 186–90, 287; World War II, 287, 287 n. See also Bismarckian System

Peace of Karlowitz, 50

Peace of Westphalia, 31, 39, 40, 41, 65, 82

Pearl Harbor, 269

Persia, 128

Pétain, Henri, 262, 263, 315

Peter I, Tsar of Russia, 47, 48, 49, 204

Petrarch, 28

Philosophes, 50, 52

Physiocrats, 111, 134

Pillnitz, Declaration of, 60–61, 62

Pilsudski, Józef, 195

Pius IX, Pope, 97, 100

Poincaré, Raymond, 151, 212, 213, 217, 235

Poitiers, 17

Poland, 20, 47, 47 n, 50, 64, 74, 86–87, 94, 152, 194 n, 195, 214, 270, 293; France, 215; Germany, 197, 233 n, 263; independence, 196; nationalism, 94–95; Russia, 49, 90; World War II, 259, 260

Political theory, 56, 59, 60, 76–78; Congress of Vienna, 85–86. See Sovereignty

Politics, 328

Pope, 22–23

Portugal, 301

Power, 102, 129, 133, 163, 190, 211, 218, 246–47, 311–12; America, 2, 183, 184, 199, 222, 274, 275, 307, 310, 323; bipolarization of, 165; characteristics, 83, 159, 246, 262, 322; Congress of Vienna, 86; "dumbbell" solution, 329–30; England, 26, 43, 45, 300–1, 305, 308; ethics, 328; Europe, 4–5, 36, 222–23; France, 43, 57, 217; Germany, 177, 202, 209 (see Hegemony); imbalance, 231; levels of, 152; operation of, 179; recognition of, 151; relationships, 144, 320–27; Russia, 213, 250; significance, 192. See Balance of power; Realpolitik

Powers, the: Eastern Question, 147–52; relationships, fluidity in, 164–65; unity of action, 145–47, 151

Propaganda, 186, 267

Protestantism, 29, 34, 83, 141

Prussia, 43, 51, 55, 60–61, 99, 143, 154; France, 67, 70, 72, 154; nationalism, 75; Poland, 47 n, 94. See Bismarck

Ptolemy, 31

Quadruple Alliance, 143

Rabelais, François, 28

Rational faculty, 8–9, 32, 53, 56

Realpolitik, 101, 102, 102 n, 250

Reason, use of, 8

Reconstruction, 282–96; Common Market, 296–302. See Integration

Reformation, ix, 31, 65, 76, 82; divisive effect, 29–33

Religion, 34, 66, 82, 141

Renaissance, 27–28, 31

Reparations, 198–99, 211–12, 213, 226

Restoration, 134, 143

Revisionism, 215

Revolution(s): 56–57, 58 ff, 60–61, 153–

54, 185, 255; defined, 332; impact of, 56–79; world, 214, 258, 277
Revolutionary principle, 61–62, 64, 75, 76–77, 78, 79, 88, 97
Reynaud, Paul, 268, 282; *Unite or Perish*, 282, 298
Rhine, 11, 15, 38, 41, 209
Rhineland, 219, 226, 229; remilitarization, 239, 240, 241
Richelieu, 39
Riga, 27
Robespierre, 66 n
Romanovs, 50
Rome Agreements, 297, 298–99, 301
Rome: ancient, 5, 8, 11, 13, 15, 21, 21 n, 22, 253; legacy of, 10–12, 22, 23, 81
Rome (church of), 65, 76, 141. See Reformation
Rome-Berlin Axis, 243, 244
Rome-Berlin-Tokyo Axis, 269
Roosevelt, Franklin D., 268, 271, 283; De Gaulle, 317, 318
Rousseau, Jean Jacques, 54–55
Ruhr, 212, 213, 217, 218
Rumania, 20, 178, 215–16, 262
Russia, 20, 26–67, 48–49, 50, 69, 106, 110, 119, 133, 140, 143, 151, 181, 192 n, 195; America, 184–85; distinctness, 26–27, 132; Europe, 47, 48, 49; France, 64, 70–71, 74, 75, 77, 81, 119, 125; geography, viii, 26–27, 48, 81; Germany, 57, 159–60; Holy, 132; Hungary, 99; imperialism, 48, 49, 121, 124, 128, 204; Poland, 47, 47 n, 49; Straits, 165, 178; World War I, 180–82, 189, 204. See Soviet Union
Russian Revolution, 27, 49, 139 n, 181–82, 184, 195, 255
Russo-Finnish War, 260
Russo-Japanese War, 129 n
Russo-Polish War, 213

Saar, 194 n, 288
St. Augustine, 31
St. Helena, 84
St. Paul, 13, 31
St. Simon, *The New Christianity*, 134
San Stefano, Treaty of, 149
Sardinia, 96, 97, 99, 100
Satellites, 95, 264, 331
Scandinavia, 20, 133, 264, 286, 301
Schleswig-Holstein, 101
Schlieffen Plan, 173, 260
Schuman Plan, 288–89, 290, 295–96, 297
Schuman, Robert, 289, 290
Schwarzenberg, Felix von, 99
Science, 8–9, 28, 31–32, 33, 52; internationalism, 133
Scotland, 42
Secularism, 20, 30
Self-determination, 20, 89, 106–7, 138, 187, 195, 253, 271
Separation, assertion of, 106, 107
Serbia, 105 n, 150, 151, 172
Siam, 125
Siberia, 48, 94
Sicily, 18 n, 95, 97
Sick Man of Europe, 147, 168. See Turks; Ottoman Empire
Six, the. See Common Market
Slavery, 10
Slavs, 264, 264 n, 265
Smith, Adam, 134; *Wealth of Nations*, 111

Socialism, 140, 179–80; international, 141, 179–80; scientific, 134, 136; utopian, 134–42
Socialist, defined, 139 n
Social science, 136
Society, stucture of, 133–34
South Africa, 307–8
Southeast Asia, 125–26; Treaty Organization (SEATO), 282 n
Sovereigns, 40–41
Sovereign state, 33–50, 253
Sovereignty, 46, 224, 225; democratic, 76; popular, 60, 62, 63, 79, 89; principle of, 82–83
Soviet Union, x–xi, 217, 222–23, 224 n, 228, 244, 282 n, 330–31; America, 280, 292–93; Germany, 236, 250–51, 257–58, 264–66; ideology, 213; integration of, 222, 263, 334; potential, 256; power bid, 277–82; purges, 244 n; Red Army, 277, 278; satellites, 71; World War II, vii, 264–65, 276–77
Spaak, Paul-Henri, 296–97, 304; Report, 297
Spain, 16, 18 n, 20, 33, 35, 36, 67, 71–72, 73, 92–93, 111, 129, 144–45; Armada, 36; Civil War, 242–43; "Spanish century," 36; Spanish Succession, War of the, 41, 43, 48, 51
Stalin, Josef, 214, 258–59, 271, 283
State, the: -church conflict, 22–23, 30, 62 n; sovereign, 33–50, 102 n; structure, 63; system, 40, 82–83, 142–43, 204
Strasbourg, 286
Stresa front, 239
Stresemann, Gustav, 212–13, 219, 221, 224, 226, 287, 294
Sudetenland, 195, 245, 293
Suez Canal, 122, 123, 124
Sweden, 48, 106–7
Switzerland, 20, 180, 301, 333

Talleyrand, 86, 87, 89, 146, 203
Tawney, R. H., 32
Taylor, A. J. P., 245, 251
Teheran, 271
Teschen dispute, 216
Teutonic peoples, 20, 132
Thiers, Louis, 148, 153
Thirty Years War, 31, 39, 46; second, vii
Tibet, 128
Tilsit, 70, 258
Tirpitz, Alfred von, 160
Tito, 330
Trade, 118, 152; free (see Free trade)
Trafalgar, 70, 261
Transvaal, 127
Treaties, 201–2
Treitschke, Heinrich von, 103
Triple Alliance, 102, 157, 164, 166 n
Triple Entente, 162, 163, 165
Tripolitan War, 150
Trotsky, Leon, 214
Truman, Harry S., 280
Tunisia, 125, 314
Turkey, 179, 224 n, 228; Truman Doctrine, 280
Turks, 15, 16, 17, 35, 37, 47, 50, 104–6, 105 n, 124. See Eastern Question
Tyrol, 74 n

Unconditional surrender, 254, 272, 272 n
Union, European, 221–28, 298. *See* Unity
United Nations, 86, 273, 274–75, 283, 307, 308, 311
Unity (of Europe), viii–ix, 6, 17, 27 ff, 33 ff, 128, 141, 145–47, 151; America, 255, 310; attempts at, 35–36, 38; Christianity and, 142, 334–35; by conquest, 72, 77, 247; cultural, 81, 83, 168; diversity, strength of, 169; England, 252; France, 320–21; Germany, 263, 263 n; ideal of, 22; key to, 320–27; meaning, 81 ff; necessity, 298; prospects, 81 ff; Schuman Plan, 289. *See also* European Union; Integration
University of Berlin, 75
Uprisings, 94, 98–100
Utopian socialism, 134–41

Vatican Council (1870), 141
Venice, 34, 87
Versailles, Treaty of, 109, 198, 203, 205, 209–10, 239, 272
Vichy France, 263, 270, 292, 311, 315
Victoria, Queen of England, 123, 153
Vienna, 17, 50, 98, 99. *See also* Congress of Vienna
Vietnam, 313–14
Vinci, Leonardo da, 28
Voltaire, 22, 39, 50, 52, 53–54, 55; democracy, 67

War, 45, 51, 63, 120, 154, 176, 247, 325; Bismarck on, 158; deterrent, 220, 231; fate of, 251; guerrilla, 313; -guilt clause, 198–99; impact, 204; Locarno, 219; renouncement, 220; revulsion against, 200, 222, 276
Wars of Religion, 30, 31, 36, 62, 66
Waterloo, 84
Weimar Republic, 229–30, 236, 262, 326
Wellington, Duke of, 73
West, the, 7, 10, 12, 23, 82
William of Orange, 43, 93, 94
William II, Kaiser of Germany, 159, 160, 161, 208, 305
Wilson, Woodrow, 1–2, 184, 187, 188, 188 n, 190, 193, 199, 205; Fourteen Points, 187–88, 196, 270
World War I, vii, 1, 95, 104, 110, 117, 120, 175–79, 184, 193, 197 ff, 254; Armistice, 189, 189 n, 190; Europeanness, 177; ideologies, 179–91; meaning, 171–99; peace, critique of, 192–202, 272; results, 192, 217, 256, 276; significance, 202; slogan, 200
World War II, vii, 6, 196, 259 ff, 261–76; character of, 265; ideological rift, 271; "phoney war," 260

Yalta, 271
Young Plan, 221, 226
Yugoslavia, 215, 237, 264, 270; defection, 330

Zollverein, 115, 117, 298, 299, 301